THE ESSENTIAL GUIDE TO FOOD HYGIENE

Graham Aston M.I.E.H., F.I.H., F.R.S.H., F.B.I.M.
Graham Aston and Associates

Since qualifying as an Environmental Health Officer in the early 1960s, he has held a number of posts in local authorities in the Midlands and the South East. He was Borough Environmental Health and Housing Officer to the Epsom and Ewell Borough Council. He was awarded an Institution of Environmental Health Officers Travelling Scholarship to study food hygiene in Spain. He is a Short Course Training Consultant at the North East Surrey College of Technology and an examiner for various Awarding Bodies. He now heads his own consultancy specialising in food hygiene and health and safety.

John Tiffney F.I.E.H., F.B.I.M.
Chief Environmental Health Officer,
Mole Valley District Council

Since qualifying as an Environmental Health Officer in the early 1960s, he has worked for authorities in London, Surrey and Sussex. He represented Surrey on the General Council of the Institution of Environmental Health Officers from 1977 to 1987 and was Chairman in 1985. He has been a lecturer at Crawley Technical College and at the North East Surrey College of Technology. Since 1977, he has been co-organiser of the South-West Thames Regional Health Authority's Clean Catering Competition for hospitals. He was appointed President of the Institution of Environmental Health Officers in 1991.

The Essential Guide to Food Hygiene

Graham Aston
Graham Aston and Associates

John Tiffney
Chief Environmental Health Officer
Mole Valley District Council

Charles Knight Publishing
Croydon · 1991

First (1977) and second (1981) editions published by
Northwood Publications Limited.
Third (1989) and fourth (1991) revised editions
published by Charles Knight Publishing
Tolley House, 2 Addiscombe Road, Croydon CR9 5AF

A United Newspapers publication

ISBN 0 85314 438-9

Phototypeset by Letterpart Ltd, Reigate, Surrey.

Printed and bound in Great Britain by Dotesios Ltd, Trowbridge, Wiltshire.

The front cover photographs were reproduced with the kind permission of British Gas plc and Spectrum Colour Library.

Preface

This book was published in its First (1977) and Second (1981) Editions under the title "A Guide to Improving Food Hygiene" by Northwood Publications Limited. A completely revised Third Edition under its new title "The Essential Guide to Food Hygiene" was brought out by Charles Knight Publishing in 1989 after a lapse of eight years and we are encouraged that sales since have been such that we have been invited to prepare this Fourth Edition.

Much has happened since the last Edition, both in terms of developments within the food industry and through the dramatic changes in the regulatory legislation. The industry has an enormous task in coping with both of these, so in preparing additions for this book (including a completely new Chapter 3 on Food Hygiene Management) and in revising earlier contents, we have had very much in mind this challenge and how we might help.

Perhaps most gratifying of all is that we recognise the ready acceptance by the industry that food hygiene is fundamental and that only good food hygiene standards will ensure a truly successful industry. We are pleased, therefore, to be able to make our contribution simply by helping food handlers to understand what food hygiene is all about.

Graham Aston & John Tiffney
June 1991

Introduction

An awareness of the need for food hygiene has existed from the time when man first realised that unless he handled his food in a certain way it would make him ill. Today those lessons that were learned by trial and error by early man still form the basis for good practice by food handlers.

We know from early writings that man realised that food kept better when in cool surroundings and that unclean hands could contaminate food to make him ill. We know too that eating certain animals and birds was frowned upon because they had long been associated with illness and, although the precise reasons for the illness were unknown, early man soon realised that good sound food, properly prepared, was essential to good health.

Communal feeding in the early days probably gave rise to an increased interest in food hygiene, for careless handling by one person could suddenly effect a great number of people. The Industrial Revolution saw for the first time a great influx from the country to the larger towns or newly founded industrial centres and as these people needed to be housed, so they needed to be fed. Bad drainage, poor refuse disposal, squalid housing and doubtful water supplies all accompanied the high incidence of food poisoning which resulted in many deaths and an overwhelming amount of general sickness.

Doctors of yesteryear had little knowledge of diagnosis and, moreover, lacked the invaluable laboratory facilities for testing that we have today. 'Collick and winde, griping of the guts and rising of the lights' all took their toll in large measure of the population in those early days and as these are all associated with the digestive system, we can confidently assume that most often unsound food was the cause.

From the simple experiments by the likes of Louis Pasteur, who proved that those invisible organisms or bacteria that cause spoilage could be killed by the application of heat, there emerged a whole new scientific approach to the preservation of food. The process of pasteurisation stands as a memorial to the French scientist. His work, for sure, has probably done more to ensure the safety of our food than any other single development. Later, the introduction of laboratory techniques to grow and isolate different types of bacteria and the development of more sophisticated microscopes ensured that man could identify those invisible enemies, thereby making the task of controlling them much easier.

Perhaps above all, food as a subject began to exercise the minds of eminent scientists who studied the nutritive qualities of food, saw the emergence of the field of dietetics and tackled the question of how food should be preserved with commendable diligence. The German, Liebig, is an example of a chemist whose special interest in food first gave rise to a restorative for the sick and then a substantial preservation industry which gave us today's canned or corned beef.

Today, legislation exists to help to prevent food poisoning and those who subject the consumer to risk can be punished. The fact remains that food poisoning continues to cause much illness and because of this an efficient system operates to deal with cases once they arise. When a person feels ill he or she will probably visit the doctor. Given certain symptoms the doctor will diagnose what he believes to be food poisoning. To confirm his diagnosis the patient may be asked to provide a faecal specimen in a special container. This will be sent for bacteriological examination to one of the Public Health Laboratories located throughout the country. Staffed by specialist chemists and bacteriologists, they have the skills and facilities to confirm and identify the type of poisoning. Once confirmation of the cause of the poisoning is received, the doctor is then able to embark upon a course of treatment to restore the patient to health. It may be that at the same time the Environmental Health Officer will carry out an investigation into how the food poisoning might have arisen, first and foremost to ensure that it doesn't happen again.

During the investigation it may be established that the patient visited a particular restaurant or cafe and ate unsound food. It may be that a number of people were affected – or it may be just a case of a private person forgetting the basic requirements of food hygiene.

After a thorough investigation, often involving very many people being interviewed, the Environmental Health Officer would hope finally to identify the cause.

Each week District Councils send a summary of notifications of all notifiable diseases, including food poisoning, to the Office of Population, Censuses and Surveys where they are collated to provide a national picture of disease. This is subsequently published to provide vital statistics on the health of the nation generally.

Unfortunately, most cases of food poisoning arise through carelessness and often it is not possible to isolate the cause of the sickness. Nonetheless, the Environmental Health Officer would doubtless take the opportunity to question food handlers thoroughly about their methods of operation to see if there is room for improvement.

The health of the population, especially in connection with food borne illnesses, is very much the concern of both the Health Service and Local Government. So far as England and Wales are concerned, 14 Regional Health Authorities exist and within each Region there are a number of District Health Authorities whose more immediate task is to manage the hospitals and other facilities provided within their areas.

All District Councils employ Environmental Health Officers who, amongst their many duties and responsibilities, are responsible for investigating outbreaks of infectious diseases, inspecting all food premises and food stuffs, monitoring the health and safety of employees in all offices, shops and many industrial premises and licensing numerous businesses. In the case of infectious diseases, the Environmental Health Officer's point of contact with the District Health Authority is through the Director of Public Health.

There are some 6,000 Environmental Health Officers employed by District Councils in England and Wales with a further 1,000 in Scotland, Northern Ireland and Eire. An increasing number of commercial companies are employing Environmental Health Officers to deal with food hygiene and health and safety matters.

CONTENTS

Chapter 1

The Law and the Food Trade

The principal Act of Parliament governing the food trade is the Food Safety Act 1990 which sets down rules concerning the storage, manufacture and sale of all foodstuffs and provides for regulations to be made which set down guidance on, for example, colouring matter, preservatives and the composition of food. Every person involved in food preparation or manufacture should be familiar with the legal requirements in the country. Since joining the European Economic Community there have been progressive moves to harmonise the legislation of the various nations and food manufacturers now need to have regard to the food laws in member states if they are to export their products successfully.

Our principal interest lies in the legislation in England, Scotland and Wales concerning food hygiene standards in food premises.

The Food Safety Act 1990 is a consolidating piece of legislation and makes reference, for example, to:–

1 Offences as to the preparation and sale of injurious foods.

2 The general protection for purchasers of food.

3 Offences in connection with the sale of unfit food.

4 The procedure whereby an authorised officer of a Council may 'seize' food if he considers it to be unfit for human consumption.

5 Ministers making regulations in connection with the sale of food for human consumption.

6 Registration of premises for sale or manufacture of food.

7 The action that a Local Authority may take if food premises are so bad that there is a danger to health.

Of particular importance to the food industry generally are the Food Hygiene (General) Regulations 1970. These are of prime importance to everyone engaged in the food industry and a copy of the Regulations should be available for all to read. Staff should be given instructions on their obligations to ensure clean food production, whilst remembering that these Regulations only prescribe a minimum standard. Many food premises and their staff maintain a far higher standard of hygiene which sets a target for the remainder to try to achieve.

The following notes provide, in simple terms, practical advice on what is required in connection with the main provisions and what is the reasoning behind any particular instruction.

The Food Hygiene (General) Regulations 1970 were originally introduced as subsiduary legislation under Section 13 of the Food and Drugs Act 1955. That Act has now been superseded by the Food Safety Act 1990 as referred to earlier.

Regulations and Explanatory Notes

S.I. 1970 No 1172

The Food Hygiene (General) Regulations 1970

Made ....3rd August 1970
Laid before Parliament......................18th August 1970
Coming into Operation......................1st March 1971

The Minister of Agriculture, Fisheries and Food and the Secretary of State for Social Services, acting jointly, in exercise of the powers conferred on them by sections 13 and 123 of the Food and Drugs Act 1955, as read with the Secretary of State for Social Services Order 1968 [S.I. 1968 No. 1699], and of all other powers enabling them in that behalf, after consultation with such organisation, as appear to them to be representative of interests substantially affected by the regulations and after reference to the Food Hygiene Advisory Council under section 82 of that Act, hereby make the following regulations:–

PART I

PRELIMINARY

Regulation 1

Citation and commencement

1 These regulations may be cited as the Food Hygiene (General) Regulations 1970, and shall come into operation on 1st March 1971.

Regulation 2

Interpretation

2 (1) In these regulations, unless the context otherwise requires

'the Act' means the Food and Drugs Act 1955;

'animal feed' means feed for sale for consumption by animals, fish or birds, but does not include food fit for and commonly used for human consumption;

'business' includes the undertaking of a canteen, club, school, hospital or institution, whether carried on for profit or not, and any undertaking or activity carried on by a public or local authority:

'catering business' means a food business consisting wholly or partly of the supply of food intended by the supplier for immediate consumption;

'certificate of exemption' in relation to food premises, means a certificate for the time being in force in relation to the premises for the purposes of regulation 28;

'container' includes any basket, pail, tray, box, package or receptacle of any kind, whether open or closed;

'equipment' includes apparatus, furnishings and utensils;

'fish' includes whalemeat;

'food' means food intended for sale or sold for human consumption and includes drink, chewing gum and other products of a like nature and use, and articles and substances used as ingredients in the preparation of food or drink or of such products, but does not include –

(a) milk:

(b) water, live animals or birds: or

(c) articles or substances used only as drugs;

'food business' has the meaning assigned to it by regulation 3;

'food premises' means any premises in or from which there is carried on any food business;

'food room' means any room (being, or being part of, any food premises), in which any person engages in the handling of food for the purposes of a food business, but does not include –

(a) a room used as a sleeping place if the only handling of food which occurs in a room is in the course of serving food there to, or at the request of, any person occupying it as a sleeping place;

(b) a room communicating with a room used as a sleeping place if the only handling of food which occurs in the room is in the course of serving food there to, or at the request of, any person (not being a person carrying on a food business at the premises which include the room or a person employed by him) by whom the room is occupied as a sleeping place; or

(c) a day room in a hospital or in a home for the reception of aged or disabled persons;

'home-going ship' means a boat or craft plying exclusively in inland waters or engaged in coastal excursions; and for the purposes of this definition 'inland waters' means any canal, river, lake, navigation or estuary and 'coastal excursion' means an excursion lasting not more than one day which starts and ends in Great Britain and does not involve calling at any place outside Great Britain;

'hospital' means any premises for the reception and treatment of persons suffering from illness (including mental disorder within the meaning of the Mental Health Act 1959), any maternity home and any institution for the reception and treatment of persons during convalescence or of persons requiring medical rehabilitation;

'local authority' means –

(a) as respects any borough and any urban district or rural district, the council of the borough or district;

(b) as respects the City of London, the Common Council;

(c) as respects the Inner Temple and Middle Temple, the respective overseers thereof:

'meat' means the flesh (including edible offal and fat) of animals and birds which is sold or intended for sale for human consumption;

'milk' includes cream and separated milk but does not include dried milk or condensed milk or food containing milk;

'open food' means food which is not in a container of such materials and so closed as to exclude the risk of contamination, but does not include any food mentioned in column (1) of the Schedule to these regulations which has been wrapped in the manner described opposite thereto in column (2);

'premises' means a building or part of a building and any forecourt, yard or place of storage used in connection with a building or part of a building;

'preparation' in relation to food includes manufacture and any form of treatment; and 'prepared' shall be construed accordingly;

'sanitary convenience' means a water closet, urinal, chemical closet or similar convenience;

'ship' means –

(a) a home-going ship; and

(b) any other boat or craft which is moored in any place, on or from which there is carried on any catering business or other retail food business.

(2) In these regulations, unless the context otherwise requires, the handling of food means the carrying out or assisting in the carrying out for the purposes of a food business of any process or operation in the sale of food or in the preparation, transport, storage, packaging, wrapping, exposure for sale, service or delivery of food, and includes the cleaning of articles or equipment with which food comes into contact.

(3) For the purposes of these regulations, the supply of food otherwise than by sale at, in or from any place where food is supplied in the course of a business, shall be deemed to be a sale of that food, and references to purchasing and purchasers shall be construed accordingly; and where in connection with any business in the course of which food is supplied the place where the food is served to the customers is different from the place where the food is consumed, both those places shall be deemed to be places in which food is sold.

(4) In determining for the purposes of these regulations whether any matter

involves a risk of contamination to any food, regard shall be had to the extent to which such contamination is immaterial because of –

(a) the nature of the food;
(b) the manner in which the food is packed; or
(c) any process to which the food is to be subjected before sale to the consumer, being a process to which food of that nature is normally so subjected.

(5) The Interpretation Act 1889 shall apply to the interpretation of these regulations as it applies to the interpretation of an Act of Parliament and as if these regulations and the regulations hereby revoked were Acts of Parliament.

(6) Unless the context otherwise requires, references in these regulations to the provisions of any enactment or regulations shall be construed as references thereto as amended by any subsequent enactment or regulations.

(7) Any reference in these regulations to a numbered regulation or Part shall be construed as a reference to the regulation or Part bearing that number in these regulations.

(8) Any reference in these regulations to a numbered paragraph shall, unless the reference is to a paragraph of a specified regulation, be construed as a reference to the paragraph bearing that number in the first-mentioned regulation.

Regulation 3

Meaning of 'food business'

3 (1) In these regulations, unless the context otherwise requires, the expression 'food business' means, subject to the succeeding provisions of this regulation, any trade or business for the purposes of which any person engages in the handling of food.

(2) The expression 'food business' does not include so much of any trade or business as consists of the handling of food –

(a) in the course of any agricultural activity, except as provided by Part VII;
(b) at any premises or place to which the Food Hygiene (Docks, Carriers, etc.) Regulations 1960 [S.I. 1960 No 1602], as amended, or the Slaughterhouses (Hygiene) Regulations 1958 [S.I. 1958 No. 2168], as amended, apply;
(c) at or upon any premises, place, market, stall or delivery vehicle to which the Food Hygiene (Markets, Stalls and Delivery Vehicles) Regulations 1966 [S.I. 1966 No. 791], as amended [S.I. 1986 No. 1487] apply; or
(d) on any ship upon which food is handled solely with a view to its consumption by the crew of the ship or by persons permanently resident thereon.

(3) In this regulation, 'agricultural activity' includes horticulture, fruit growing, dairy farming, the use of land as market gardens and nursery grounds and the breeding and keeping of livestock but not its slaughtering and subsequent processing.

Regulation 4
Application to ships and to certain agricultural activities
4 The regulations shall apply in relation to ships to the extent and in the manner provided by Part VI, and shall apply in relation to agricultural activities to the extent and in the manner provided by Part VII.

Regulation 5
Enforcement
5 Except as provided in Part VI each local authority shall enforce and execute the provision of these regulations in their district:

PART II

GENERAL REQUIREMENTS

Regulation 6
Food business not to be carried on at insanitary premises or place
6 No food business shall be carried on at any insanitary premises or place or at any premises or place the condition, situation or construction of which is such that food is exposed to the risk of contamination.

Notes to Regulation 6

The term 'insanitary premises' suggests conditions that affect health adversely. This generally refers to the presence of dirt and/or infection. The issue to be determined by the Environmental Health Officer is – what constitutes insanitary premises or place? In deciding this point it is worth remembering the medical logic behind the Regulation. Dirty premises can be insanitary on the basis that dirt can harbour bacteria. The fact that pathogenic or harmful bacteria exist or not is immaterial. Dirty or unclean conditions clearly encourage bacteria and given this, we can assume that sooner or later those bacteria may be pathogenic and present a danger.

The presence of visible dirt – of whatever origin – is therefore unacceptable, especially if allowed to accumulate (see Regulation 7).

Regular inspections by management is important and to ensure thorough and periodic cleaning of all parts a comprehensive cleaning schedule needs to be drawn up. This is best achieved as a joint Caterer/Environmental Health Officer exercise and is necessary whether cleaning is carried out in-house, by contractors or as a combination of both.

Regulation 6 also refers to the condition, situation or construction of premises and the fact that it is an offence where these are such that food is exposed to the risk of contamination.

The 'condition' of the premises relates to the basic structure. If, for example, the wall or floor surfaces are such that they cannot be readily cleaned, there could be an offence. Plaster that is perished and flaking cannot be properly cleaned. Moreover that plaster could harbour dirt and bacteria which one way or the other could find its way on to the food. A concrete floor that is not properly sealed could give rise to dust in the atmosphere which would settle on the food. That dust could – though need not necessarily – be contaminated by dirt and possibly pathogenic bacteria.

The 'situation' of the premises will normally relate to land which is not adequately drained or where external influences could give rise to contamination. An area susceptible to flooding, or a former refuse tip where there could be some harmful leaching of the soil, could be situations that are not acceptable for food premises.

The 'construction' of the premises is straightforward. If food premises are poorly constructed so that they are not wind-and water-tight they could be unacceptable. If there are exposed areas allowing the ingress of wind, rain or insect or rodent pests then they could be seen as exposing the food to risk of contamination.

In the case of the condition of premises the EHO will need to draw the owner's attention to any items of disrepair and require these defects to be remedied within a reasonable time. The amount of time given will be determined by the extent of the deficiency and the degree of risk. The person normally responsible for remedying items of disrepair will be the person carrying on the food business.

Regulation 7

Cleanliness of articles or equipment

7 (1) Articles or equipment with which food comes into contact, or is liable to come into contact, in the course of a food business shall be kept clean, and with the exception of non-returnable containers, shall be so constructed, be of such materials and be kept in such good order, repair and condition as to:

(a) enable them to be thoroughly cleaned;

(b) prevent, so far as is reasonably practicable, any matter being absorbed by them; and

(c) prevent, so far as is reasonably practicable, any risk of contamination of the food.

(2) Without prejudice to paragraph (1), all containers intended for containing food in the course of a food business, whether or not they come into contact, or are liable to come into contact, with food, shall so far as is reasonably practicable, be protected and kept free from contamination.

(3) In determining for the purposes of this regulation whether any article or equipment is clean, regard shall be had to the nature and packing of the food for which the article or equipment is required and to the use which is made of the article or equipment.

Notes to Regulation 7

This Regulation deals in the main with the dangers of cross-contamination – that is the transfer of bacteria to the food via an article or piece of equipment. A table top or a storage tray can come into contact with food and, if dirty and contaminated with pathogenic bacteria, these can be transferred to the food. Such items of equipment must be kept clean. At this point we should look at what is meant by the term 'clean'.

One definition refers to cleanliness in factory workplaces with the qualification that it is a question of fact which depends largely upon the class of work carried out. This being the case the same standard of cleanliness would not be applied in a foundry as in a television assembly shop, regard being had to the nature of the work and the inevitable dust generated in the former. Deciding, therefore, on acceptable or unacceptable cleanliness is not so difficult in most cases particularly where a visual assessment is sufficient. In a foundry, for example, a two inch covering of sand would be unacceptable whilst a lightcovering might not.

Cleanliness is equally important in catering areas and one has to draw the line not only between clean and dirty equipment or premises but also sometimes between degrees of cleanliness.

The *Oxford Dictionary* defines 'sanitary' 'as . . . aimed at or helping or not impeding protection of health against dirt and infection . . . and we assume therefore that insanitary premises are those in which there is a danger to health through dirt or infection being present. This being the case the Environmental Health Officer will not only be looking for the obvious visible dirt but also for the hidden dirt beneath tables, cupboards and equipment. In addition he will have regard to that invisible dirt – invisible, that is, to the naked eye – which articles and equipment may be harbouring.

Environmental Health Officers, however, will not lose sight of the fact that food premises are workplaces and workplaces generate waste. In assessing degrees of cleanliness they will therefore have regard to the nature of the work being carried out. This being so one can accept that in any busy kitchen or food preparation area some dirt is going to arise whether from dirty vegetables that are being prepared or from dirt brought in on the shoes of staff. The situation therefore that the Environmental Health Officer is going to find unacceptable is where there are accumulations – possibly over a long period – as opposed to dirt which has arisen from the normal carrying on of the food preparation process and which will be cleared at least at the end of the working day.

Of additional significance is the fact that bacteria need time to multiply and given the dirt in which to do so they will have the time in those places where dirt remains and is allowed to accumulate.

A further definition of 'clean' implies an absence of dirt. Where, however, a different type of cleanliness is introduced is a situation in which an Environmental Health Officer has to consider bacteriological as opposed to visual cleanliness. This applies especially where defective equipment is concerned, because although it may look clean to the naked eye, through its defective construction it may not be capable of being readily cleaned to that standard. A typical example is where a soft wood table is used for food preparation. The wood, by its very nature, is absorbent and although it may, after scrubbing, be clean to the naked eye, it is very difficult to ensure that it is bacteriologically clean at all times. It would be possible for the Environmental Health Officer to take swabs from the wood to show a colony count which could confirm a high degree of uncleanliness.

Cleanliness, therefore, is clearly a matter of opinion for there is no standard against which one might compare it. One obviously has to put the situation into perspective but what emerges is that where a lack of cleanliness in food premises is used as a basis for a prosecution, it will normally be because dirt has been allowed to accumulate to such an extent that those bacteria that cause food poisoning are being or could be harboured.

It would be an unreasonable Environmental Health Officer who looked for sterile conditions but at the same time he/she has an obligation to see that obvious sources of contamination are removed.

The Regulation takes account of the fact that equipment made of certain materials cannot be thoroughly cleaned. Often those materials will be absorbent to some extent. This particularly applies to the use of wood. Whether in new condition or whether of a less absorbent type, all wood will be absorbent to some degree and it follows therefore that bacteria can be harboured within the surface texture of the wood. This is known as the 'absorbency' layer of the wood and its depth will depend on both the type of the wood (hard or soft) and on its condition.

Whilst a wooden table top could be soaked with a bactericidal solution to destroy any pathogenic bacteria, the fact that it cannot be readily cleaned and the fact that there will always be some absorbency renders it unacceptable.

Some articles of equipment used in connection with food may be of a non-absorbent material. Plastic or similar material is a typical example, as is aluminium or other stainless metal. Metals likely to rust introduce a secondary type of contamination and they also render an article incapable of being readily cleaned.

A good example is a storage tray. Even though it may be made of non-absorbent material it may be cracked and broken to the extent that it cannot be readily cleaned. The term 'readily' can be applied if it takes a person an unreasonably long time to clean the article. If the cleaning process is not realistic having regard to its normal usage then it is reasonable to reject the article. If it takes an hour, for example, to clean the article thoroughly – however bacteriologically acceptable it may be at the end– then this is unacceptable.

An article of equipment used in connection with food may itself contaminate the food by virtue of the material from which it is constructed. A lead lined tray, for example, would be unacceptable because of the danger of the lead being transferred to the food. A poorly cured plastic type tray may also be unacceptable if it exudes a chemical used in its manufacture. Poor quality enamelware can cause a problem if used to store acid food.

The matter of absorbency does not apply to containers such as trays if they are non-returnable and intended for 'one trip' only. The need to have a clean non-returnable item still applies, however. One-trip absorbent cardboard or paper containers can be used provided they are clean.

Environmental Health Officers will need to satisfy themselves that such containers are not only clean but that they are stored so that cleanliness can be ensured. It is not unknown for one-trip containers including wrapping paper to become contaminated on premises as a result of poor storage.

Regulation 8

Restriction on preparation and packing of food on domestic premises

8 (1) Except as this regulation provides, a person carrying on a food business shall not for the purposes of that business give out any food or permit any food to be given out for preparation or packing or another person at any domestic premises other than those of the person carrying on the business.

(2) This regulation shall not apply in relation to shrimps or prawns which are given out for the purpose of peeling, if the premises at which the peeling is to be carried out (in this regulation called 'the relevant premises'), are registered under section 16 of the Act for the preparation of the food in question and provided that the requirements of sub-paragraphs (a), (b) and (c) of this paragraph are complied with by the person carrying on the food business.

- (a) Before making the arrangements for giving out the food the person carrying on the food business –
  - (i) shall satisfy himself that the person to whom he proposes to give out the food is aware of the requirements mentioned in paragraph (3) of this regulation and is able to comply with them; and
  - (ii) shall give notice of his intention to make the arrangement to the local authority for the area in which the relevant premises are situated;
- (b) shall personally or by an authorised agent visit the relevant premises at intervals of not more than three months and satisfy himself that the person to whom the food has been given out remains able to comply with the paragraph (3) of this regulation; and
- (c) shall at intervals of not more than six months send to each local authority within whose area any relevant premises are situated a list showing for each of those premises the names of all persons who work there for the purposes of the arrangement.

(3) Any person carrying out any peeling under any such arrangement shall be subject, in addition to the requirements imposed by Part III on persons engaged in the handling of food –

- (a) to the same requirements with respect to articles and equipment used in carrying out the peeling as are applicable under regulation 7 with respect to articles and equipment used in the course of a food business; and
- (b) to the same requirements with respect to the relevant premises as are applicable under regulations 17 and 18 with respect to the provisions of a water supply and wash-hand basins in food premises and under regulations 25 with respect to a food room.

Notes to Regulation 8

The Regulation is intended to safeguard food that is handled on premises that would not necessarily be covered by the provisions of the legislation. It seeks to effect some control over food which is put out or sub-contracted by a main handler to small – often self-employed – suppliers.

It is often the case that hygienic standards in domestic kitchens fall well short of acceptable standards from the point of view of facilities provided, practices, personal hygiene and cleanliness. To safeguard certain cottage industries and/or traditional practices, however, the Regulation exempts certain processes, for example, involving shrimps or prawns, subject to certain conditions.

PART III

REQUIREMENTS RELATING TO FOOD HANDLERS AND THE HANDLING OF FOOD

Regulation 9
Food to be protected from risk of contamination
9 A person who engages in the handling of food shall, while so engaged, take all such steps as may be reasonably necessary to protect the food from risk of contamination, and in particular (without prejudice to the generality of the foregoing) –

(a) shall not so place the food as to involve any risk of contamination;
(b) shall, before offering any food for sale, ensure that any food which is unfit for human consumption is kept apart from any other food;
(c) shall not in or about any forecourt or yard, place any food lower than eighteen inches from the ground unless it is adequately protected from risk of contamination;
(d) shall ensure where reasonably necessary that open food while exposed for sale or during sale or delivery is kept covered or is otherwise effectively screened from possible sources of contamination;
(e) shall not keep in any food room any animal feed unless it is in a container of such material and so closed as to prevent the risk of contaminating the food in the room:

Provided that paragraph (b) shall not apply where food is intended to be sold by wholesale either by sample or description.

Notes to Regulation 9

The Environmental Health Officer will sometimes be required to consider the term 'reasonably necessary' when it comes to protecting food from the risk of contamination. Food placed in the open air to cool clearly exposes it to risk of contamination by insects, dust, etc. (see also Regulation 27). Food placed within a perspex type cover or within a suitable fly screen will receive some protection. It will depend on both the food and the environmental conditions. Unfit food can cross-contaminate fit food either by direct contact, via equipment or by personal handling. This will mean that once food is known to be unfit for human consumption it should be put aside and covered. It should be placed away from food that is fit for human consumption and should be clearly labelled as unfit.

The Regulation (see 9(c)) talks in terms of food not being placed any lower than 18 inches (46 cm) from the ground in any forecourt or yard unless it is adequately protected from risk of contamination. This is more frequently found in, for example, retail outlets such as greengrocers' premises where displays of food are often placed at the front of the premises on pavements. The provision equally applies to non-public parts of the premises and is intended as a safeguard against animals – and in particular dogs – gaining access to the food. If food is placed lower than 18 inches from the ground then it should normally be in suitable boxes which are enclosed on all sides though leaving the top open for display purposes.

Regulation 9(d) refers to the need to ensure 'where reasonably necessary' that food is kept covered from possible sources of contamination. This will generally refer to atmospheric contamination and could refer, for example, to food that is exposed to dust in the atmosphere without being adequately covered. The Environmental Health Officer will clearly have regard to the nature of the food and how vulnerable it is.

The Regulation also raises the question of how far one should go in asking the caterer to protect the food by way of screens, for example, sneeze guards. The decision whether to ask for such screening to be provided will depend on basically two considerations, namely the particular food and its vulnerability and also the degree of the hazard or potential hazard. Certain foods are more vulnerable in that they are more conducive to bacterial growth. In addition much will depend on the degree of hazard presented, for example, by way of hands or by people breathing or sneezing on the food. If a queue of customers finds it difficult not to breathe on food which is displayed at or below eye level then it would be reasonable for the Environmental Health Officer to ask for screening to be provided. Where in doubt the trader should consult the Environmental Health Officer.

Some Environmental Health Officers use this regulation to require caterers to wrap the food where customers are offered the opportunity to select their own food. Observations by one local authority lead to the conclusion that there can be a high degree of contamination through people 'picking over' such consumables as apples, peaches and plums.

Regulation 10
Personal cleanliness
10 A person who engages in the handling of food, shall while so engaged –
(a) keep as clean as may be reasonably practicable all parts of his person which are liable to come into contact with the food;
(b) keep as clean as may be reasonably practicable all parts of his clothing or overclothing which are liable to come into contact with the food;
(c) keep any open cut or abrasion on any exposed part of his person covered with a suitable waterproof dressing;
(d) refrain from spitting;
(e) refrain from the use of tobacco or any other smoking mixture or snuff while he is handling any open food or is in any food room in which there is open food.

Notes to Regulation 10

10 (a) The food handler is responsible for ensuring that those parts of his person that come into contact with the food are kept as clean as possible. In reality this will normally refer to the hands and forearms but could quite easily include upper arms. It would be unreasonable in a working situation to expect the whole time a high standard bacteriologically having regard to hands, etc., but the least that the Environmental Health Officer can expect is that they are visually clean.

Hands can sweat and in the process certain bacteria may be transferred either to equipment or to the food direct. The pores and creases in the hands can harbour bacteria and it is very easy for the areas behind the nails to hold particles of dirt. Rings can also harbour bacteria and nail varnish can chip off.

Supervisors and Environmental Health Officers should be prepared to look at the hands of food handlers to see that they are clean. It is not always easy but the point needs to be made direct to the handler. See also Regulation 29 in relation to the responsibility of management.

There is a good case for providing shower facilities for staff, thereby encouraging good overall personal hygiene.

10(b) This is intended to temper desirable standards with reality. In most working situations in the catering industry there is an amount of 'dirt' involved. Almost inevitably this will find its way onto the overclothing. The Environmental Health Officer may have regard to the cleanliness being 'reasonably practicable'. His decision will depend on both the extent of the dirt and/or the length of time that the dirt has been on the overclothing. A heavily soiled overall dirtied 10 minutes ago could be unacceptable. Equally a lightly soiled overall dirtied three weeks ago could also be unacceptable on the basis that dirt, however limited, can harbour bacteria and those bacteria can multiply to dangerous proportions if given time. Accumulated dirt, even in small amounts, must be regarded as potentially dangerous.

The Regulation refers to parts of clothing or overclothing 'which are liable to come into contact with the food'. Sleeves and fronts of coats or aprons are most implicated and clearly will be the Environmental Health Officer's first priority.

10(c) The medical logic behind the Regulation is demonstrated clearly here. Cuts, abrasions, spots, sores and certain other skin complaints harbour bacteria. These bacteria may give rise to food poisoning. Therefore any cut or abrasion, on the assumption that pathogenic bacteria are present, must be covered with a suitable waterproof dressing to prevent the outflow of infected matter. The choice of a suitable waterproof dressing is important, for it must completely cover the source of infection and be such that water/moisture cannot gain entry to ooze out and contaminate food.

If a bandage dressing is thought to be more appropriate this is acceptable provided it is covered with a suitable waterproof (usually rubberised) finger stall. It is important to ensure that the stall completely covers the bandage and renders it waterproof.

Coloured dressings are recommended for ease of recognition in the unfortunate event of their becoming detached and falling into the food.

10(d) Harmful bacteria can be harboured in the nose, ear and throat regions. These can be transferred directly or indirectly to food through coughing, sneezing or spitting. An individual's control over coughing or sneezing is limited. This is not the case with spitting which is an entirely voluntary action.

The strongest disciplinary action should be taken with staff found to be spitting. Besides the health objection, it is an indication of lack of self-control on the part of the individual.

10(e) Although ash in food is a contaminant in itself, and is equally unacceptable aesthetically, the main reason why smoking is not permitted is because harmful bacteria that may be present in the mouth and throat regions can be transferred to the food through the act of removing the cigarette, etc., from the mouth, contaminating the fingers which in turn touch the food. The same harmful bacteria found in the mouth and throat regions are often to be found in the nose and for this reason the use of snuff is also an offence.

Besides prohibiting smoking in food rooms, it is recommended to set aside areas, other than in food areas, where staff who smoke can do so.

Areas within restaurants and canteens are being increasingly designated as no smoking areas, in this way responding to the increasing objection from non-smokers.

One should be mindful of the effect of secondary smoking – that is, smoke inhaled by one person that was generated by the act of smoking by another person (also known as passive smoking).

Regulation 11

Persons handling open food to wear overclothing, etc.

11 A person who engages in the handling of open food, other than raw vegetables, intoxicating liquor or soft drinks, shall while so engaged wear sufficient clean and washable overclothing, and every person who carries meat which is open food and which is liable to come into contact with his neck or head shall, while so engaged, also wear a clean and washable neck and head covering:

Provided that this regulation shall not apply –

(a) to waiters in catering businesses,

(b) to any person so long as he is engaged only in the carrying of unskinned rabbits or hares or unplucked game or poultry;

(c) to transport of food –

(i) by railway undertakers; or

(ii) in the course of the business of a carrier other than a railway undertaker in which the vehicle used for the transport of food is not ordinarily used;

if in either case the person carrying the food takes all such other precautions as are reasonable and practicable to prevent the food from coming into contact with any exposed part of his person or with any clothing other than overclothing.

Notes to Regulation 11

In general, anyone who handles open food needs to wear clean and washable overclothing. The term 'washable' does not apply where disposable overclothing is used (providing it is clean). If, however, the handler is only handling raw vegetables, intoxicating liquor or soft drinks this provision does not apply. Once other foods, however, such as sandwiches or pies are introduced then suitable overclothing is necessary. This would be the case where there are licensed facilities in, for example, social clubs or pubs.

Carriers of meat – and one has in mind here mainly those involved in meat deliveries by vehicle – must wear suitable protective clothing if they carry it on their shoulders so that both the neck and hair regions are covered. What has become known as the 'Foreign Legion' type hat is often used and is wholly suitable.

The requirement for staff to wear protective clothing does not apply to railway or other transport personnel provided in the case of the latter the vehicle is a general duty vehicle and in both cases precautions are taken to prevent the food being contaminated through contact with normal dress. In practice it means that a carrier of general merchandise, including food, does not have to wear special protective clothing subject to certain precautions being taken.

Disposable clothing is used to an increasing extent. A ready supply must be made available so that replacements can be provided as and when necessary. Overclothing of whatever type should not be rationed to one or more every week. To prevent the danger of cross-contamination they need to be replaced as often as necessary. The use of disposable outerclothing, for example, aprons, can be a sensible way of protecting main coats and overalls.

If protective clothing is laundered, care should be taken by the staff to ensure that the end product is clean and germ free. Whether the laundry is carried out in-house, or by outside contractors, it is important to ensure bacteriologically acceptable clothing.

The storage of protective clothing is important. There is no point in having clean clothing if it is kept in a place where it may become contaminated.

Regulation 12
Carriage and wrapping of food
12 A person who engages in the handling of food shall not while so engaged –
(a) carry any food in a container together with any article from which there

is a risk of contamination of the food, or with any live animal or live poultry, without taking all such precautions as are reasonably practicable to avoid risk of contamination, and in particular, (without prejudice to the generality of the foregoing), shall not allow any live animal or live poultry to come into contact with any food;

(b) use for wrapping or containing any open food any paper or other wrapping material or container which is not clean or which is liable to contaminate the food, and shall not allow any printed material, other than printed material designed exclusively for wrapping or containing food, to come into contact with any food other than uncooked vegetables or unskinned rabbits or hares or unplucked game or poultry.

Notes to Regulation 12

12(a) The essential requirement here is to prevent 'safe' and 'less safe' foods, including live animals and poultry, coming into contact with each other so that harmful bacteria may be transferred. Food that is decomposing or otherwise unfit should not be placed in the same container as clean food unless there is adequate separation. This separation will normally be achieved by one or the other food being adequately covered.

12(b) Materials used to contain open food must be clean and incapable of contaminating the food.

Wrapping paper specifically manufactured for use with food should be used whilst newspaper or similarly printed paper must not be used except for uncooked vegetables, unskinned rabbits or hares or unplucked game or poultry.

One should ensure that wrapping materials, cartons or other containers are stored in a clean place.

Regulation 13

Persons suffering from certain infections

13 (1) Immediately a person engaged in the handling of food becomes aware that he is suffering from, or is the carrier of, typhoid, paratyphoid or any other salmonella infection or amoebic or bacillary dysentery or any staphylococcal infection likely to cause food poisoning, he shall inform the person carrying on the food business and that person shall immediately notify the appropriate medical officer of health accordingly:

Provided that where the person required to give such information is himself the person carrying on the food business he shall give the information immediately to the appropriate medical officer of health.

(2) In this regulation –

'appropriate medical officer of health' means –

(a) in the case of a person engaged in the handling of food at or from food premises, the medical officer of health of the district in which the premises are situated; and

(b) in any other cases, either the medical officer of health of the district in which the person resides or the medical officer of health of the district in which the food business is situated.

Notes to Regulation 13

In reality is is invariably the patient's doctor, having diagnosed food poisoning, who notifies the local authority. In most cases the Medical Officer will be the District Community Physician employed by the District Health Authority.

PART IV

REQUIREMENTS RELATING TO FOOD PREMISES

Regulation 14

Soil drainage systems

14 (1) No fresh air intake of any ventilation pipe included in the soil drainage system of food premises shall be situated in a food room.

(2) Every inlet into any such system situated in any such room shall be trapped.

Notes to Regulation 14

Fresh air intakes can give rise to smells and allow rodent and insect pests access into premises, especially if not properly maintained.

It is not uncommon to have drainage gullies in food rooms to enable floors to be washed down. Sometimes a system of channels may be used which lead to a central gully. Gullies should be properly trapped with a water seal to prevent the ingress of smells or rodent and insect pests.

Depending on the food process being caried out it may be sensible to install a grease trap to prevent grease gaining access to the main system where it can solidify and cause an obstruction. Grids to channels and gullies should be readily removable for cleaning purposes. To prevent smaller particles from falling into the system there is merit in placing a finer grid or mesh over the cast or plastic grid.

Regular cleaning of gullies and grids in essential, since a build-up of debris can readily take place which can create a harbourage for pests.

Remember, too, that access points such as rodding eyes or manholes should be of such a type that smells, etc., cannot pass. Covers to such access points will usually be of a screw down type incorporating grease seals.

Regulation 15
Cisterns for supplying water for food rooms.
15 No cistern for the supply of water to a food room shall supply a sanitary convenience otherwise than through an efficient flushing cistern or some other flushing apparatus equally efficient and suitable for preventing contamination of water supplies.

Notes to Regulation 15

Although water supplies for food preparation purposes should desirably be taken direct from the mains supply there are occasions where it needs to be taken via a storage tank. This will be usually situated at a high level so that a sufficient pressure can be maintained. It should be covered to prevent contamination by birds and other pests. If the same tank or cistern also supplies water to a water closet there must be a flushing system which disconnects the supply and prevents any backflow of water.

Operators are well advised to be familiar with the water supply systems. If there is any doubt regarding the wholesomeness of the water supply ask the local Environmental Health Officer to arrange for samples to be taken for examination.

Regulation 16
Sanitary conveniences
16 (1) Every sanitary convenience situated in, or regularly used in connection with, any food premises –
- (a) shall be kept clean and in efficient order;
- (b) shall be so placed that no offensive odours therefrom can penetrate into any food room.

(2) Any room or other place which contains a sanitary convenience shall be suitably and sufficiently lighted and ventilated and shall be kept clean.

(3) No room which contains a sanitary convenience shall be used as a food room.
(4) No food room which communicates directly with a room or other place which contains a sanitary convenience shall be used for the handling of open food.
(5) There shall be fixed and maintained in a prominent and suitable position near every sanitary convenience provided or made regularly available for use by persons employed in the handling of food in or about food premises, a clearly legible notice requesting users to wash their hands after using the convenience.

Notes to Regulation 16

16(1)(a) Any sanitary convenience, whether in the form of a water or chemical closet or a urinal, must be kept clean. Failure to do so will result in a deposition of faecal matter as well as urine which not only can provide a harbourage for bacteria but which can give rise to contamination through direct contact with individuals.

Sanitary conveniences must be kept in efficient order so that they operate correctly. A cistern that does not deliver a sufficient flush is not acceptable. The convenience must be in good condition. Broken glazing to a pedestal or a string/cord substitute for a chain are unacceptable because they cannot be readily cleaned and can provide a harbourage for bacteria. A worn or cracked lavatory seat is unhygienic and unacceptable too.

A heavy build-up of lime or other salts is also unacceptable because it means that the unit itself cannot be properly cleaned.

16(1)(b) Effective means must be provided to prevent any offensive odours from passing from the W.C. compartment to any food room. This requires some positive disconnection between the room containing the convenience and the food room. In reality, an intervening space which is suitably ventilated needs to be provided, the size of the intervening space and the ventilation thereto being such that odours from the W.C. compartment cannot penetrate to the food room. An openable window in the intervening space is not acceptable if it is kept closed. Though not as good as the permanent air vent, a window kept in the open or louvred position could be acceptable.

In exceptional circumstances in may be physically impossible to install a suitable intervening space. In such circumstances it is acceptable to install an extractor fan to the W.C. compartment itself with the discharge to the outside air. Alternatively this could be via a proper ventilation system such that it is automatically activated when a person uses the convenience. Such systems incorporate a carry over arrangement which enables the exhaust to continue for 2–3 minutes after the user has left the compartment. Deodorisers are not an acceptable alternative to a suitable intervening space.

16(2) The room or compartment containing the convenience must be kept clean and this applies to all parts whether floor, walls, ceiling or fitments.

The room should be adequately lighted and ventilated to enable the user to see clearly, to enable cleaning to be readily undertaken and to ensure that there is no build-up of offensive odours. Ventilation will generally be to the outside air and desirably should be permanent.

16(3) Open food must not be handled or stored in a sanitary compartment or room.

16(4) This Regulation is quite clear in stating that food handling must not take place in any room which communicates directly with a W.C. compartment.

16(5) Two points are of note, namely the 'Now Wash Your Hands' notice itself must be clear and it must be situated so that it is readily seen by the person using the convenience.

Regulation 17
Water supply to be provided
17 (1) Subject to the provisions of any certificate of exemption, a supply of water sufficient in quantity to enable these regulations to be complied with shall be provided at all food premises.
(2) Any such supply of water shall –
(a) be clean and wholesome;
(b) be constant, if the provision of a constant supply is reasonably practicable and is in accordance with good practice at premises used for business of a similar class.

Notes to Regulation 17

17(1) A sufficient supply of water needs to be provided for the food premises. This applies to both hot and cold supplies.

17(2)(a) The water supply must be clean and wholesome. Routine sampling can be undertaken to check this from time to time. Water must be free from pathogenic bacteria and free from extraneous and particularly harmful matter – for example, chemicals, metals.

Supplies obtained direct from the mains are less likely to be affected but supplies obtained via storage tanks or long pipe runs may give rise to contamination. Tanks should be regularly checked and should be properly covered to prevent contamination. If tanks and pipework become contaminated they should be flushed through with a suitable disinfectant.

Water obtained from wells should be thoroughly checked from time to time for both bacteriological and chemical quality.

17(2)(b) Adequacy of water supply not only applies to total volume but also to constancy of supply. The demands made by the business must be met so that there is a sufficient supply for washing up and cleaning at all times. It is not acceptable, for example, to use a kettle of hot water for washing purposes.

Regulation 18
Wash-hand basins to be provided
18 (1) There shall be provided in all food premises suitable and sufficient wash-hand basins for the use of all persons engaged in the handling of food in or about those premises and such basins shall be placed in a position conveniently accessible to such persons.
(2) There shall be provided for every such wash-hand basin an adequate supply of hot and cold water or of hot water at a suitably controlled temperature, or in the case of food premises where no open food is handled, of cold water.
(3) There shall be provided for use at every such wash-hand basin an adequate supply of soap or other suitable detergent, nail-brushes and clean towels or other suitable drying facilities.
(4) Every such wash-basin shall be kept clean and in good working condition.
(5) The washing facilities provided under this regulation shall not be used for any purpose other than for securing the personal cleanliness of the user.

Notes to Regulation 18

18(1) The Regulation first and foremost refers to wash-hand basins. This is regarded by some as an anomaly because it is often necessary to wash the forearms which cannot be readily accommodated in a small basin. A wash-hand basin in reality can be too small. Nonetheless the Regulation does refer to 'suitability' and the Environmental Health Officer can ask for a larger one to be provided if it is felt that there is a need to wash forearms too.

A sufficiency of basins means that all staff must have reasonable access to a basin at all times. Given the need to wash hands, for example, between handling cooked and uncooked foods, a basin must be within easy reach. A basin situated within or near to the food room would usually be acceptable. Access which may involve passing through various doors or involve climbing or descending stairs to another floor is not. A point to be considered is the lack of accessibility of the basin likely to discourage a food handler from washing hands? If this is so, then there is a case for providing additional basins.

18(2) Each basin needs to be provided with an adequate supply of hot and cold water or hot water at a suitably controlled temperature. The water temperature required for hand washing should be in the region of 50–60°C. Hot water from a normal hot water cylinder will be in the region of 80°C – hence the need for cold water to lower the temperature to an acceptable level.

18(3) Each wash-hand basin needs to be provided with an adequate supply of soap or other detergent. This may be in the form of powder, liquid, tablet or gel and should be capable of helping to remove dirt and grease. Some soaps, gels, etc., incorporate a bactericidal agent. Their use should be encouraged.

A nail-brush should also be provided, preferably of non-absorbent plastic bristles and base. The nail-brush needs to be regularly cleaned.

Clean towels or other suitable drying facilities are necessary. Disposable towels of paper or other material are to be recommended. Proper storage is important.

Continuous roller cabinet towels are acceptable but are not as good as paper or hot air dryers.

18(4) Basins, including taps, must be kept clean and should be properly connected to the drainage system to enable an efficient removal of waste water. A plug must be provided. Caterers are using elbow type taps to an increasing extent and these do have a number of advantages, including that the hands do not touch them.

18(5) Only personal washing (not laundry!) shall be carried out using a basin. Food or equipment must not be placed in the basin.

Regulation 19
First-aid materials to be provided
19 There shall be provided at all food premises a sufficient supply of suitable bandages, dressings (including waterproof dressings) for first-aid treatment of persons engaged in the handling of food in or about those premises and such supply shall be kept in a place readily accessible to those persons.

Notes to Regulation 19

A suitably equipped first-aid box/kit should be readily available. If the catering facilities are spread over a wide area it could mean that a box/kit should be situated at several locations.

A member of staff should be detailed to ensure that it is properly maintained and it should be readily identifiable, with the standard first-aid sign on the outer face.

It is not good practice for the first-aid equipment to be kept in an office on the basis that it may not always be accessible.

Regulation 20
Accommodation for clothing, etc.
20 (1) Subject to the provisions of any certificate of exemption, there shall be provided in all food premises where open food is handled suitable and sufficient accommodation for outdoor or other clothing and footwear not being worn during working hours by persons engaged in the handling of food in or about those premises; and such clothing and footwear shall not be kept in any place on or about thc premises other than in the accommodation so provided.
(2)Where such accommodation is situated in a food room it shall be in the form of lockers or cupboards.

Notes to Regulation 20

20(1) Overclothing, whether in the form of coats, overcoats, macintoshes, hats and shoes or other footwear must not be kept in the food room. The reason behind this is that dirt and/or bacteria can be brought into the food premises from outside on the overclothing. Besides any aerial contamination of the overclothing, bacteria could be present on the overclothing through having been in contact with, for example, domestic animals.

20(2) Where there is no separate staff changing room and where there is little alternative but to keep overclothing and footwear in a food room, then it must be in a locker or cupboard. This is unlikely to be necessary in premises where separate staff changing facilities/rest room are usually provided.

Regulation 21

Facilities for washing food and equipment

21 (1) There shall be provided in all food premises where open food is handled sinks or other washing facilities suitable and sufficient for any necessary washing of food and equipment used in the food business; and in this regulation reference to a sink shall include a reference to any other suitable washing facility.

(2) There shall be provided for every such sink an adequate supply of hot and cold water or of hot water at a suitably controlled temperature, or cold water only where the sink is used –

(a) only for washing fish, fruit or vegetables; or

(b) for washing with a suitable bactericidal agent only drinking vessels, or only ice-cream formers or servers.

(3) Every such sink shall be kept clean and in good working condition.

Notes to Regulation 21

21(1) The vast majority of larger businesses will have mechanised washing facilities. Whether manual or mechanical the facility for washing food and equipment must be adequate in terms of number and capacity.

It is not good practice to use the same sink for food and equipment. Much will depend on the size of the catering concern and the availability of space. If in doubt the Caterer should consult the Environmental Health Officer for advice.

21(2) Hot and cold water supplies or hot water at a suitably controlled temperature must be provided, the reason being that grease/dirt can only be removed by the application of heat.

An adequate supply of hot water must be available at all times. With a central boiler system this is unlikely to be a problem but if an independent water heater is being used it should be of sufficient capacity to ensure an adequate supply of hot water at the correct temperature.

Washing facilities can incorporate a tap proportioner/measure which has the effect of introducing into the hot water supply a pre-determined dose of detergent/bactericidal agent. This eliminates the less effective manual dosing of water in the sink. Such an arrangement is not a requirement in law but is to be highly recommended.

Only a cold water supply need be provided to a sink used for washing fish, fruit or vegetables. Provided a bactericidal agent is used, cold water need only be provided for washing drinking vessels or with ice cream scoops or servers. In practice it is easy for the water to become contaminated through prolonged use in spite of the bactericidal agent being present. It is important for the Caterer to ensure that the water is regularly changed and that the correct amount of bactericidal agent is introduced at the outset.

21(3) Every sink or washing machine needs to be kept clean and in good working order. Sinks can normally be maintained by catering personnel whilst mechanical washers will require periodic servicing by trained engineers. The efficiency of machines can fall dramatically if proper water temperatures and circulation are not maintained. Machines normally rely on a high temperature to provide a sterilising effect. Blockage of water lines from scaling or accumulation of debris must be avoided by regular maintenance of the equipment.

Where the 'two-sink system' for washing up is used it is important to ensure that the temperature in the second sink is sufficient to destroy harmful bacteria. Regular checks are important when in use. The temperature of the water in the first sink should be in the region of 50–60°C whilst the temperature in the second sink should be around 80°C.

Regulation 22
Lighting of food rooms
22 Suitable and sufficient means of lighting shall be provided in every food room and every such room shall be suitably and sufficiently lighted.

Notes to Regulation 22

Lighting needs to be sufficient in terms of capacity of providing enough light to all parts. It must also be suitable in terms of providing a light that is agreeable to staff. The Caterer should consult the Environmental Health Officer in terms of what is 'suitable and sufficient' in any particular part of the premises. The positioning of light fittings is important – staff should not, for example, be expected to work in their own shadow.

Adequate lighting is necessary to provide safe working conditions, to prevent eye strain and glare and to enable all parts of the food room to be clearly seen and thus adequately cleaned. A figure of 400 lux is considered to be a reasonable level for all general areas.

Lighting fittings themselves should be capable of being readily cleaned. Fittings, including switches, which are simpler in design are easier to clean and are less likely to collect dirt and grease. Fittings and switches should comply where necessary with the appropriate safety standard having regard to any exposure to moisture and steam.

Regulation 23
Ventilation of food rooms
23 Except in the case of a room in which the humidity or temperature is controlled, suitable and sufficient means of ventilation shall be provided in every food room and suitable and sufficient ventilation shall be maintained there.

Notes to Regulation 23

Ventilation is necessary to provide an adequate supply of clean fresh air to the food room. It is dependent on the removal of old stale air and replacement with fresh air, usually from the outside. In catering premises adequate ventilation is essential because:

(i) high temperatures can promote the growth of bacteria;
(ii) hot steamy conditions are less comfortable for staff and can give rise to accidents;
(iii) grease and steam can build up on surfaces adding to the need for cleaning.

Although natural ventilation, through open windows, can be used it is not to be recommended because of the possibility of contamination being introduced from the outside in the form of dust, insects, etc.

Ventilation is best provided artificially through a system designed to remove stale air quickly. More sophisticated systems not only remove stale air at a pre-determined rate but also replace it with filtered fresh air.

Food production often gives rise to considerable quantities of steam, grease, etc. Good overall ventilation is essential whilst special ventilation may need to be provided to those particular sources of steam. Cookers, ovens, steamers, etc., will almost certainly be situated in a ventilated area, usually beneath a ventilation or exhaust hood. In this way steam and grease-laden air can be removed, filtered and discharged to the outside air. Care should be taken to ensure that discharge points are not going to give rise to a secondary nuisance and should not be situated near to, for example, windows.

Filters need regular attention and should be thoroughly cleaned or replaced.

The positioning of hoods, filters, ducting and discharge points is important for an efficient system. Caterers would be well advised to consult a ventilation engineer when new equipment is to be installed or where a reasonable working atmosphere cannot be achieved with existing equipment.

Regulation 24
Food room not to be, or communicate with, a sleeping place
24 (1) No food food room shall be used as a sleeping place.
(2) Subject to the provisions of any certificate of exemption, no food room which communicates directly with a sleeping place shall be used for the handling of open food.

Notes to Regulation 24

Wards and day rooms in hospitals or homes for the aged and disabled are exempt from this Regulation. Otherwise sleeping must not be permitted where food is handled nor must a room which communicates directly be used for handling open food.

Regulation 25
Cleanliness and repair of food rooms
25 The walls, floors, doors, windows, ceiling, woodwork and all other parts of the structure of every food room shall be kept clean and shall be kept in such good order, repair and condition as to –

(a) enable them to be effectively cleaned; and
(b) prevent, so far as is reasonably practicable, any risk of infestation by rats, birds, mice or insects.

Notes to Regulation 25

This Regulation should be read in conjunction with Regulation 6, so far as it relates to insanitary premises.

It is necessary for all parts of the food room to be in good condition such that they can be readily cleaned. A part of the structure such as a window, door or floor may be in sound condition. If, however, it is of such material that it cannot be effectively cleaned then it could be an offence. The Regulation is making the point that if parts of the premises are of such material that they cannot be easily cleaned then there is always the danger of bacteria and dirt building up.

In terms of materials, Environmental Health Officers will be looking for those that are smooth and impervious. Tiles or other ceramic finishes or stainless metal are widely used, though the location within the premises will determine which material is best. Tiles are not recommended near sources of heat or where they are likely to suffer impact damage. A stainless metal, however, firmly bonded to the wall behind, would be acceptable in such places.

Other types of finish may be acceptable such as smooth gloss paint but this should only be used in less vulnerable areas. Gloss paint for example may be acceptable in a ward kitchen of a hospital. It is unlikely to be acceptable in a main preparation kitchen, except at higher levels.

A further consideration for the food operator and the Environmental Health Officer is the 'construction' of parts of the premises. A window may be in good condition and may be of impervious material. If, however, it is of a complicated pattern, then it may be difficult to clean effectively. Simplicity of design therefore is important, as is the avoidance of hidden corners and dirt traps.

Although specifically relating to the main features of food rooms, that is, walls and floors, the Regulation also refers to 'all other parts'. Drainage channels, grids, ceilings, joists and other exposed beams are also included.

Regulation 25(b) specifically relates to preventative pest control having regard to cleanliness and the need to avoid infestation. Some parts of kitchens can easily become infested, for example, with cockroaches if certain measures are not taken. Voids behind tiling or beneath floors can provide a harbourage. These should be filled in and treatment carried out if there is an infestation. If rodents are gaining access to food rooms through holes in woodwork or around pipework, then these need to be filled or sealed.

Similarly, netting and other measures may need to be installed to prevent access by birds. This is often necessary where there are high ceilings with rooflights or louvres which are sometimes left open or where control mechanisms have failed so that they cannot be properly closed.

Metal plates can be placed at the base of doors if rodents are gaining access through the gap below and mesh can be effectively used to prevent the ingress of birds and insects through windows and roof lights.

Food operators need to arrange for regular checks of all parts of the catering facility for signs of infestation. Immediate action is necessary where there is evidence. Many businesses engage pest control operators for the purpose. It is important that specifications for pest control are drawn up with great care and that equal attention is given both to control measures and preventative measures. It is essential to specify requirements very clearly.

> **Regulation 26**
> *Accumulation of refuse, etc.*
> **26** (1) The layout of food premises shall be such as to provide adequate space, suitably sited, for the purpose of the removal of waste from food and the separation of unfit food in compliance with the requirements of regulation 9(b), and the storage of any such waste and unfit food prior to disposal.
> (2) No refuse or filth, whether solid or liquid, shall be deposited or allowed to accumulate in a food room except so far as may be unavoidable for the proper carrying on of the trade or business.

Notes to Regulation 26

26(1) Adequate waste storage facilities must be provided in all food premises. Often depending on the scale of the catering these may range from small individual bins or sacks to larger bulk containers and compaction units. These must be capable of containing the refuse generated by the business and must be regularly emptied/removed.

Containers need to be of such material that they can be easily cleaned to prevent any build-up of food which would give rise to smells and encourage pests. Periodic steam cleaning is recommended. Containers should have suitable tight-fitting lids/covers to prevent access by insects and vermin and to minimise any smell nuisance.

The area where containers are situated should be readily accessible and should be so constructed that it can be easily cleaned so that it discourages the harbourage of pests. If should also be properly ventilated and provided with adequate artificial lighting.

Refuse should not be burned in containers. Various disinfectants/deodorisers can be applied to control smells, etc., but these are cosmetic. There is no substitute for thorough and regular cleaning by, for example, high pressure hot water/steam.

Refuse will often need to be segregated depending on its nature. Boxes and paper may need to be kept separate. Baling is sometimes used to render bulky material easier to handle.

If food waste is collected for animal food, special procedures need to be adopted. The Environmental Health Officer will advise in this connection.

26(2) Refuse or waste generated within the premises can be stored within those premises so long as it is not allowed to accumulate unreasonably and so long as it is removed regularly to the facilities referred to in the notes of Regulation 26(1) above.

Waste is continually being generated in every food business. This can be temporarily stored in a bin or sack within the food room so long as it is removed at least daily to the main storage area. Where bins (as opposed to disposable sacks) are used these should be regularly cleaned and maintained in good condition. They should be of such material that they can be easily cleaned, that is, smooth and impervious.

Regulation 27

This regulation has been replaced. Please see reference to Food Hygiene (Amendment) Regulations 1990 (pp. 37–39).

PART V

ADMINISTRATIVE PROVISIONS

Regulation 28

Exemption of premises from certain requirements

28 (1) The appropriate authority for the purposes of this regulation shall be the local authority in whose district the food premises are situated.

(2) While there is in force in relation to any food premises a certificate of the appropriate authority to the effect that compliance with any provisions specified in paragraph (6) cannot reasonably be required with respect to those premises or any activities carried on therein, those premises shall be exempt from the provisions mentioned in the certificate.
(3) A certificate of exemption shall not be granted by the appropriate authority with respect to any food premises unless the authority is satisfied that by reason of restricted accommodation or other special circumstances affecting the premises it is reasonable that such a certificate should be in force.
(4) A certificate of exemption shall be withdrawn by the authority if at any time they cease to be satisfied as aforesaid.
(5) If the person carrying on a food business is aggrieved by the refusal or withdrawal of a certificate of exemption he may appeal to a magistrates' court and that court may make such order concerning the certificate as appears to the court, having regard to the matters with respect to which the authority are required to be satisfied as aforesaid, to be just and equitable.
(6) The provision referred to in paragraph (2) are regulation 17 (water supply to be provided), regulation 20 (accommodation for clothing, etc.), and regulation 24(2) (food room not to be, or communicate with, a sleeping place).
(7) Section 120 of the Act (which relates to the right to carry on business while an appeal is pending), shall apply for the purposes of these regulations, with the modification that references therein to refusing or revoking a licence shall include references to refusing or withdrawing a certificate of exemption.

Note to Regulation 28

In certain circumstances exemptions may be granted to the provisions of the Regulations in connection with, for example, the provision of water supply.

Regulation 29
Offences
29 (1) A person engaged in the handling of food shall be guilty of an offence against these regulations if he fails to comply with any provision of these regulations which imposes obligations on a person so engaged.
(2) A person carrying on a food business shall be guilty of an offence against these regulations if –

(a) as respects that food business, any provision of these regulations (other than the requirements imposed by regulations 10 and 13 on persons engaged in the handling of food) is contravened; or
(b) he fails to take all reasonable steps to secure the compliance by any person employed by him or under his control with the provisions of regulations 10 and 13.

(3) Any person for the time being having the control or management of persons engaged in the handling of food, not being himself a person carrying on a food business, shall be guilty of an offence against these regulations if he fails to take all reasonable steps to secure the compliance by any person under his control or management with any provision of the regulations which impose obligations on a person engaged in the handling of food.
(4) Section 113 (which relates to a contravention due to some person other than the person charged), section 115(2) (which relates to conditions under which a warranty may be pleaded as a defence) and section 116 (which relates to offences in relation to warranties and certificates of analysis) of the Act shall apply for the purposes of these regulations in references therein to proceedings taken or brought under the Act shall include references to proceedings taken or brought for an offence under these regulations.

Notes to Regulation 29

29(1) This especially refers to the provisions of Regulation 10 which require food handlers to take certain precautions. If the food handler, for example, smokes or spits whilst handling food, or does not maintain clean hands, then he is guilty of an offence.

29(2)(a) Other than where the food handler is responsible, the person carrying on the food business is guilty of an offence if the requirements of the Regulations generally are contravened. This would usually be where the condition of premises and equipment are involved.

29(2)(b) The person carrying on the business can be guilty of an offence if he condones or does nothing to prevent an offence by a food handler as mentioned in 29(1) above. In practice, therefore, if a supervisor condones a food handler smoking or failing to keep hands clean he/she too may be guilty of an offence.

29(3) & (4) These merely extend the responsibility set out in 29(2) above and sets out possible defences.

Regulation 30
Penalties
30 Any person guilty of an offence against these regulations shall be [liable –
- (a) on summary conviction, to a fine not exceeding {£2000}*; and
- (b) on conviction or indictment, to a fine or imprisonment for a term not exceeding two years or both.]

* The amount of fine shown in curly brackets represents an amendment made by the Food (Revision of Penalties) Regulations 1985 (S.I. 1985 No. 67).

Note to Regulation 30

The penalties have been increased substantially since 1970. The maximum of £2000 on summary conviction applies in theory to each offence of which a person is found guilty.

PART VI

SHIPS

Regulation 31
Application and enforcement
31 (1) The provisions of these regulations shall apply in relation to ships, and to food businesses carried on in ships, as they apply in relation to food premises and to food businesses carried on therein, subject to the modifications and further provisions specified in this regulation and in regulation 32.
(2) Subject to paragraph (3) of this regulation, the authority responsible for enforcing and executing the provisions of these regulations in relation to ships shall be each port health authority, in relation to any ships in their district.
(3) In relation to a ship requiring annual survey pursuant to section 271 of the Merchant Shipping Act 1894, the authority responsible for enforcing and executing the provisions as to structural and other requirements specified in paragraph (7) of this regulation shall be the port health authority for the port in which the survey is being, or was last, carried out or if there is no such port health authority, the local authority for the port.
(4) Except as otherwise provided in paragraphs (2) and (3) of this regulation each local authority will enforce and execute the provisions of these regulations in relation to any ship in their district.
(5) A local authority or port health authority shall furnish any authority responsible under paragraph (3) of this regulation with any information in their possession which will be likely to assist that authority in their duties.
(6) The person having command or charge of any ship described in paragraph (3) of this regulation shall, on being requested to do so, furnish any authorised officer of the authority responsible under that paragraph with the name of the authority in whose area the survey mentioned therein is being, or was last, carried out.
(7) The provisions referred to in paragaph (3) of this regulation are –
- (a) regulation 6 (food business not to be carried on at insanitary premises or place) and regulation 15 (cisterns for supplying water to food rooms);
- (b) so much of paragraphs (1) and (2) of regulation 16 (sanitary conveniences) as relates to the placing of sanitary conveniences and to the lighting and ventilation of rooms containing them; and
- (c) regulation 17 (water supply to be provided),

paragraphs (1) and (2) of regulation 18 (wash-hand basins to be provided),
regulation 20 (accommodation of clothing, etc.),
paragraphs (1) and (2) of regulation 21 (facilities for washing food and equipment),
regulation 22 (lighting of food rooms),
regulation 23 (ventilation of food rooms),
paragraph (1) of regulation 26 (provisions of adequate space for sorting food).

Regulation 32

Modification of the regulations in relation to ships

32 (1) For the purposes of the definition of 'food room' as contained in regulation 2(1), reference to any room shall be construed as references to any room or space.

(2) For the purposes of regulation 13(2), a food business which is carried on from or on a ship shall be deemed to be situated in the district or port health district in which the ship is for the time being moored.

(3) The reference in regulation 17(2)(b) to premises used for business of a similar class shall be construed as a reference to ships of a similar type.

(4) The appropriate authority for the purposes of regulation 28 shall be –

(a) in relation to any ship described in regulation 31(3), the port health authority or, if there is no port health authority, the local authority for the port in which the survey mentioned therein is being, or was last, carried out; and

(b) in relation to any other ship the authority for the time being responsible under regulation 31(2).

(5) The reference in regulation 28(5) to a person carrying on a food business shall be construed as a reference to the owner of a ship.

(6) The owner of a ship shall be guilty of an offence if as respects the food business carried on there any provision of the regualtions mentioned in regulation 31(7) is contravened.

PART VII

AGRICULTURAL ACTIVITIES

Regulation 33

33 (1) The provisions specified in paragraph (2) shall apply in relation to premises comprised in an agricultural unit (within the meaning of section 109(2) of the Agriculture Act 1947) and in which is carried on the business of packing or storing eggs, fruit or vegetables, as they apply in relation to food premises and to food businesses carried on there.

(2) The provisions referred to in paragraph (1) are –

regulation 7 (cleanliness of articles or equipment),
paragraphs (a) and (b) of and the proviso to regulation 9 (food to be

protected from risk of contamination),
regulation 10 (personal cleanliness),
regulation 12 (carriage and wrapping of food),
regulation 13 (person suffering from certain infections),
regulation 17 (water supply to be provided).

SCHEDULE **Regulation 2(1)**

FOOD NOT TO BE REGARDED AS OPEN FOOD

(1) *Food*	(2) *Mode of wrapping or enclosure*
Butter, margarine and cooking fat	Any total enclosure of greaseproof paper or foil.
Meat, except meat which has been cooked or otherwise prepared for sale by any similar process	Any total wrapping of mutton cloth, hessian, jute, paper or film.
Fish	Any total enclosure of greaseproof paper or film.
Vegetables	Any box, bag, sack, string container or pliable film pack.
Flour confectionery and bakery goods	Any total enclosure.
Ice-cream	Any total greaseproof enclosure of paper, foil, film, cardboard, carton, cup or similar wrapping.
Ice lollies	Any total greaseproof enclosure of paper, foil, film or similar wrapping; or any bag made of such materials to contain the ice lolly and which may or may not be sealed at the end from which the stick or holder protrudes.

Food Hygiene (Amendment) Regulations 1990

Temperature Control of Certain Foods

Largely as a reaction to the public outcry about Salmonellosis and Listeriosis in food in the late 1980s the UK Government introduced the Food Hygiene (Amendment) Regulations 1990. The aim of the new Regulations is to secure consistent standards of temperature control throughout the food chain (from production to retail sale). Because of the major investment in new refrigeration equipment which the food trade have had to make in order to comply with the new rules, the Government decided to phase them in over 2 years. We will only deal with the ultimate requirements which will take effect from 1 April 1993. From that date the following types of food will have to be stored, transported and displayed *at or below 5°C*:-

- Mould ripened soft cheese which has been cut from the whole cheese.
- Cooked products containing meat, fish, eggs (or their substitutes), cheese, cereals, pulses and vegetables which are intended to be eaten without reheating, e.g. pâté, pies, egg mayonnaise, cooked meats
- Cured or smoked fish
- Cured or smoked meat
- Pasta salad
- Sandwiches, filled rolls and bread products containing soft cheese, smoked or cured fish or meat, not intended for sale within 24 hours.

The following foods will have to be stored, transported and displayed *at or below 8°C*:-

- Mould ripened soft cheese (whole)
- Cooked products intended for further heating before eating, e.g. pizzas, ready-made meals
- Dairy-based desserts with a pH over 4.5, e.g. fromage frais, mousse
- Prepared vegetable salads
- Uncooked or partly cooked pastry and dough products containing meat, fish or their substitutes, e.g. pizzas
- Sandwiches, filled rolls and bread products containing any other relevant foods (not covered by 5°C) and intended to be sold within 24 hours
- Dairy cream cakes

These Regulations apply to all food traders, including market stallholders and mobile vehicles, snack bars and outdoor caterers. The Local Authority Environmental Health Officers are responsible for enforcing the Regulations and are empowered to take temperature readings, ask for copies of recording charts, etc. All food proprietors need to equip their premises and vehicles with refrigeration equipment which can maintain these low temperatures and to use thermometers which will accurately record the temperature of the food.

The authors are surprised that a wide range of "at risk" foods such as cooked pies, pasties and sausage rolls which are intended to be sold on the day of production or the following day are exempt from temperature controls. In view of the potential for food poisoning organisms to multiply in a few hours (see pp. 50–53) we urge all proprietors and retailers of such products to refrigerate these products at all times regardless of the law.

Similarly, any food which is intended to be sold or eaten within 2 hours (if hot) or 4 hours (if cold) of being made does not legally need to be kept at the stipulated temperatures. This means that restaurant sweet trolleys, cheese boards and pub snack cabinets need not be chilled or heated. However, in such cases only a minimum display is permitted of each type of food being sold/offered. We nonetheless reiterate our view that good practice demands the highest standards of temperature control.

As far as hot food is concerned, the Regulations quite simply require a minimum temperature of 63°C to be maintained in the vehicle or on the premises for all foods listed on the previous pages if they are to be served hot (except within 2 hours of being produced).

Since January 1991 all quick frozen foods (except ice-cream) must be stored, transported and displayed for sale at a temperature of −18°C. These foods must be labelled with basic information relating to the shelf-life of the product, storage instructions and conditions of use. The Regulations are designed to maintain the quality of quick frozen foods.

THE FOOD SAFETY ACT 1990: Relevant Sections with Notes

This Act is the result of a major review of the legislation which was a collection of 7 Acts stretching back over 30 years. The UK Government also had to change its approach to food law because of the harmonisation programme required by the European Community's Single Market initiative. This means that by 1992 all Member States must have matching legislation and controls which do not restrict trade between each other.

The new Act recognises the modern methods of food production and distribution; provides more efficient powers to deal with unfit food and unhygienic food premises and introduces the concept of training for food handlers for the first time. The definition of food business covers every conceivable thing done to food in the course of producing, storing, delivering, selling, importing or exporting it – in other words, from the farm to the table. The contents of the Act can be summarised as follows:

Part I Definitions and responsibilities for enforcement.

Part II Powers to ensure food safety – methods of enforcement – consumer protection – power to make regulations for hygiene, registration, training – defences.

Part III Appointment of Public Analyst – sampling – powers of entry – appeals.

Part IV Codes of Practice and miscellaneous matters.

We decided to reproduce at this point a precis of certain sections of the Act which refer especially to food hygiene.

Section 9
Inspection and Seizure of Suspected Food
An Authorised Officer of a Local Authority can inspect, seize and detain suspected food if the Officer considers that the food does not conform to food safety requirements or is likely to cause food poisoning. A Justice of the Peace must decide whether the food is unfit for human consumption. If a JP refuses to condemn the food, the Local Authority is liable to pay compensation to the owner.

Section 10
Improvement Notices
An Authorised Officer can serve an "Improvement Notice" where he has reasonable grounds for believing that the Proprietor of a food business is failing to comply with the Regulations (e.g. Food Hygiene Regulations). The Improvement Notice must state:

(a) The Officer's grounds for believing that the Proprietor is failing to comply with the Regulations;
(b) The precise reasons why the Regulations are being contravened;
(c) The measures which need to be taken to rectify the problem/criticism and the time within which the Proprietor must complete the work.

Local Authorities have been advised to consider any request for an extension of time in order to comply with an Improvement Notice. There is a right of appeal against the service of an Improvement Notice by way of a complaint to the local Magistrates Court within the period stated in the Notice or one month if that is shorter. The service of an Improvement Notice does not preclude a Local Authority from issuing a summons for contravening one or more of the relevant Regulations. A Notice is likely to be served if the Environmental Health Officer wishes to ensure that serious matters are remedied quickly.

Section 11
Prohibition Orders
This power enables a Local Authority to apply to a Magistrates Court for a Prohibition Order to prevent a piece of equipment, a process or the complete premises being used for food production where there is a serious risk of injury to health. Once the health risk is removed the Local Authority must apply to the Court for the Order to be lifted.
An Order can also be applied by the Court, on conviction for an offence, to the Manager or Proprietor of a food business which would prohibit that individual from working in a food business until the Order is lifted by the Court.

Section 12
Emergency Prohibition Notices
If an Environmental Health Officer believes that there is an imminent risk of injury to health because of a piece of equipment, a process or the premises as a whole, he may serve an Emergency Prohibition Notice. This has the effect of prohibiting the continued use of the equipment or premises. The Officer must then apply to the Magistrates Court within 3 days for an Emergency Prohibition Order. The Notice should explain the reasons for serving the Notice and specify the measures required to remedy the defects. The Notice would usually be served personally by the Officer on the Proprietor or the senior member of staff. The Proprietor must be given details of the rights to attend the Magistrates Court hearing.

If the Magistrates Court decides to confirm the Notice by making an Emergency Prohibition Order, the Order must be displayed on the premises so that the public can easily read it. A similar provision applies to the making of a Prohibition Order by a Court when a business has been prosecuted for breaching the Hygiene Regulations and the Court feels that public health is at risk.

The Proprietor can apply to the Local Authority for the Prohibition Order to be removed once the defects have been remedied and the Environmental Health Officer is satisfied with the remedial works. There are procedures to enable a Proprietor to appeal against a Local Authority's refusal to remove a Prohibition Order and on the contrary for a Proprietor to be prosecuted for ignoring the terms of a Prohibition Order. If a Local Authority's Officer serves an Emergency Prohibition Notice which is not upheld by the Court the

Proprietor can claim compensation for losses incurred whilst the business was closed.

The Court also has the power to prohibit the Proprietor or Manager of a business from running another food business. This would probably be considered following two or more separate convictions for contravening the Hygiene Regulations. After a minimum period of 6 months the individual can apply to the Court for the Order to be lifted.

Section 32

Powers of Entry

An Authorised Officer of the Council is entitled to enter any food premises at all reasonable hours on production of an authorisation if it is requested; before entering domestic premises an Officer must give 24 hours notice unless a Warrant has been obtained from the Court. Officers are empowered to inspect everything including files, interview personnel and take photographic and video evidence. It is an offence to obstruct an Officer in the course of his duty. On the other hand, it is unlawful for an Officer to disclose information about a food business obtained whilst performing his or her statutory duties.

Section 7

Anyone who renders food injurious to health with intent that it should be sold for human consumption is liable to prosecution.

Section 8

Similarly, anyone who supplies food for human consumption which has been rendered injurious to health, or is unfit for human consumption or is so contaminated that it is not suitable for use for human consumption, is liable to prosecution.

Section 14

Makes it an offence to supply to the purchasers prejudice food which is not of the nature or substance or quality demanded by the purchaser.

The maximum fine a Magistrates Court can impose for any of these offences is £20,000 per offence.

Section 19

Registration of Food Businesses

This enables the Minister to make Regulations which came into force on 1st July 1991 requiring premises, including certain vehicles and stalls, used for food businesses to be registered with the Local Authority. The main purpose is to assist the Council with identifying the food premises in their area to enable it to organise inspections effectively and to provide up to four weeks notice of a new food business opening. Registration is free of charge and a Local Authority cannot refuse to register premises.

From 1 November 1991 it is an offence to operate a food business from premises which are not registered. There are various exemptions from the registration requirements such as premises only used occasionally for 'one-off' events; premises which are already registered or licensed such as Slaughterhouses and Dairies; ships unless they are permanently moored and individual stalls which operate only within an established market which will be registered as a whole.

Section 23
Training Courses for Food Handlers
By the autumn of 1991 there will be Regulations governing the training requirements for food handlers.

Codes of Practice have been published by the Department of Health and the Ministry of Agriculture, Fisheries and Food for the guidance of Local Authorities and their Enforcement Officers. The Codes recognise that food safety is no longer just a local enforcement matter because many manufacturers and retailers operate on a national and international scale and they are sometimes unwilling to accept the local officials interpretation of the legislation.

Codes of Practice have been issued to Food Authorities to try to secure greater uniformity of enforcement of the new laws. Although the Codes have been written for Enforcement Officers they can be purchased from Her Majesty's Stationery Office by any one who is interested in such matters as food inspection procedures, sampling, training, food hygiene inspections and related subjects.

Defence of Due Diligence

Through the Food Safety Act 1990 there is a clearer definition of the various defences that a defendant might rely upon if legal proceedings are instituted by an enforcement authority. Though most traders are law abiding people, very many are not familiar with the details of the legislation and it is important that they should know what defences are available to them. Certain offences – known as absolute offences – are where there is no defence for the person accused to indicate that . . . he did not intend to break the law. The fact that there is clear evidence of a contravention is sufficient for a conviction to be inevitable.

On the other hand, there are many circumstances where a defendant can demonstrate all good intentions in the course of his business yet where a contravention has emerged. In mitigation, therefore, the defendant can use various aspects of . . . due diligence . . . which in effect are areas of defence that he might rely upon given that he did not commit any contravention knowingly and other than in good faith.

The areas of due diligence, though complex, are intended to help a defendant, and food traders who may find themselves at variance with the food authorities should pay due regard to how they might help in any defence. It must be stressed that the food trader must prove to the Court that, on the balance of probabilities, he has taken all reasonable precautions and exercised all due diligence. Written records of his system and controls – specifications, training records, instructions, cleaning regimes and corrective action – are all important evidence. Above all the Court will scrutinise the methods used to secure proper standards of hygiene, safety and food composition whenever due diligence is claimed.

Contaminated Food

One result of the lack of attention to food hygiene is the increased likelihood of the food being contaminated and, therefore, failing to reach or maintain the accepted standard. In legal terminology the Food Safety Act 1990 requires food to be sold or offered for sale without prejudice to the purchaser by reason of its nature, substance and quality.

Without going into too much detail the courts have held that the person or company which sells the product is responsible for ensuring that the commodity is up to the required standard unless they can produce a warranty from the manufacturer or supplier of the product who accepts that liability. The presence of a 'foreign body' i.e. an article or substance which is not normally present in the product is considered to be not of the substance (examples: a cigarette end in a loaf of bread, a nail in a boiled sweet or a piece of glass in a bun). A piece of cod sold as halibut, on the other hand, would be not of the nature demanded.

There are many 'horror' stories which can be used to illustrate the range of foreign bodies which have been found in food by consumers. One recent example concerned the end of a human finger which was in some tossed salad bought with a 'take-home' pizza! Other examples can be found in the list taken from the Institution of Environmental Health Officers recent Annual Reports for England and Wales (Table 1, pp. 45 & 46).

TABLE 1

Out of Condition and Unfit Food, Foreign Matter and Mould and Dirty Containers 1989/90

Type of food	*Extraneous matter*	*Unfit*	*Out of condition*	*Mouldy*	*Dirty bottles or containers*
Fresh food					
Eggs	70	127	252	21	–
Fish	323	129	227	16	–
Fruit and vegetables	600	295	383	390	2
Meat (inc. frozen)	751	941	1,083	82	16
Milk	1,473	246	650	36	1,763
Manufactured food					
Bread and confectionery	3,335	220	527	804	38
Biscuits	414	25	89	14	1
Butter, margarine & cooking fats	155	31	131	67	3
Cocoa and chocolate	395	37	158	15	1
Fruit and vegetables (frozen)	496	29	75	17	2
Fruit and vegetables (canned, bottled, dried)	2,285	197	449	148	41
Jams, marmalade, jellies, etc.	334	20	44	56	1
Meat and fish products (frozen)	493	139	219	59	2
Meat and fish products (other processed)	2,663	619	1,008	548	16
Milk products	1,086	292	631	402	48
Sugar confectionery	1,073	122	265	63	3
Tea and coffee	129	4	20	3	1

(continued overleaf)

Table 1 (*continued*)

Type of food	*Extraneous matter*	*Unfit*	*Out of condition*	*Mouldy*	*Dirty bottles or containers*
Drink					
Beer	88	60	52	3	3
Soft drinks	473	110	323	75	24
Spirits	21	–	19	4	–
Wines, cider, perry	109	13	62	6	1
Other food and drink	2,464	420	804	181	28
Totals	19,230	4,076	7,471	3,010	1,993

Reproduced from the Annual Report of the Institution of Environmental Health Officers with permission.

Only a small proportion of all such complaints are received by the Environmental Health Departments of local authorities. The vast majority of consumers just throw the offending food away, some take it back to the shop or supermarket and receive an apology and a replacement, whilst others respond to the manufacturer's request to return it to the factory or head office.

If the local authority receives the complaint its officers will almost always investigate the cause of the problem, contact the officers of the authority where the food was produced and quite often prosecute the retailer or manufacturer for committing an offence for which the maximum fine is currently £2000. In order to proceed the council must be satisfied with the complainant's evidence as to the purchase and subsequent discovery of the offending object or contamination. Their willingness to be a witness in court is also important.

The other aspect of quality control which is exercised by the authorities concerns the numerous regulations about composition of food and these are enforced by the Trading Standards Officers employed by county councils, London boroughs and Metropolitan boroughs in England and Wales. In Scotland the district councils do the work through their health departments. These officers are responsible for monitoring the composition and labelling of all home produced and imported food to ensure that there is no attempted fraud. All sorts of attempts have been made over the years to cheat the public by watering down milk and scotch or substituting margarine for butter and the chemists tend to be more and more skilful at their work. Sometimes it can go seriously wrong and people die as with the contaminated cooking oil in Spain. The public analysts are chemists who are specially employed to check on all these aspects of quality assurance.

Of course the food trade is not generally unscrupulous, indeed many firms take great care to produce food of the highest quality and use their own quality control staff to monitor their products at all stages, from the farm to the factory and to the retailer. Many smaller companies use the services of specialist laboratories to sample the products and advise them on quality control matters.

Another important task performed by local councils concerns the inspection of fresh meat and poultry. All food animals which are slaughtered for human consumption must be treated humanely and slaughtered hygienically. The meat and edible offal (liver, lungs, heart and kidneys) must be inspected for evidence of disease or harmful conditions and passed as fit for human consumption or rejected. Environmental Health Officers and Authorised Meat Inspectors carry out this work at about 600 licensed abattoirs/slaughterhouses in the United Kingdom. The reader will appreciate the importance of both quality control and good hygienic practices despite the fairly unpleasant duties which slaughtering animals involves. Enormous quantities of poultry are slaughtered and the trade takes prime responsibility for quality control with supervision from Poultry Meat Inspectors and Veterinary Surgeons employed by the local council.

To complete the picture we must mention the work of the Port Health Officers who work at the sea ports and airports in the United Kingdom alongside H.M. Customs and Excise Officers to check the quality of all imported food. This is normally a 24-hour-year round task which is rarely mentioned or appreciated as part of the system of official surveillance of the food we eat.

Chapter 2

Food Borne Illness

Food poisoning has been recognised as a disease of man since the days of Hippocrates (460–377 BC). Murder by poisoning was rife during the Roman Empire, oysters being a popular vehicle for removing the unwanted. In the Middle Ages poisoning was so common that official food tasters were familiar members of all Royal Courts. The sale of diseased and contaminated food was commonplace until the introduction of sanitary measures during the nineteenth century. These were slowly developed at the end of the last century and the early part of this century into the food inspection and hygiene system we operate in Britain today.

In 1990 it was estimated that food borne illness caused the loss of 8 million working days and food scares cost the UK food industry more than £350 million annually through plant closures and £250 million in lost sales.

In order to understand the different types of food poisoning, particularly of a bacterial origin, it is necessary to examine the basic fundamentals of bacteriology. Bacteria or germs in the popular sense of the word are an essential part of human life, as we would not live without them. The vast majority of bacteria are harmless, many are beneficial and indeed some are exploited by man in various industrial processes. Examples of this are in the treatment of sewage and the production of cheese, beer and yoghurt. Those which are responsible for causing illness are called pathogenic bacteria.

Bacteria differ in shape, size and habitat but unfortunately are invisible except under a powerful microscope; it is therefore impossible to identify the source of an infection either quickly or easily.

TEMPERATURE DANGER ZONES

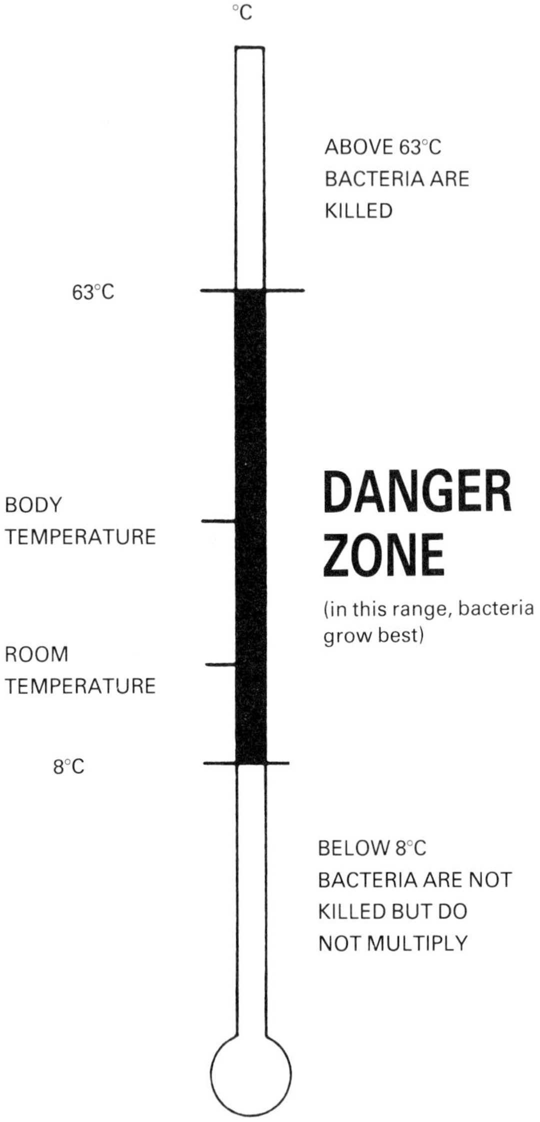

BACTERIAL BINARY FISSION

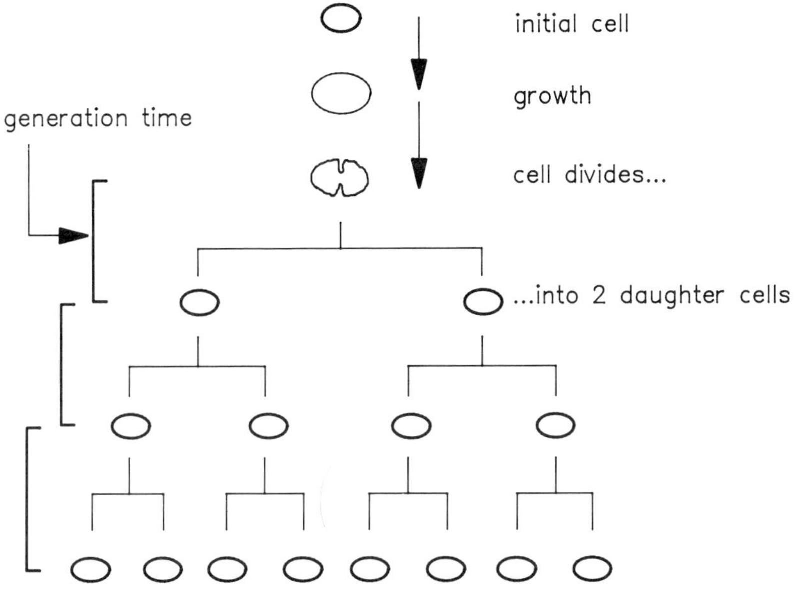

If generation time is 15 minutes...		
TIME	NUMBER OF CELLS	
0	1	1×10^{0}
1 hr	16	1.6×10^{1}
2 hrs	256	2.5×10^{2}
3 hrs	4,096	4×10^{3}
4 hrs	65,536	6.5×10^{4}
6 hrs	16,777,216	1.6×10^{7}
8 hrs	4,294,967,296	4.2×10^{9}

Food poisoning bacteria multiply at a phenomenal rate given certain conditions, the most important of these being:

1. Temperature (the 'Danger Zone' range) (see diagram on page 50)
2. Moisture
3. Nutrients (food)
4. Time

The acidity (pH) of the medium, its salt or sugar content and the presence or absence of air are also important factors determining the rate of bacterial growth.

There are types of bacteria which like cold temperatures, ambient temperatures and even temperatures up to 75°C but none survive the entire range. It is a common but erroneous belief that cold temperatures will kill bacteria – they are merely slowed down! Exposure to heat, on the other hand, will kill bacteria provided a sufficiently high temperature is maintained for long enough. Moisture is essential to all bacteria as their outer cell protoplasm contains a high percentage of water. This explains why the primitive method of preserving food was to dry it. All bacteria need food in some form, such as blood, serum, dirt, meat, eggs, etc. Bacteria can be classified according to their chemical status: i.e. whether they prefer acid, alkaline or neutral environments in which to live. Most bacteria thrive on acidic (meat and fruit) or neutral food substances. Finally, most bacteria dislike light, especially ultra violet light (radiation from the sun or artificially induced).

Bacteria reproduce by each cell dividing into two identical parts – a process known as *binary fission* (see diagram on page 51). The daughter cells then grow until they too reach the right size for division. Under optimal conditions this *generation time* may be as short as 10–12 minutes, hence many thousand cells may be produced in a few hours.

Four *phases of growth* are recognised in a population of bacteria:

Lag phase: Little or no multiplication occurs during this phase which can last for several hours. During that time the cells become accustomed to their environment, and having done this, they increase in size. Since they are fewer in number at this stage, they are easier to destroy. Because this is a phase when the bacteria are merely adapting to their new surroundings, it follows that the more suitable the food as a medium for bacterial growth, then the shorter the lag phase will be. The less 'accommodating' the medium then the longer will be the lag phase as the bacteria adapt to their surroundings.

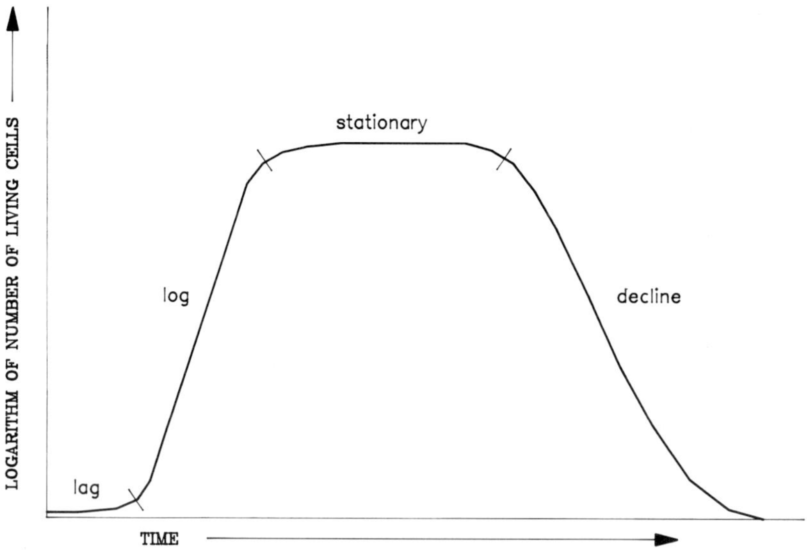

The phases of population growth

Log phase: During this period bacteria multiply rapidly at regular intervals until the maximum number is reached that can be supported by the medium. If you prepare a graph and plot the logarithm of the number of bacteria against time, it usually results in a straight line, hence the term log phase. This is the more dangerous phase, where substantial multiplications take place where food is held at warm temperatures.

Stationary phase: Growth slows down during this stage since the food supply is exhausted, the amount of waste matter produced by the bacteria has increased, the cells are overcrowded and so on. A stable situation is reached where the number of cells dying roughly equates with the number of new cells produced.

Decline phase: As the same suggests, as the environment becomes less hospitable to the bacteria – because of the lack of nutrient, build-up of toxic wastes, etc. – so the number of cells progressively age and die. The decline phase continues until such time as a fresh boost is given, e.g. when fresh food/medium is added.

Unfortunately some pathogenic bacteria can survive for up to 14 weeks out of contact with the human or animal body – just lying in dust or

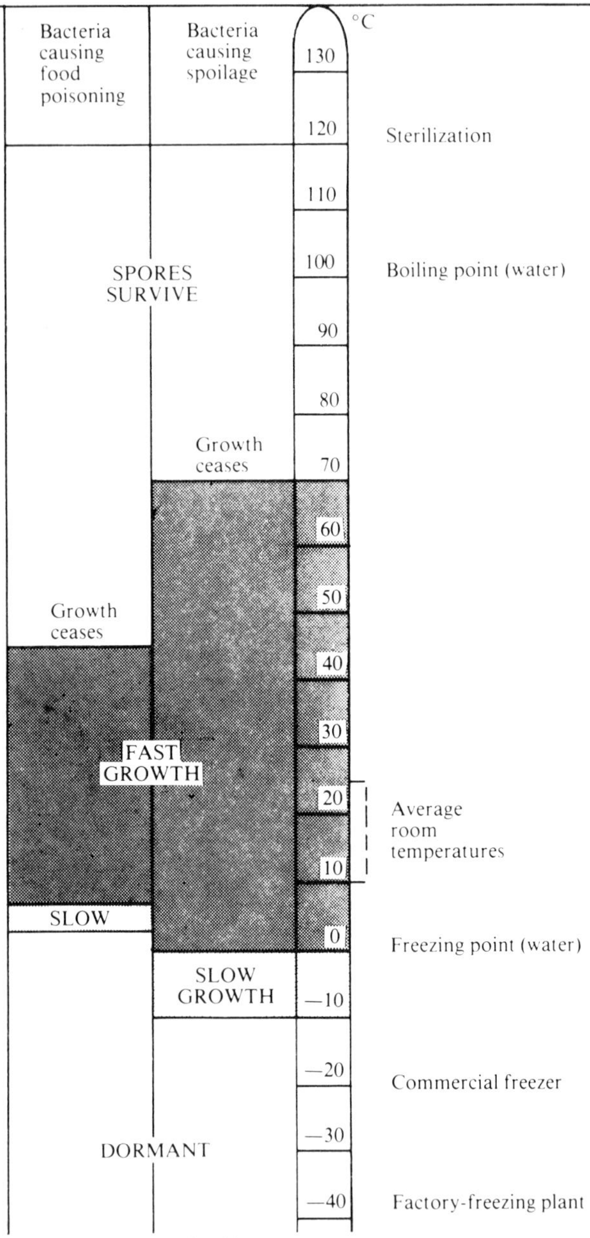

Influence of temperature on growth of bacteria

floating in the air. There are also certain bacteria which can produce spores which are particularly resistant. Tetanus and anthrax, for example, can live for several hundred years in the soil.

Some bacteria are harmful by producing poisons or toxins which cause illness in humans. These may be released from the cells (exotoxins) so that they mix with the surroundings. While they can be particularly lethal, heat rapidly kills them with the important exception of *Staphylococcus* exotoxin. On the other hand, endotoxins are produced within the bacterial cell and are not usually released until the germ dies. These endotoxins are more resistant to heat and tend to take much longer to cause illness because it takes longer for sufficient numbers to build up in the bowel.

Fortunately, pathogenic (harmful) bacteria represent less than two per cent of all species, and to cause disease there needs to be two important circumstances, namely:

1. lowering of body resistance; and
2. contact with the harmful bacteria and/or their toxins.

Our bodies operate a number of defensive systems starting with the unbroken skin, which is a complete barrier to bacteria. If the skin is grazed or cut then white blood cells attack the invading bacteria. If that fails then the lymph glands act as filters, so causing the familiar swelling when infection is present. If the bacteria get past the glands into the blood stream, they can be attacked by white blood cells in the blood vessels, liver or spleen. The mucous membrane linings to most organs also attack bacteria as do substances known as antibodies which are formed in the body to resist a particular disease organism by natural or artificial immunisation. One of the most difficult control problems concerns people who have been infected, recover (often after a mild illness) but are not free of the bacteria. For obvious reasons they are called 'carriers'. Thereafter such people may unknowingly continue to contaminate articles and food which subsequently can cause illness in other people.

There are six major groups of organisms responsible for bacterial food poisoning in Britain: *Salmonella, Staphylococcus, Clostridium, Bacillus cereus, Campylobacter* and *Listeria* (for illustrations of the food poisoning chains for *Salmonella*, *Staphylococcus aureus*, *Clostridium perfringens*, and *Campylobacter* see pages 59, 60, 61 and 62 respectively).

Salmonella

Salmonella organisms are intestinal bacteria found in humans, animals and birds and are widely distributed throughout the world. To date over two thousand different types have been identified. The table below gives an indication of the more common types of *Salmonella* known to cause food poisoning, together with their common hosts. *Salmonella*, together with *Campylobacter*, are by far the greatest cause of food poisoning in Great Britain, and in many other countries. Indeed, West Germany has a much higher incidence rate – around 50 cases per 100,000 population per year, as opposed to 16 cases per 100,000 in Britain. As can be seen from the table, *Salmonella* organisms are commonly associated with all food animals, animal feeding stuffs, domestic animals and vermin. Unfortunately the task of eradicating the infection from these sources is so daunting in terms of scale and cost, that it is unlikely to be tackled.

TABLE 1 Salmonella Hosts

Salmonella serotypes	*Host*
S. typhimurium	Rats, mice, dogs, cats, birds, ducks, turkeys, hens and their eggs, cattle, calves, pigs, sheep, game
S. enteritidis	Cows, calves, pigs, sheep, turkeys, ducks, water birds, rats, mice, hens and their eggs, feeding stuffs
S. panama	Poultry, calves, pigs, feeding stuffs
S. agona	Poultry, cattle, eggs, pigs, feeding stuffs
S. heidelberg	Poultry, cattle, eggs, pigs
S. virchow	Poultry, cattle, eggs, pigs, feeding stuffs
S. indiana	Poultry, pigs, feeding stuffs
S. hadar	Cattle, poultry, game, sheep, pigs, feeding stuffs

The lack of hygienic practices has contributed to the rapid spread of *Salmonella* infections from the live animal, raw meat and on to meat products through cross-contamination. Canned meats are reasonably safe, because efficient processing at high temperatures will destroy Salmonellae.

Pasteurised milk is safe, but untreated milk is still sold at the farm gate and this product has caused a number of outbreaks of *Salmonella* food

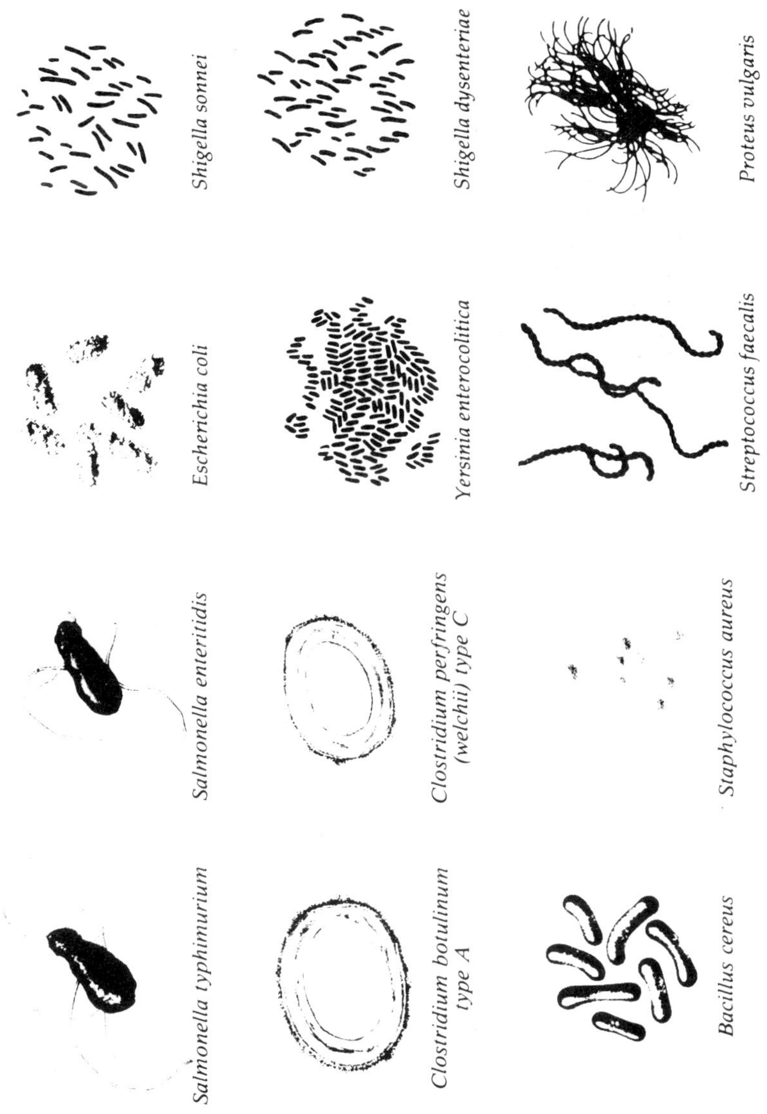

Artist's impression of some bacteria – drawings not to same scale (by permission of Lever Industrial Ltd)

poisoning in this country. The sale of untreated milk to shops, schools and catering establishments was banned from 1 May 1985 in England and Wales.

Duck's eggs are almost invariably contaminated with *Salmonella* and this is one of the main reasons for giving them an extended period of boiling before consumption. Hen's eggs are also likely to be infected and for some years Regulations have prohibited the importation of foreign or powdered egg unless it has been subjected to pasteurisation.

Staphylococci

It has been suggested that up to 50 per cent of all people carry *Staphylococcus aureus* in their noses, throats, ears and on their hands, so common is the bacterium. Outbreaks of food poisoning due to this organism are caused by poor hygienic practices which result in food being contaminated by people, for example, sneezing over it; allowing food to come into contact with uncovered septic cuts or boils; or from healthy carriers. The bacterial enterotoxins can resist temperatures of 121°C for 10 minutes, so they are not easily killed.

Clostridium perfringens

This particular species of bacteria is commonly found in human and animal faecal matter and is frequently present in low numbers in raw meat. The organism forms spores which may survive boiling for several hours. Outbreaks of *Clostridium perfringens* food poisoning are associated with meat which may have been insufficiently cooked, cooled slowly, stored at room temperature rather than in a refrigerator, and either eaten cold or inadequately reheated the following day. High standards of personal hygiene assist in minimising the chances of contamination. Prevention of this type of food poisoning depends entirely on the suppression of growth of the organisms in the meat after cooking. Meat should be thoroughly cooked, cooled rapidly and stored in a refrigerator. If reheating is essential, it must be done thoroughly.

Bacillus cereus

This is a spore-forming bacterium commonly found in soil, on vegetation and in many raw and processed foods. In Britain many outbreaks of food poisoning caused by *B. cereus* have involved fried rice from Chinese

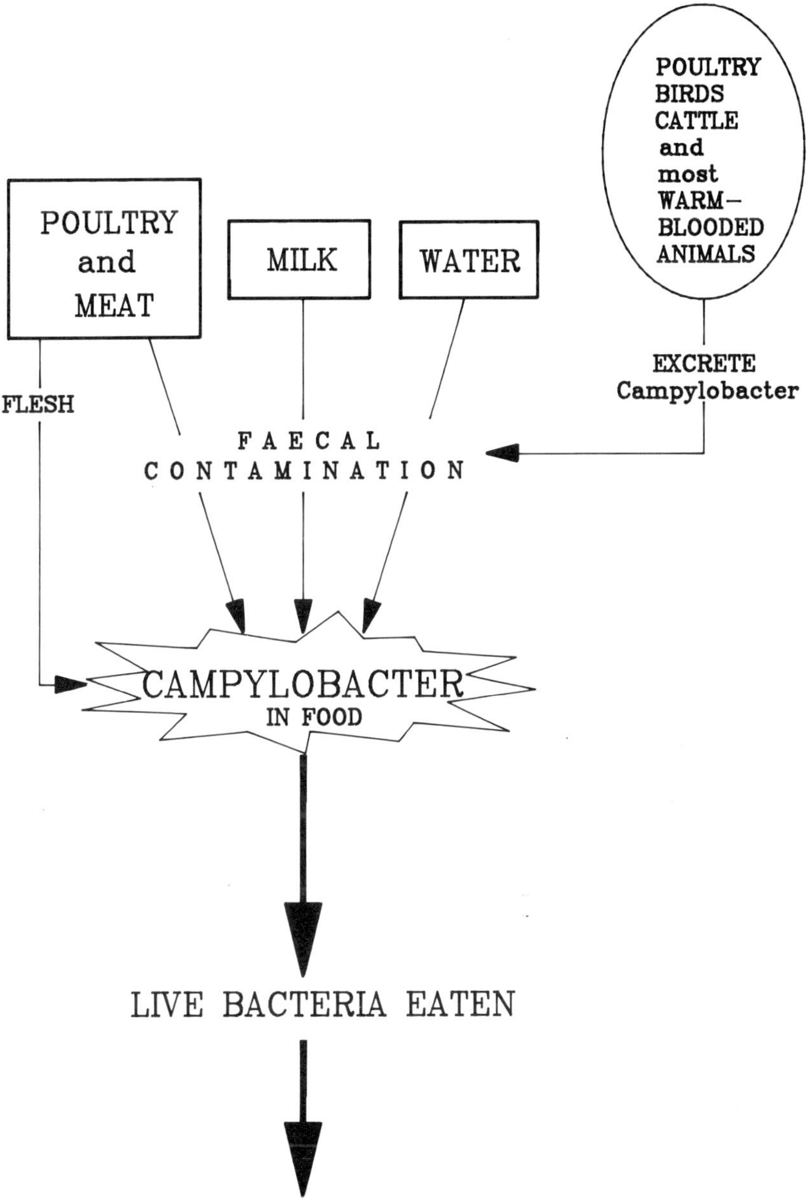

FOOD POISONING – CAMPYLOBACTER

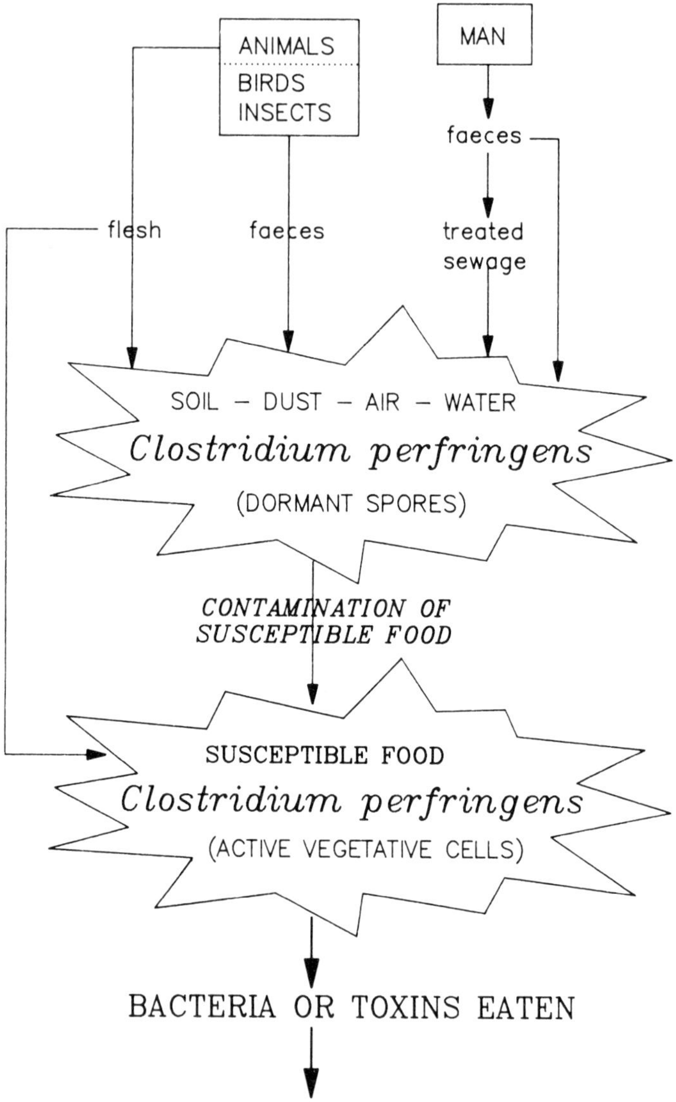

FOOD POISONING – CLOSTRIDIUM PERFRINGENS

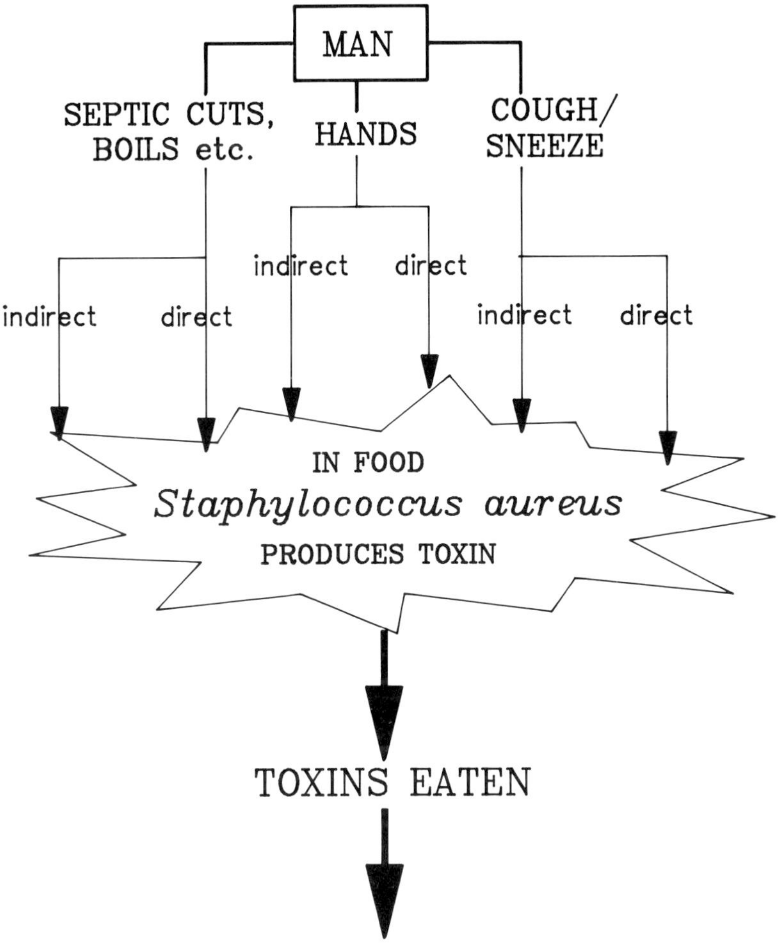

direct = direct contact of bacteria onto food
indirect = via surfaces, utensils etc. onto food

FOOD POISONING – STAPHYLOCOCCUS AUREUS

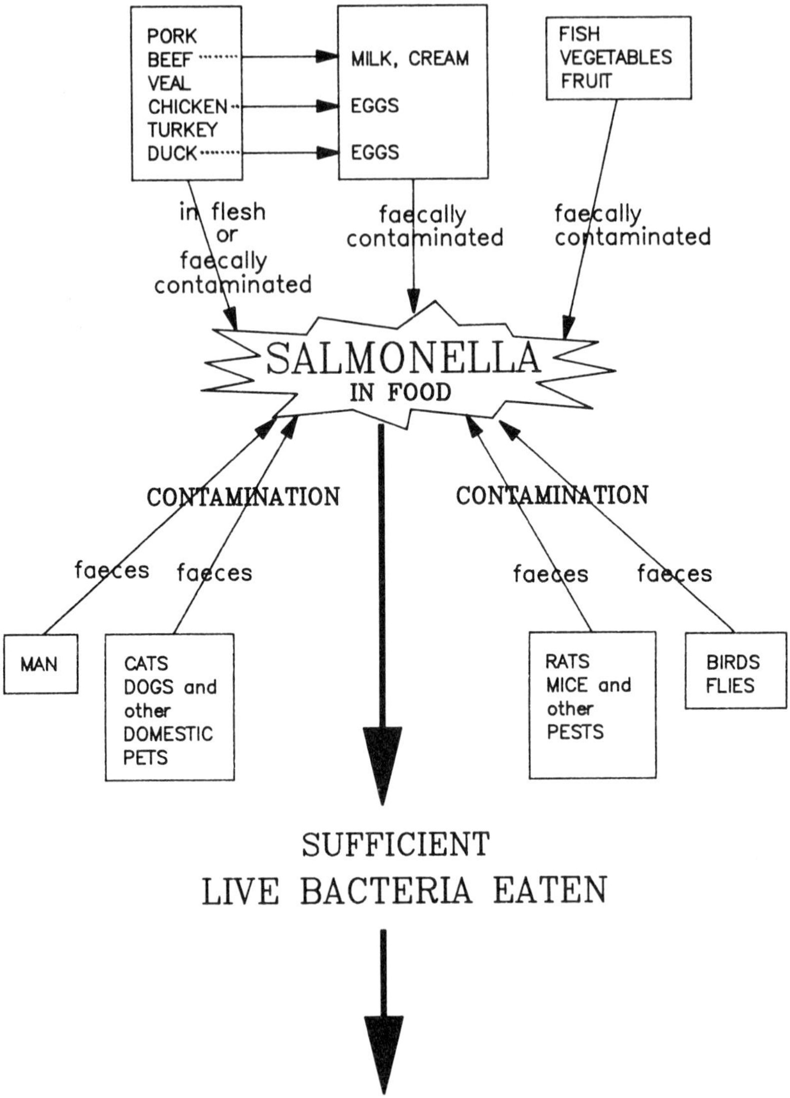

FOOD POISONING – SALMONELLA

restaurants. In these instances the incubation period varies, according to the quantity of infected food consumed, between thirty minutes and five hours. Symptoms include severe nausea and vomiting. The practice of boiling quantities of rice, subsequently allowing it to cool and remain at room temperature and then frying in beaten egg and oil appears to be the main cause of this form of poisoning. The answer is to boil the rice thoroughly and then chill it quickly and store in the refrigerator.

Vibrio parahaemolyticus

Vibrio parahaemolyticus is a common cause of food poisoning from seafoods. The organism is found in shellfish, fish and sea water worldwide. Whilst raw food is naturally suspect, cooked seafood which has been contaminated during processing is equally dangerous. The incubation period for the disease varies from six to twenty hours.

Campylobacter

These bacteria were known to cause several diseases in animals but since 1974 the organism has been identified as the cause of acute enteritis (headache, nausea, diarrhoea and severe abdominal pain) in large numbers of patients. The incubation period varies from two to seven days and the illness lasts from a few days to three weeks.

Campylobacters of the type that affect man have been isolated from cows, sheep, pigs, horses, chickens, cats, dogs, monkeys, gulls, pigeons and rodents. Raw water in streams, untreated milk, salad, raw mushrooms and sea food, and eggs have also been implicated in outbreaks of the illness in the UK and USA, but the food only acts as a conveyor of the organism as a passive carrier having been contaminated or infected. It is not strictly a food-poisoning organism. *Campylobacter* now causes more cases of gastrointestinal infections than *Salmonella* and it has been estimated that at least 3 million working days are lost in the United Kingdom each year due to this infection. Worse still it has been suggested that for every laboratory diagnosed case there are at least 10 others, i.e. 340,000 cases or more each year. Fortunately *Campylobacter* enteritis is not usually life threatening but it is a serious problem of ever increasing proportions. Unlike *Salmonella* the Campylobacters do not multiply in food but relatively small numbers cause infection if the food is not cooked sufficiently to kill the organisms.

Scombrotoxin poisoning

Another relatively modern cause of illness which results in sickness and diarrhoea is through the consumption of fish, particularly smoked mackerel, although sprats, tuna and whitebait, and canned sardines and pilchards have also been implicated. The illness is attributed to high levels of histamine in the fish flesh. Normal levels are less than 5 mg per 100 grams (0.0002oz per 3.5oz) and levels of 20 mg (0.0007oz) or more have been known to cause illness. The fish industry has been taking steps to maintain a careful control over temperatures at all stages of processing and transportation.

TABLE 2 Food Poisoning Characteristics

Organism	*Average incubation period*	*Symptoms*	*Average duration*	*Mortality rate*
Salmonella	12–24 hours Usually 18–24 hours	Nausea (with or without headache), abdominal pain, vomiting, diarrhoea, fever	1–7 days, but may last several weeks	Low 1.0%
Staphylococcus aureus	½–6 hours	Nausea, frequent vomiting, abdominal pain, persistent diarrhoea, prostration	Usually 6–24 hours after onset	Low 0.2%
Cl. perfringens	8 hours up to 24 hours	Diarrhoea, vomiting and abdominal cramp	2 days	Low

(continued opposite)

Organism	*Average incubation period*	*Symptoms*	*Average duration*	*Mortality rate*
B.cereus	1–6 hours	Nausea and vomiting	1–2 days	Nil
Campylobacter	1–7 days usually 2–4 days	Acute diarrhoea, headache, fever, muscle pain	7–14 days or longer	Nil
Listeria monocytogenes	4–21 days	Influenza-like meningitis with septicaemia	Variable	25%
Vibrio para-haemolyticus	Usually 12–18 hours	Diarrhoea, abdominal pain, vomiting	2–5 days	Nil

Botulism

Fortunately this serious disease is rare in Britain. However the death of two pensioners in Birmingham in 1978, following a canned salmon and salad meal, reminded everyone that the risk is still there. In 1989 another outbreak was traced to hazelnut purée used to flavour yoghurt and 27 people were hospitalised and one person died. Outbreaks in 1922 (eight fishermen died after eating duck paste), 1935, 1947 and 1955, reveal the extent of botulism in the UK. However many cases occur around the world, particularly in the USSR and USA, as a result of home canning of vegetables and fish. *Clostridium botulinum* is widespread in the soil and it is the cause of disease in animals and birds throughout the world. Fortunately some types of the organism only affect animals and not humans. The organism produces heat resistant spores which can only be destroyed by prolonged heat treatment; they are also affected by the pH of the food being processed. Faulty canning or processing leads to the risk of illness, which is caused by a potent exotoxin. In the Birmingham incident, the salmon was processed in Alaska. As no other people were affected before the batch of nearly 500,000 cans were traced and withdrawn from sale, it is likely that a minute hole found in the can was the cause of the contamination and not the failure of the heat treatment.

Listeria monocytogenes

Listeria monocytogenes is a dangerous pathogen causing septicaemia and meningitis in infants, pregnant women and elderly people. It can cause deaths in up to 30% of those affected depending on how long it takes to diagnose the cause of the symptoms. The organism is widely distributed throughout the environment in soil, water, vegetation and animals. It was first isolated in 1926 but started to be reported in increasing numbers from 1976 (39 cases), 1987 (259 cases) and 1989 (244 cases) in the United Kingdom. The organism can grow at low temperatures (+2.5°C) and consequently chilled foods can become a health risk unless they are subjected to sufficiently high temperatures for at least the following periods: 65°C – 40 seconds; 75°C – 10 seconds.

There have been serious outbreaks in Canada – coleslaw, 41 cases (9 deaths) 1981; United States of America – Mexican soft cheese, 108 cases (34 deaths) 1985; Switzerland – vaccherin Mont D'or cheese (60 deaths) 1988, all of which reflected poor manufacturing practices. A survey of chilled foods by the Public Health Laboratory Service in 1989 revealed that 18% of chilled meals, mainly poultry, were contaminated with *Listeria* and 12% of pre-cooked ready-to-eat poultry dishes were also contaminated.

Yersinia enterocolitica

This organism is also found in chilled foods with infection more common in the autumn and winter months. The main symptoms are diarrhoea and severe abdominal pain similar to appendicitis. It has been isolated from raw and pasteurised milk, fresh and synthetic cream cakes, ice-cream, liquid eggs, vegetables, cooked prawns, mackerel and many raw meat products, particularly pork.

Viruses

An increasing number of food poisoning cases are caused by viruses rather than by bacteria or toxins. Unfortunately, the laboratory diagnosis of viruses is very difficult and expensive and consequently the experts at

TABLE 3
Cases of Bacterial Food Poisoning and Salmonella Infection

According to year and causal agent

Salmonellas			*Clostridium perfringens*		*Staphylococcus aureus*		*Bacillus cereus*		*Vibrio parahaemolyticus*		*Other organisms*		*All bacterial causes*
Year	*No.*	*%*	*No.*	*%*	*No.*	*%*	*No.*	*%*	*No.*	*%*	*No.*	*%*	*No.*
1970	6,848	79	1,263	15	523	6	–	–	–	–	–	–	8,634
1971	6,784	84	978	12	302	4	15	–	–	–	–	–	8,079
1972	4,849	81	1,026	17	116	2	16	–	13	–	–	–	6,020
1973	6,871	80	1,311	15	168	2	66	1	17	–	141	2	8,574
1974	5,663	66	2,769	32	103	1	51	1	5	–	–	–	8,591
1975	8,894	74	2,418	20	443	4	82	1	96	1	10	–	11,943
1976	7,465	68	2,924	27	510	5	54	–	44	–	–	–	10,997
1977	6,501	71	2,576	28	81	1	37	–	9	–	–	–	9,204
1978	9,086	86	1,042	10	301	3	143	1	9	–	9	–	10,590
1979	9,912	83	1,607	14	328	3	22	–	6	–	6	–	11,881
1980	9,540	88	1,056	10	189	2	64	–	–	–	7	–	10,856
1981	9,532	89	918	9	143	1	72	–	–	–	–	–	10,665
1982	11,099	87	1,455	11	89	1	41	–	–	–	–	–	12,684
1983	13,250	87	1,624	11	160	1	134	0.8	–	–	–	–	15,163
1984	13,201	86	1,716	11	181	1	214	1.5	–	–	76	0.5	15,312
1985	11,172	86	1,466	11	118	1	81	0.7	12	–	–	–	12,837
1986	14,177	93	906	6	76	0.5	65	0.5	15	–	–	–	15,244
1987	16,991	91.5	1,266	6.5	176	1	137	0.7	18	–	–	–	18,572
1988	23,200	93.6	1,312	5	111	0.4	418	1.0	5	–	–	–	24,941
1989	25,831						Other details						
1990	34,552						not available at date of publication						

the Public Health Laboratories are frequently unable to confirm the precise cause of the illness. One such virus is *Norwalk* which causes winter vomiting disease and is responsible for numerous food poisoning-type outbreaks. The virus thrives in refrigerators and chilled display units but it is killed by heat, so cold food is the most vulnerable host. The modern open buffet bars in self-service restaurants and hotels are particularly vulnerable to this virus. Fortunately the symptoms of nausea, sickness and mild diarrhoea are relatively short lived. In two outbreaks in 1987 over 800 people in England and Wales were affected after eating cockles. The contamination of foods by faecally soiled hands is the most common mode of infection.

Food poisoning can be fatal, especially in the young and the elderly. The symptoms are very unpleasant in most instances; severe vomiting and stomach pains are frequently experienced and are commonly mistaken for appendicitis or even heart attacks. Diarrhoea and headaches are almost always a feature of the illness. In 1988, 71 people died with *Salmonella* infection being the underlying cause.

Host foods

Readers will have already observed the classes of food identified with the various types of bacteria and it will probably suffice to list the most common 'danger' foods under broad headings.

TABLE 4 Foods Commonly Associated with Food Poisoning

Meat and meat products	*Dairy products*	*Other foods*
Beef	Milk	Fish
Veal	Cream	Crabs
Pork	Artificial cream	Oysters
Mutton	Cream cakes	Prawns
Chicken	Custard	Other shellfish
Duck	Cheese	Rice
Turkey	Eggs	Red kidney beans
Goose	Meringue	Eggs
Game	Ice-cream	Desiccated coconut
Rabbit	Mayonnaise	Black pepper
Meat Pies		Frogs legs
Ham and boiled bacon		Eels

(continued opposite)

Meat and meat products	*Dairy products*	*Other foods*
Sausages		Beansprouts
Canned meats		Yeast
Cooked meats		
Brawn		
Tripe		
Pâté		
Gravy and stock		

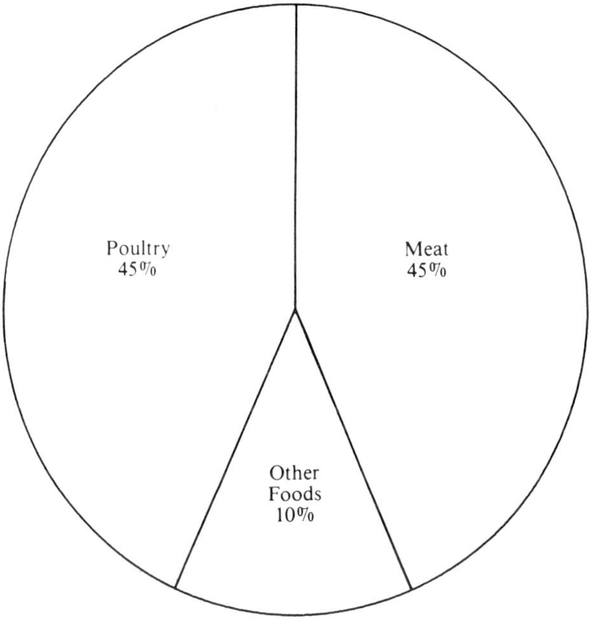

Proportions of sources of food poisoning , 1986–1988

Other types of food poisoning

Apart from bacteria, food poisoning can be caused by protozoan parasites, fungal or vegetable toxins or chemical contamination.

Illness can result from the consumption of meat, fish and shellfish infected with the cystic stage of one of several parasites. Pork containing the cysts of *Trichinella spiralis* is responsible for Trichinosis, which is a painful disease affecting the eyes and face. Thorough cooking of food will kill any such cysts.

A number of exotic fish notably from Japan, such as 'puffer fish' have occasionally been imported into this country and resulted in poisoning outbreaks, while the consumption of the roe of pike, sturgeon, carp, bream and turbot in the breeding season has also caused violent poisoning.

Vegetable poisoning is primarily due to the consumption of a poisonous fungus which is mistaken for a mushroom. This frequently results in death, especially if the death cap fungus is involved. Certain moulds can also produce lethal toxins – therefore avoid mouldy foods!

Poisonous weeds such as hemlock and monkshood have been mistaken for parsley and horseradish, while every country child is warned not to mistake deadly nightshade berries for cherries or redcurrants. Belladona leaves were mixed with comfrey leaves in a herbal tea imported from West Germany and several cases of poisoning occurred before the cause was traced and the tea was withdrawn from sale. The presence of oxalic acid in rhubarb leaves when used as a vegetable can lead to poisoning. Even potatoes have been the cause of illness due to the presence of excess glycoalkaloids in the skin of baked potatoes. In 1979, for instance, 78 children at a school in South London were poisoned by substandard potatoes with 17 requiring hospital treatment for apathy, drowsiness and visual disturbance. In recent years, red kidney beans have caused gastro-enteritis and vomiting within a few hours of consumption. The precise cause of the illness is unclear at present, although high levels of haemagglutinin were isolated from the beans.

Because of their close contact with the soil, many vegetables are potential carriers of pathogenic bacteria such as Salmonellae and Streptococci. A survey in the Netherlands revealed that 10 per cent of all vegetables sampled were contaminated by such bacteria. Cabbages, cauliflower, celery, courgettes, lettuce, paprika, aubergine and endives were all implicated. The results serve to emphasise the importance of careful washing and cooking and the avoidance of cross-contamination by hands, utensils, sinks and equipment.

Chemical poisoning is usually attributable to metallic concentrations in food following prolonged storage in cadmium, lead or copper pipes or containers. This is a particular problem with acid foods such as fruit,

Allergy

tomatoes and vinegar-based products. Consumption of contaminated food is likely to result in severe vomiting within two minutes to two hours. Food which has been contaminated with pesticides might also give rise to food poisoning type symptoms if eaten.

Some people are known to be allergic to certain food such as plums, strawberries, oysters or eggs; consumption of these will cause food poisoning type symptoms of sickness, nausea and headache, often accompanied by a skin rash. Once the sensitive food has been identified the only precaution is to avoid eating it.

Methods of preservation

One age-old method of prolonging the shelf life of food has been the preservation of a variety of foods by drying. This originated with natural drying in the sun which removed the moisture which was vital to the growth of bacteria. This has developed into the accelerated freeze drying of food today.

Preservation by curing in salt has a long history, and also smoking to dry out the flesh. Sugar is another substance which bacteria dislike and which is used successfully as a preservative. In more recent times chemicals such as sulphur dioxide, benzoic acid and sodium nitrite and gases such as carbon dioxide, have been used to store or preserve fruit in particular. Even antibiotics are being used in poultry, fish and cheese to prevent spoilage.

Canning was developed as a convenient packaging and preserving method during the nineteenth century and remains a popular and important part of the food industry. It should be realised that 'sterile' products have received sufficient heat treatment to destroy *C. botulinum* and most spoilage organisms and that not all canned foods are commercially sterile and may need refrigeration, e.g. large hams. Faulty canning can still, however, result in spoilage and waste.

The bottling of food has been carried out for many years, not least in connection with the pasteurisation and sterilisation of milk. In the former the milk is heated to a temperature that destroys any pathogenic organisms, whilst in sterilisation the milk is heated to a higher temperature which also destroys a range of food spoilage bacteria.

Sprays, lacquers and waxes are used for the preservation of fruits whilst vacuum packing is used for certain foods following heat treatment. One should not forget either the long established use of vinegar for pickling food.

Ultrasound and high pressure methods are also being used increasingly.

There has been enormous growth in the use of freezing techniques to preserve a wide variety of foodstuffs. One important factor which must not be overlooked in this last method is that freezing does not always kill bacteria but merely suspends the growth and reproduction until thawing occurs.

An all too common occurrence is food poisoning which has resulted from frozen poultry not being thawed properly prior to cooking. If the poultry is contaminated, unless it is thoroughly thawed, it will have the effect of countering the heat so that whilst the outer meat is cooked, the inner meat will not be subjected to a sufficiently high temperature to kill any bacteria present.

Irradiation of food has been the subject of controversy in the United Kingdom. However, the Food Safety Act 1990 enabled the Government to issue Regulations to control the technique and these became law in 1991. The Ministry of Agriculture, Fisheries and Food issue licences to food companies which satisfy the strict conditions laid down in the Food

(Control of Irradiation) Regulations 1990. Only the foods approved by the European Community Scientific Committee for Food as being suitable for irradiation from a public health standpoint can be subjected to the radiation process, namely fruit, vegetables, cereals, spices and condiments, fish and shellfish, fresh meat and poultry. There are many countries where irradiation of foodstuffs has been carried out for years, notably Holland, the United States of America and some in South America. The principal reason is to retard ripening or ageing whilst the food is being stored or transported for long distances. Exposing the food to ionising radiation basically kills most pathogenic and spoilage organisms but it does not make the food radioactive! Some food like cereals, nuts and spices are ideally suited to this method of preservation, whilst others would be ruined. Unfortunately, there is no simple test to identify irradiated food so it must be clearly labelled and there is always the possibility of unscrupulous people deliberately withholding that information.

Reducing the risk of food poisoning

Other chapters will deal in detail with the techniques of food handling and cleansing of equipment, but the links between bacterial food poisoning and food processing (see Table 5 overleaf) are so fundamental that some reference should be made to the subject in this section.

One of the basic links in the chain of infection is the food handler, whether as a result of being a carrier, either knowingly or unknowingly, or as an intermediary responsible for transferring bacteria from one food or surface to another. One of the golden rules of catering is to avoid handling food more than absolutely necessary. Of equal importance is to observe strict personal hygiene, particularly keeping the hands scrupulously clean at all times, and not indulging in bad habits such as nose-picking, scratching and smoking. Clearly the state of the premises and the equipment play a part in good hygiene, so there is no substitute for the highest standards of cleanliness prevailing at all times. Above all, there is no doubt that safe practices and methods of food handling play a major part in preventing or avoiding outbreaks of food poisoning.

Reference has already been made to the large numbers of foods which can be potentially dangerous if allowed to be contaminated by bacteria. Basically *food should be safely stored at the correct temperature* and then *carefully prepared* for sale or for consumption, *thoroughly cooked* and

TABLE 5 Food Practices in Relation to Food Poisoning Outbreaks

Factor	*Type of organism involved*							*Total number of outbreaks*	
	Salmonella	*C. perfringens*	*Staph. aureus*	*B. cereus*	*Other bacteria*	*Non bacteria*	*Not known*		
Preparation too far in advance	173	338	66	49	4	–	3	633	60%
Storage at room temperature	115	208	54	32	1	2	1	413	39%
Inadequate cooling	71	236	10	16	–	–	–	333	31%
Inadequate reheating	47	215	4	29	3	–	2	300	28%
Contaminated processed food	105	9	25	4	9	46	1	199	19%
Under cooking	91	62	1	1	1	4	1	161	15%
Inadequate thawing	42	22	–	–	–	–	–	64	6%
Cross-contamination	57	3	2	–	–	–	–	62	5.9%
								2165	

served immediately. Ideally food should not be kept hot for more than one hour, and during that time a temperature of over 66°C should be maintained.

In an effort to provide the public with more information on food hygiene, the UK Government distributed 12 million leaflets in 1989.

Legal responsibilities

Food poisoning is a notifiable infectious disease, which means that a doctor is required by law (The Public Health Infectious Diseases Regulations, 1968) to notify the local authority of any case with which he is dealing. Many people who suffer from mild symptoms of food poisoning, such as diarrhoea, put it down to 'having eaten too much fruit', or recover sufficiently not to trouble the hard-pressed doctor. So many cases of food poisoning go unreported and undetected every day.

Unfortunately, there is no easy diagnosis of food poisoning and the only method of identifying the offending bacteria is to take a faecal specimen from the sufferer and samples of suspected foodstuffs for examination in

Characteristic symptoms

the laboratory. The examination is an involved and highly technical laboratory investigation which can take several days and even weeks if a particular *Salmonella* has to be identified from the 2,000 different types. When the species of bacterium has been identified it is possible to subject the strain to further tests which will indicate which drugs will destroy the bacterium and which will be ineffective. This information is then reported to the doctor to enable a suitable course of treatment to be prescribed. Once the treatment is over, further faecal specimens will be necessary in order to ensure that the treatment was effective. In the case of *Salmonella* infections the incidence of cross-resistance effectively precludes any effective treatment.

Occasionally doctors fail to arrange for the necessary laboratory examination and prescribe a drug which may be ineffectual or even produce an immunity in the bacteria. This may result in the person becoming a 'healthy carrier' for lengthy periods of time. It is probable that persons not troubling the doctor will also become healthy carriers who can remain undetected for months, possibly years in the case of typhoid carriers. If these carriers are also food handlers who are not careful of their personal hygiene, there is a very real risk that the bacteria will be spread via food to other people.

When a general practitioner notifies the local authority, the sufferer will usually receive a visit from an Environmental Health Officer who will not only arrange for the submission of faecal specimens before and after treatment, if prescribed, but will also investigate the likely cause of the food poisoning. Skilful detective work will often lead to an offending food handler or food premises and ultimately to the elimination of food poisoning to the public at large. If the sufferer is a person engaged in the food trade the local authority has the legal power to prevent that person resuming work until satisfied that the person is free from infection. This procedure may involve the individual in several weeks' absence and in such cases the person may claim compensation for loss of earnings during that period of time. However, many local authorities will allow food handlers to return to work once they have been symptom free for 48 hours.

The law also prohibits any person from working in a food business when suffering from any infectious disease or a bowel disorder, skin infection, nose or throat infection, and requires the person and/or proprietor to notify the local authority of any such occurrence.

In addition to requiring employees to be symptom free before allowing them to resume work after illness, many companies now require staff to submit routine faecal specimens for examination. The purpose of these checks is to identify carriers of food poisoning or gastro-enteritis bacteria, especially following a holiday abroad or an unspecified bout of illness. At least one large medical company offers a service to the food industry in which the staff are screened for *Salmonella* organisms and the results are notified to the company's medical adviser or the employee's general practitioner.

Finally, if an outbreak of food poisoning should occur in premises under your control, the following action should be taken:

1. Telephone the local Environmental Health Department (unless they bring the bad news). Outside normal office hours there is usually an emergency number in the telephone directory.
2. If customers are ill on the premises, call an ambulance or local doctor.
3. If possible keep any food similar to that eaten by them.
4. Do not throw anything away or start cleaning until advised to do so.
5. Make a list of the staff on duty and the names and addresses of any staff off duty, together with the reason for their absence.
6. Prepare a list of your food suppliers: e.g. butcher, wholesale grocer, baker.
7. Prepare a set of menu cards for the past 48 hours. Ideally a sample dish from each type of meal served in the previous 48 hours should be available for examination.

This information and assistance will be invaluable to the Environmental Health Officer in order to identify the cause of the outbreak and to advise on ways of preventing a recurrence.

Some case histories

Salmonella spoils the birthday party

On Friday 15 July a private birthday party at which 60–70 people were present was held in a local public house. During the weekend of 16 and 17 July, more than 40 people developed symptoms of food poisoning, mainly diarrhoea and vomiting. The symptoms were apparently mild as few people consulted their doctors and none were admitted to hospital.

Suspicion fell on the chicken portions as the source of infection because all persons who were ill had eaten them, and the four infected persons who had not attended the party had eaten chicken from the same source. In addition to the chicken, there were ham, beef and egg mayonnaise sandwiches, cocktail sausages, vol-au-vents, and black forest and lemon gâteaus. Several of those ill had not eaten one or more of these additional items. The chickens had been purchased cooked from a local butcher on the morning of the day of the party. The butcher had obtained frozen Belgian birds of a standard weight of 2lb 10oz. At the end of the previous working day Thursday, they were removed from the freezer and laid out individually on a stainless steel table to thaw overnight. On the day of the party they were placed on spits, five per spit, and cooked in a barbecue oven equipped with thermostat control and timer. After roasting for 1 hour 40 minutes at 49°C the spits were removed from the oven, the birds drained of grease and slid off the spit onto three polypropylene trays. Cooking was completed by 11 am and the cooked chickens were then left to cool at an ambient temperature of about 25°C. At 2.30 pm the batch of cooked chickens was divided into three orders, quartered and boxed. Two of these orders were sent to local public houses where they were subjected to refrigeration and then further cooking. No reports of illness arose from these premises.

Chickens belonging to the third consignment were quartered with a pair of scissors and packed in a box in which the raw poultry had been delivered, the box being lined with grease-proof paper. At approximately 3.30 pm the order was taken to the home of the host and the chicken portions were placed on separate serving dishes, and covered with cling film. They remained at the house at ambient temperature until the early evening, when they were taken to the public house which was to be the venue of the party. They remained there, covered, until 9.30 pm when the buffet was served. It should be noted that this was a very warm day with the 10.00 am ambient temperature recorded at 24.7°C. The public house staff did not handle the chicken.

It seems likely that the chickens were contaminated after cooking within the butcher's premises by the surfaces of the container in which they were placed for delivery. There were other opportunities for cross-contamination in the butcher's shop from surfaces and equipment. The chicken was not then refrigerated until the time of consumption. The owners of the butcher's shop were advised by the Environmental Health Department of the faulty food handling practices and have since decided to discontinue the preparation and sale of cooked chickens.

Clostridial food poisoning in a general hospital

On the night of 26/27 October, an outbreak of gastro-enteritis occurred at a small general hospital. There were 147 patients in the hospital, 34 of whom developed diarrhoea and abdominal pain but no pyrexia. None was seriously ill and most recovered in 24 hours. On the advice of the Control of Infection Committee the hospital was closed to all admissions for 24 hours whilst the extent and nature of the outbreak was determined.

The beef stew was freshly prepared in the hospital kitchen on the morning of 26 October. The stew was cooked in a five gallon pan by simmering, and regularly turning the pan, on the edge of a hot plate for 3 hours. About 30 minutes before the end of the cooking fresh mushrooms were added to the stew. The meals were plated at 11 am and put into heated trolleys. The trolleys were distributed to the wards at 11.30 am and plugged in on arrival at the ward.

The isolation of *C. perfringens* from 20 of 23 affected patients as well as from the food samples confirms that the outbreak was one of clostridial food poisoning. It is suspected that the method of simmering and turning the stew on the edge of the hotplate resulted in inadequate temperature penetration and subsequent germination of spores and bacterial growth. It was noted that on the ward with the lowest attack rate the food was served within minutes of arrival, whilst on the ward with the highest attack rate the food was served about 30 minutes after arrival. The other practices and hygiene in the kitchen were, as far as could be ascertained, of an acceptable standard. In this outbreak the food samples provided useful confirmatory evidence and we believe that this adds to the case for maintaining the practice of keeping food samples.

It was recommended that the kitchen should be provided with convection fan ovens or pressure cookers.

Outbreak of Campylobacter enteritis associated with unpasteurised milk

During a two week period in February – March, about 90 of approximately 300 people in a village on the edge of the North Yorkshire Moors became ill with abdominal pain and diarrhoea.

On 2 March the Environmental Health Department was contacted by a general practitioner who reported that a number of his patients had acute diarrhoea accompanied by severe abdominal pain. Some patients complained of diarrhoea containing blood. The first cases had presented themselves in the latter half of the previous week. Sixteen cases were seen from 26 February to 1 March of which 2 were admitted to hospital; 8 were males and 8 females with ages ranging from 21 months to 64 years. One case was not a resident of the village and had only been there for 24 hours before the onset of symptoms. It became apparent during the initial enquiries that a number of other people in the village were similarly affected.

All dwellings in the village were serviced by a mains water supply and mains sewage disposal. Most villagers drank untreated milk, mainly from one farm in the village, but a few drank milk from their own cows. The two local shops sold only pre-packaged food and most people did their main shopping outside the village. The Health Centre in a nearby village served most of the households.

The only feature common to the cases visited was the consumption of water and untreated milk. The affected households did not obtain their food from the same sources and they had not attended any communal functions in recent weeks. Samples of water taken by the Environmental Health Department and the Northumbrian Water Authority showed no evidence of faecal contamination.

Stool samples were obtained from those affected people who consulted their general practitioner and samples of untreated milk from the suspect supply were also obtained for examination. On 6 March Middlesborough PHL reported that 9 of the stool specimens were positive for *Campylobacter*.

On 6 March a house to house survey was carried out by the Environmental Health Department. Access was gained to 139 of 207 houses in the village. Sixty-eight premises were either vacant or the investigating officers were unable to gain access. All people in the premises visited were questioned about recent gastro-intestinal symptoms, their consumption of milk and the source of that milk.

Eighty-six of 243 persons interviewed had recently experienced symptoms compatible with *Campylobacter* enteritis. The median onset date for 82 persons who could remember it was 27 February; 77 became ill between 20 February and 9 March, although one of the confirmed cases apparently had symptoms on 11 February. However, the first isolate was not made until 4 March making this onset date unlikely.

Males and females were affected to the same extent. Those under 15 years comprised 31 (36%) of the 86 cases, compared with 54 (28%) of 243, the total population surveyed.

Eighty-four of 222 who drank the suspect unpasteurised milk complained of symptoms of *Campylobacter* enteritis compared with 2 of 21 who did not drink this milk. The 2 whose specimens were negative for *Campylobacter* may in fact have consumed untreated milk at a friend's house. Of 139 premises visited 130 obtained untreated milk from the suspect farm. The other 9 premises, with 29 well persons, used alternative milk supplies with 13 of 21 people in these houses drinking untreated milk from other sources, and the remaining 8, UHT milk. No stool specimens were obtained from those who were asymptomatic but there is a statistically significant difference between the numbers of clinical cases in those who did or did not drink the untreated milk. Untreated milk from this farm was not supplied to any other community.

Norwalk virus at a Christmas lunch

The chief executive of a local district council held his staff Christmas party at the Council's community centre on 18 December. A buffet lunch was prepared by outside caterers. Of the 39 partygoers, 27 developed gastro-intestinal symptoms after an interval of 42 hours. On 19 December about an hour before the first of the chief executive's guests became ill, another lunch, for an engineering firm, was prepared at the community centre by the same caterers. Of the 19 people attending the second function, 14 ate lunch and 5 developed gastro-intestinal illness after an interval of 44 hours.

The illness was similar in both groups. Seventeen of the 32 who experienced symptoms complained of a severe disabling illness characterised by nausea, recurrent vomiting and diarrhoea. The remaining 15 reported milder symptoms of nausea, abdominal colic and diarrhoea in various combinations. A minority also complained of headache (12), myalgia (4) and mild fever (5) and the occurrence of these symptoms was not related to the seriousness of the gastrointestinal symptoms. One of the guests with severe symptoms was a vegetarian.

The first lunch consisted primarily of pre-cooked foods bought in or defrosted that morning: 3 varieties of meat, quiche, gâteau, profiterole pastries and mince pies. Two frozen foods – a boneless turkey joint and sausage rolls – were defrosted overnight and cooked by the caterers.

There were seven varieties of salads freshly prepared on the morning of the lunch including a potato salad which was prepared with a bottled mayonnaise dressing and a waldorf salad mixed with bottled mayonnaise and yoghurt.

The second lunch was less extensive and included sandwiches made from meat served on the previous day and some leftover sausage rolls. Pre-cooked quiche, turkey pie, gâteau and mince pies were defrosted overnight. The sandwiches were served with lettuce, tomato and cucumber, but no other salads were available.

Each lunch was prepared by two catering assistants, only one of whom was present on both occasions. This assistant experienced headache and nausea (but denied diarrhoea or vomiting) during preparation of the council lunch; she was given a gin and tonic to 'settle her stomach'. The mother and sister of the catering assistant experienced episodes of vomiting and diarrhoea on 20 and 21 December which at first were attributed to excitement over a pop concert.

There was no clear division of specific food preparation between the catering assistants although the young woman who experienced symptoms was employed as an apprentice and was expected to perform the basic preparation chores, rather than the more sophisticated tasks. These certainly involved cutting the quiche into 1 inch squares and 'reconstructing' the turkey pie which had crumbled on slicing. We believe that she was involved in slicing the turkey (the other meats were pre-sliced) and hand-chopping the apples and walnuts for the waldorf salad – although we were unable to obtain a definite statement from the caterers on the latter point. Some items for the green salad would also have been hand sliced (e.g. tomatoes) but in general preparation of the other salads and desserts did not required hand contact.

Circumstantial evidence strongly supports the contention that the catering assistant common to both functions was the source of infection. She denied eating any foods herself or taking any home to her family, although two of them subsequently became ill. That she could shed sufficient virus to infect 34 people without apparently displaying symptoms of vomiting or diarrhoea is worrying.

Norwalk viruses have been implicated in previous episodes of food poisoning, although to our knowledge the first reported episode of transmission by a food handler occurred in August 1982 in a bakery in

Minnesota. In that case, the source was thought to be a food handler who experienced diarrhoea and vomiting while preparing butter cream icing, and a rising antibody titre to *Norwalk* virus was demonstrated in his serum.

Food poisoning from partially cooked red kidney beans

A physician and two guests ate a slowly-cooked beef stew one evening; about 2 hours later both guests developed nausea and severe vomiting; one also had diarrhoea. The physician who had prepared the dish ate it about three hours later, because his meal was delayed by an urgent visit he had to make to hospital: he did not have any vomiting, but developed fluid non-gaseous diarrhoea after about 3 hours. None of the three had abdominal pain. The diarrhoea lasted in two persons for 8 – 12 hours.

Fresh beef had been browned that same morning at about 8.00 am. Other ingredients, including vegetables, were then added and the whole brought to boiling. The dish was then transferred to an electric slow-cooking casserole on the 'high' setting, which runs apparently at well below boiling point (up to 80°C) though no temperature readings are given, for 30 minutes. The 'cooker' was then altered to the 'low' setting where it remained until early evening. About 5.00 pm red kidney beans which had been soaked from dry all day in water, were added and the stew dish was eaten by the guests, after another 2½ hours at 'low' setting, and by the physician after another 5½ hours. The dish, except the beans, had been cooked in fact for about 11 hours in all, but the recipe had specified tinned beans.

In view of the previous reports of gastro-enteritis from uncooked red kidney beans it seems likely that these were the cause of the symptoms produced. They were not added to the casserole until much later and the low temperature was probably insufficient to cook them in the time allowed.

All reports reproduced by kind permission of the Public Health Laboratory Service.

Chapter 3

Food Hygiene Management

The Food Chain

In 1989 the government introduced the important White Paper – *Food Safety – Protecting the Consumer*. That document set out major considerations, many of which have subsequently been carried into law through various Acts and Regulations. That White Paper placed much emphasis on the Food Chain – referring to it as having . . . many links, stretching from the field to the home; ranging from farms and fishing vessels to warehouses and supermarkets to take-aways. The food industry, the White Paper says, employs over three million people and contributes nearly 10% of the Gross Domestic Product. Ensuring food safety requires co-operation and protective action at every point in this chain.

In the past, the attention of the authorities and much of the legislation has focused on certain manufacturing premises and retail outlets – often at the expense of attention not being given to even more vulnerable premises. Though it is acknowledged that there may well be especially critical points in the path that an item of food may take prior to consumption, it is equally acknowledged that contamination can occur at any stage – that is from the time at which the plant emerges from the ground to the point at which it is consumed. The Food Safety Act covers crops and live animals, which are known as food sources, and the food derived from them. This means that, for example, farmers will be affected far more by the law than they may have been in the past. Farmers will now be considered to be running food businesses although there is an exception for those who simply rear animals and sell them live.

Attention to the food chain, therefore, seeks to introduce some quality control throughout the 'life' of the food – or 'at every link' in that chain. It is worth quoting from the government's White Paper in relation to the food chain as follows. The government . . .

★ insists on stringent hygiene standards throughout the food chain.

★ controls the use of additives, such as colourings and preservatives.

- ★ monitors chemical contaminants and lays down stringent limits, often with very wide margins of safety.
- ★ aims to ensure that the danger to human health from microbiological contamination is kept to an absolute minimum.
- ★ assesses novel foods and processes to ensure their safety.

In giving attention to the food chain, one should also consider that this applies equally to imported food as to that which is home-produced. In the past, the controls on imported food have been limited, and legislation now enables tighter controls to be exerted on imported foodstuffs, whether from European Community countries or elsewhere.

Food Hygiene Policies

An encouraging development in recent years has been the adoption of Food Hygiene Policies by an increasing number of food concerns. In effect, they set down a commitment by the company or operator to encourage good food hygiene practices within the organisation. These should be seen as establishing clear guidelines and objectives for both management and other personnel and experience shows that such initiatives can only do good.

Some policies have been modelled closely on Health and Safety lines giving both a set of broad objectives whilst at the same time giving detailed guidance in relation to particular processes. In this latter connection, management must ensure that clear and accurate guidance is given if it expects personnel to comply. What is important is that the policy must be accepted by all staff. Some employers insist upon a written undertaking by staff to accept and work toward such a policy and failure to do so could lead to disciplinary action being taken. Such measures should not be seen as an imposition by management. Moreover, the introduction of a food hygiene policy should be seen as a positive move to improve and maintain standards.

Policies can be in various forms. Some companies have settled for a simple statement whilst others have taken the trouble to present it in a simple, easy to understand form illustrating the various points. The success of any policy will depend at the end of the day on the commitment of the workforce at large, and in preparing the details of any policy, management are well advised to consult staff, both on its content and practicability. A policy established with the co-operation and support of staff is far more likely to succeed than one arbitrarily introduced by the employer.

Some operators have introduced food hygiene policies used by other organisations/companies. These are less likely to succeed than one prepared with a particular company/organisation in mind which has involved staff in its preparation and relates specifically to premises with which staff are familiar.

An interesting dimension to all this is that some retailers insist upon their suppliers having an acceptable policy as a condition of their trading with them.

Role of Consultants

In recent years there has been an increasing involvement of consultants in the fields of food hygiene and food quality control. As food hygiene, particularly, has become the focus of statutory attention, making the demands on the food and catering industry wider and more complex, so there has emerged a number of consultancies that offer specialist advice. Some larger food organisations themselves have established their own advisory/consultancy sections – many of these engaging qualified Environmental Health Officers or food technicians to advise them. Most smaller concerns, however, cannot justify such people within their own organisation and increasingly are turning to private firms for advice.

The range of advice or services offered by them varies widely. Most of the larger consultancies will carry out hygiene audits of premises, liaise with local authority Environmental Health Officers, prepare maintenance programmes and contract manage as appropriate. Increasingly, consultancies are offering a range of training courses leading to recognised qualifications of the national Awarding Bodies.

It is very tempting for the caterer to be panicked into choosing the first consultant in sight when he needs help. Responding to the demands of the industry, new consultancies are emerging apace and it is important for the client first of all to establish clearly what he wants of the consultant before proceeding further. Clients should establish the credentials of a consultancy before committing themselves to it and there is merit in seeking the views of the local Environmental Health Officer who may have had experience of the consultancy before. Even though he will be unwilling to recommend any one particular consultancy, he may well be prepared to suggest several, or alternatively – and no doubt for good reason – suggest why it is not a good idea to engage a particular firm.

It should also be remembered that when it comes to offering training courses held under the auspices of the national Awarding Bodies, not all consultancies are approved to organise these – or at least the range of courses offered by each. It is important for the client to establish this at an early date. It is also useful to ask the consultant about his track record in relation to particular parts of the industry. The industry is wide and specialised and it may well be that the client is looking for specialist experience in, for example, dairy hygiene or hospital catering. As once said "You don't normally engage a brain surgeon to mend a broken leg."

Most consultancies operate on a single contract basis, that is they are called in to advise in connection with a particular project. On completion of the project the contract is ended. Some food concerns prefer to reserve the services of a consultant on a retainer basis – this is where the client enters into a contractual agreement with the consultant to – as it were – be available as and when necessary in addition to any routine inspections that take place. Such an approach has merit in that a client has ready access to 'his own advisor', besides which the consultant feels able and encouraged to build up a special interest and knowledge in relation to the company/operation.

The time is fast approaching for a regulatory body to monitor the performance of consultancies to be introduced. The expanding food industry is going to have to turn increasingly to consultancies for help and advice and such help and advice can have far reaching consequences. For this reason, clients should satisfy themselves as to the credentials of a prospective consultant. Failure to do so can be both costly and damaging to a client's standing.

Local Authority Environmental Health Departments – Advisory Services

Local authority Environmental Health Officers have invariably been willing over the years to advise those in the food industry on standards, and how to achieve them. It has been generally accepted that this is complementary to any enforcement role that they have. Some Environmental Health Departments have extended their traditional role and developed within their departments sections that have been able to offer the full range of advice to those in the food industry. This is to be commended. However, such arrangements are most likely only to be available in larger authorities where staff resources permit, but operators may wish to enquire if such facilities exist before going down the path of engaging a consultant to do the job. Local authorities may levy a charge for any such service.

Hygiene Committees

The need for special attention to be given to food hygiene is generally accepted by the food industry. It involves everyone, whether directly or indirectly involved with food handling and in order both to focus attention on the subject and also to maintain an interest throughout the workforce, an increasing number of organisations are setting up hygiene committees. These comprise those with an immediate responsibility for maintaining hygiene standards – quality control and training personnel, etc. – and will also include representatives of the staff. It is a good idea to bring in a staff representative from the various sections and there is also merit in changing those representatives from time to time – again to try and encourage an interest throughout the organisation. It is possible for such a committee or group to ensure that it sets the pace with the food hygiene standards and it can also from time to time benefit from inviting specialists in to talk about, for example, cleansing techniques, use of cleaning materials and equipment, and so on. It would also benefit from occasional attendance by the local Environmental Health Officer.

Such committees/groups, whilst most likely to operate in larger organisations, can be used with success where fewer staff are involved. Management should see such groups as a valuable means of encouraging an interest in an area crucial to the success of a company, and where these have operated thus far, management invariably reports favourably on the refreshing outlook to food hygiene that is often adopted by staff. Needless to say, the meetings need not be so long nor so frequent as to become counterproductive!

Hazard Analysis and Critical Control Point (HACCP)

Though not new in concept, attention is being focused increasingly on the application of HACCP in the food industry. Developed in the USA in the mid 1970s it is already widely used by food manufacturers and processors and increasingly it is being used by those in the wider catering industry. In the past, one has tended to leave testing the quality of the product to the end of the line. HACCP is a process whereby each stage of a process is critically examined, and where these may appear vulnerable in terms of introducing a hazard into the food, then particular attention is given at that point. It is, in effect, a process of critically examining each stage of the journey that the food takes until it is consumed. It also means that having identified potential hazards in the food's journey – whether it be within the processing plant or before – then particular attention can be given to either eliminating or minimising the hazard. One of the advantages of HACCP is that a multi-disciplinary team is involved because it covers the entire range of activities associated with the product; indeed the commitment of the entire staff is crucial to the success of the exercise.

In introducing HACCP one needs to identify various elements, namely:

(a) The need to draw up a detailed flow diagram showing the path of the food throughout its life/manufacture.

(b) Product details need to be identified so that any special characteristics are noted that could cause a problem.

(c) Each stage must then be carefully examined to see if there is the likelihood of a hazard occurring. The risks can then be assessed as high, medium or low and then monitoring and control procedures can be implemented. A simple example might be, for instance, that cans of food moving along a conveyor belt and waiting for lids to be fitted may be exposed to both air pollution and risk of contamination. Having identified this, solutions would include covering the area to minimise air pollution or the entry of 'extraneous material' or minimising the length of time the cans are on the track.

Sampling of food or taking bacterial swabs may well need to complement any HACCP programme. Though the example of the tins on the conveyor belt speaks for itself, there may be other instances where the bacterial testing of the food may be necessary to check whether a hazard is being introduced at those particular points. In addition to any bacteriological quality of the food, it may also be necessary to check on the chemical composition to see that a particular machine is blending the ingredients as it should. All of this is important in ensuring proper food quality control, whether it be bacteriological or chemical.

HACCP should not be regarded as a sophisticated programme only intended for the larger company. Every food concern has its critical control points to some extent – this is why the food industry is so vulnerable. What all food concerns should do – large or small – is to at least be aware of those stages where hazards lurk and make sure that extra attention is given to hygiene at those points. The larger operator will need to go one further by introducing a programme of periodic monitoring of those points, thus ensuring that those parts of the food chain under his control are properly monitored and safe.

Food Hygiene Audits

Increasingly, reference is now made to food hygiene audits which are intended to scrutinise any food operation with a view to recording deficiencies and areas for improvement, or simply to monitor performance at a certain point. These may be linked to any quality assurance (including BS 5750) criteria – see later reference to quality assurance. On the other hand such an approach may be used simply as good practice.

The approach to hygiene auditing varies but will generally involve a suitably qualified person carrying out an in-depth inspection of both premises and practices, and reporting to management with both observations and where necessary, recommendations. As with any other industry, food companies can change their techniques of operation without, for example, being aware of hazards that are introduced, and it is very easy for people that are familiar with premises to fail to see problem areas that are emerging. It may be that staff are beginning to be lax in connection with a certain task. It could be that through normal wear and tear, parts of the building are deteriorating and repairs are necessary. Similarly, equipment may need attention. Day to day contact with the work situation means that those close to the premises or practice simply do not notice and a hygiene audit is one way of bringing in someone who can look critically to the extent of picking up any problem areas or practices.

The frequency of hygiene audits may vary, depending on the type of premises. High intensity production will justify more frequent audits. Premises of all sizes that are involved with the preparation of more vulnerable foods will also justify more frequent audits. It is important that whatever emerges from these in-depth inspections must be properly recorded and brought to the attention of the appropriate people, either management or individual food handlers or both. Management must in turn ensure that hygiene audits are acted upon, otherwise there is little value in this regulatory exercise. Management may not always be able to respond immediately to the recommendations of an audit, especially so far as costly renovations, etc., may be involved. In such cases, those carrying out the audit should be able to prioritise whatever is required and in this way management will be able to budget for improvements or replacements. Having said this, however, it is important to ensure that when priorities are established, that these are acceptable to the local Environmental Health Officer. There is simply no point in assuming that certain works can be scheduled for two years hence if the local Environmental Health Officer considers that they are of such an urgent nature that they should be dealt with immediately.

As a general comment, hygiene audits should clearly identify the parts of the premises or equipment so that there can be no doubt on anyone's part as to what is being identified by the auditor.

In terms of carrying out audits on an on-going basis this is a matter for management themselves, and many companies have their own audit teams. Others, on the other hand, will look to outside consultants to carry out this work, probably on a regular basis.

Quality Assurance

The British Standards Institute are responsible for publishing and supervising the British Standards which manufacturers of plant and equipment, as well as commodities like food products, packaging and the like, design their production system to achieve. BS 5750 is rather different in that it lays down a standard of carrying out operations by which all materials and components are subjected to comprehensive regular checks at critical points throughout the food production process. Complying with BS 5750 is a guarantee of a quality product because the manufacturers management system is subjected to regular independent scrutiny and the accreditation certificate can be withdrawn if a company fails to adhere to the specification at any time. Several leading catering equipment manufacturers are accredited with BS 5750 so that the purchaser can be guaranteed a quality product. There are two international counterparts to the British Standards Institute, namely the International Standardisation Organisation (ISO) and the European Standards (EN) which are also quoted by some manufacturers. Large food production companies are becoming accredited for BS 5750 in order to supply a guaranteed quality product which enables them to use the 'due diligence' defence under the Food Safety Act, if there is any question of the fitness of the food at the point of sale.

Chapter 4

Design and Construction of Food Premises

The difficulty in considering the design and construction of any food premises is that so much depends on the type and volume of the anticipated business. As so often happens, this volume of business is underestimated to the extent that the premises become too small with the almost inevitable result that problems arise in connection with the storage, preparation and production of food.

In designing new premises, an accurate assessment of likely trade is essential for a proper balance to be made in the allocation of space. There is no point in planning a restaurant with seating for 200 customers, if the kitchen is only suitable for preparing fifty meals at any one time. To some extent this will be determined by the type of catering involved. The restaurant that takes advantage of convenience foods and where minimum preparation and handling is required will clearly need less room than the one which processes the different foods from the raw state. A clear definition of the type of catering is essential before any planning of premises is carried out so that the proper allocation of area between the various parts of the business can be made. In all of this it should be remembered that building costs are continually rising to the extent that it is even more necessary to get it right at the outset.

Equally there is little point in planning a shop where the anticipated retail trade far exceeds the back-up storage capacity. The economic viability of the business must be carefully calculated beforehand, in the knowledge that a food business means far more than just 'selling'.

There has been a tendency in recent years for many retail outlets to reduce their storage capacity and to rely on either more regular deliveries by suppliers or to draw stock as necessary from wholesalers. Such practices can sometimes work against any move towards 'economy of scale' but on the other hand this may be less important where the emphasis is on sales and throughput.

Perhaps most problems are experienced where existing premises, which were never originally designed as food premises, have to be adapted; although careful planning and the sensible use of materials and equipment can help to make the best use of limited space. Certainly the careful design and choice of equipment in any food premises will not only make good hygiene an easier process, but also will encourage clean habits with the staff.

The basic lay-out and construction should be designed to enable:

1. Adequate space to be provided in all food handling and associated areas for equipment and working practices; and
2. Frequent and routine cleaning to be carried out.

Food preparation rooms should be planned to allow a 'work flow', whereby food is processed through the premises from the point of delivery to the point of sale or service with the minimum obstruction. The various processes should be separated as far as possible and food intended for sale should not cross paths with waste food or refuse. Staff time is valuable and a design which reduces wasteful journeys is both efficient and cost effective.

The various preparation processes require different types of consideration depending on what food is involved. A vegetable preparation area means that water from the sinks and dirt from the vegetables are going to accumulate and therefore adequate facilities for drainage should be provided. Pastry preparation, on the other hand, entails dry processes, although flour is likely to be released into the atmosphere which can create problems with cleaning.

Whatever the process, however, there are certain basic rules that can be applied which not only make for easier working conditions but which also help in making the requirements of the Food Hygiene Regulations a reality. Given that one has an existing shell of a building, care should be taken in the very first instance to see that, before specific areas are allocated, adequate space is provided for the preparation of food, storage, sales and service, staff facilities and the storage of refuse.

The various methods of storing food are dealt with in Chapter 7, but it will suffice to say at this stage that food stuffs should not be stored in passageways or in food preparation areas where they will not only impede staff working there but also will hamper proper cleaning.

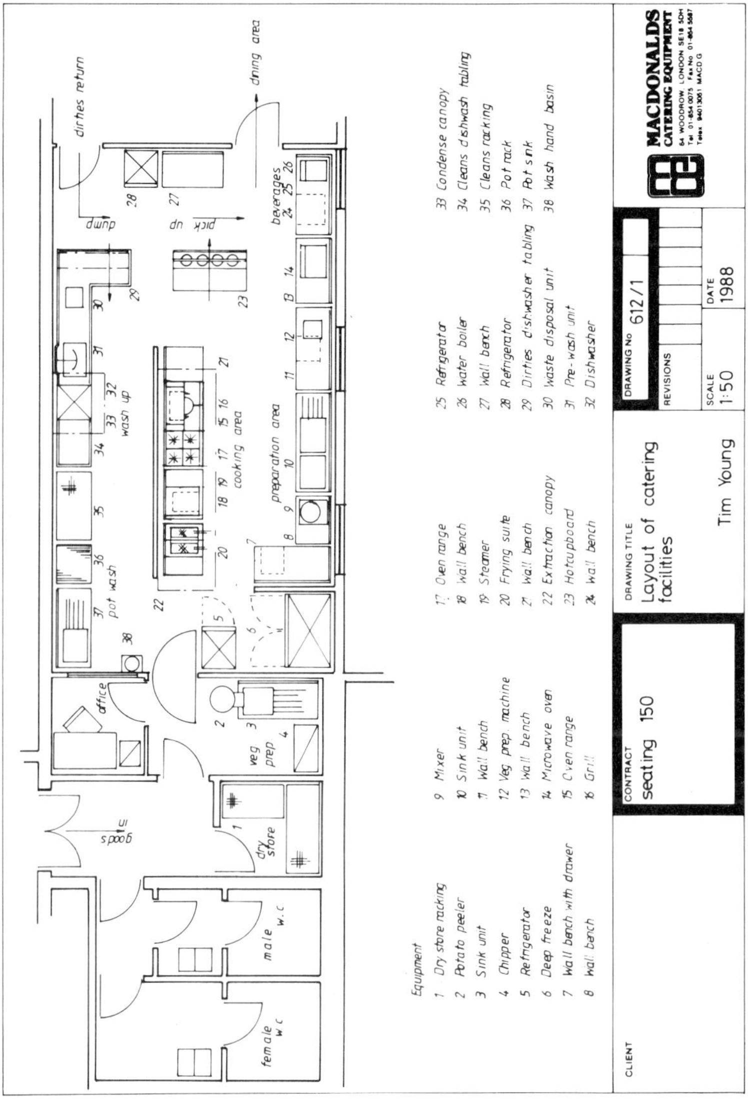

'Work flow' diagram showing optimum use of space and minimum interference from other workers

Food preparation areas

There is no doubt that the proper design and lay-out of the preparation area can make a major contribution to good food hygiene. It is also true that staff generally respond to good working conditions by taking more of a pride in themselves and in what they are doing.

Adequate space must be provided for each process and care should be taken to separate dirty and clean areas. Vegetable preparation and wash-up areas should be separate from the actual food preparation or service areas. As with the lay-out of premises, a work flow arrangement should be introduced so that staff do not hamper each other by having to cross each other's paths more than is absolutely necessary.

Actual work-top areas should be adequate in size for the preparation process and should enable the food handler to have all the necessary food and utensils near to hand. Stainless steel (18/8 quality) is an ideal material for use in catering premises for work-tops and in the construction of most pieces of equipment. An inferior alternative is a plastic laminate veneer finish, although this is far preferable to wood in any situation. Wood in whatever condition tends to be absorbent and easily damaged, with consequent cleaning difficulties.

Ensure adequate working space

Floors

The basic rule is that these should be smooth, impervious (water and grease proof), and capable of being readily cleaned. At the same time they should not be slippery or in any other way dangerous. Floors should generally be solid, whilst the choice of finish will usually depend on the type of food business. In a kitchen, quarry tiles, granolithic or terrazzo are best because they are hard-wearing, will withstand grease and water and can be easily cleaned. Floors in storerooms or retail areas may be similarly surfaced, although industrial sheet linoleum or vinyl may be acceptable where there are dry conditions, and provided a suitable adhesive is used. Many very acceptable vinyl type materials are now available often in sizes which involve fewer joints which can be a particular problem. Ensuring that the covering is firmly fixed to the floor and that the joints are properly heat or otherwise joined is essential. Quite acceptable covings are also available. Wooden floors are not acceptable as a general rule because, even if they have been sealed, dirt may collect in cracks and joints. An additional hazard, where there are wooden suspended floors, is the risk of harbourage for rodents and insects.

Concrete floors are not suitable in most food rooms because the surface can break down and cause dust. Although the surface can be sealed, concrete should not be used where there is likely to be heavy wear. It is vulnerable to attack by acids, alkalis, fats and oils, although the application of a polyurethane seal will provide some protection.

Various types of composition floors are available which incorporate the strength of concrete/cement whilst overcoming some of the disadvantages, by adding bituminous or mastic compounds. The main disadvantage is that these tend not to withstand heavy use by, for example, trolley wheels and sharp foot wear.

A good development in recent years has been in connection with polymer flooring. Though sometimes more expensive than traditional coverings, they have the advantage of being hard wearing, resistant to a range of materials/chemicals and can be trowel laid to eliminate joints. Depending on their location, different additives can be incorporated, e.g. granite or other hard wearing aggregates. Fast colours can also be introduced.

Where quantities of water are likely to find their way on to the floor, or in an area where wet cleaning is the best way of removing deposits, adequate drainage should be provided, either by a central gully to which the floor is sloped or by a channel situated along one of the walls – to which again the floor is inclined. Grids and grease traps should be provided to filter out material that might obstruct the drainage system and full access should be provided to permit proper cleaning. Where grids are provided they should not be made inaccessible through being under or behind equipment. Lighter metals are now often used in preference to cast iron to enable more ready access. Care is necessary, however, as some of the lighter metals bend under pressure which can present a safety problem. The use of newspaper, cardboard or sawdust on floors is not acceptable. In recent years there has been an increasing practice in the food industry generally of using carpeting, often supplied by contract cleaning firms, that are changed periodically. Though many Environmental Health Officers consider these unsuitable for use within kitchen areas on the basis that they are absorbent and can harbour bacteria, it is accepted that they can be used in other areas, especially for reasons of health and safety. The installation of non-slip floor tiles is recommended wherever slippery conditions are encountered.

Some food premises are adopting the use of different coloured floors for various parts. This encourages practices and personnel to be confined to specific areas, thus helping to prevent cross contamination. Personnel may also be required to wear similarly coloured overalls/hats/ties as a means of clearly identifying their work role. See also Chapter 9.

Walls

Again the general rule of being smooth, impervious and capable of being readily cleaned should be applied. The walls themselves should be surfaced to prevent any intervening gap in which insects or rodents might be harboured. Where possible, walls should be coved with the floor to enable easy cleaning.

Glazed tiles or stainless steel sheets provide the most suitable surfaces for food rooms, although the former should not be used near to sources of heat such as cookers, otherwise they will crack. In kitchens and other food preparation areas, the most vulnerable areas are those up to approximately 1.5 metres (5 ft) and it may be sufficient merely to tile to that height. Wall areas where there are likely to be special problems, for example, near cookers or where they are likely to be knocked, should be covered with stainless steel or similar sheeting. Tiles should be laid evenly on a sound base and the jointing compound should be mixed with

A typical example of wall to floor covering

gloss paint as a sealer to prevent absorption. Other areas may be covered with laminated sheeting or gloss painted, but care should be taken with the sheeting to ensure that no voids are created behind.

The choice of tiles and paint is important not only from an aesthetic point of view, but also with regard to safe working conditions. Light colours show up dirt better, besides which they make the best use of available light. The use of metal edging strips around doorways is a sensible precaution against accidental damage by trolleys, etc. Plastic or metal crash rails can also be fitted to walls to prevent damage.

Walls should be as clear of obstruction as possible to enable easy cleaning. The pinning or taping up of posters or notices should be discouraged.

Wall surfaces in retail shops may not need the attention required in a kitchen, although again smooth and impervious finishes are essential. The use of gloss paint may, however, be extended, particularly where the walls are unlikely to be exposed to either damage or extremes of temperature. Wallpaper should not be used in food preparation rooms, although there are some washable varieties which may sometimes be used in dry areas such as in retail shops.

Pipework, ducting and so on should be chased into the wall or floor, or constructed tight to the ceiling to enable an effective seal to be made. Horizontal pipework collects dust and dirt and frequently results in condensation. This causes dripping which can contaminate any uncovered food beneath. Both to prevent contamination and, for example, to insulate against heat loss or frost, pipework should be insulated. This should be firmly fixed around the pipework or ducting, otherwise fragments can become detached to fall into the food; poorly installed insulation/cladding can also become a harbourage for insect pests.

Ceilings

The choice of materials for ceilings presents particular problems because they may be exposed to extremes of temperature, fumes and steam, and are not readily accessible for cleaning. Ceilings should be capable of being easily cleaned by being smooth, but should also be partially absorbent. Otherwise, in moist conditions, condensation will arise which may result in droplets falling on to food, thus causing contamination.

The most suitable material is plasterboard sheeting, where the joints are taped and a skim coat of plaster applied to prevent harbourage of dirt. This type of surface is slightly absorbent, yet can be wiped over to remove heavy concentrations of dirt. It also has the advantage of being able to be emulsioned when it becomes discoloured.

Gloss finishes should be avoided and, where possible, fibreglass insulation should be provided behind the main surface. This will help to reduce the risk of condensation.

The height of the ceiling will often have a bearing on the conditions in the food room and particularly in a kitchen. If the ceiling is too high, it can create cold working conditions and means that the ceiling is less accessible for cleaning. On the other hand, without adequate ventilation, a low ceiling may create temperatures that are too high for comfortable working.

Much will depend on the extent of the food preparation but, in an average size kitchen, a ceiling of approximately 3–3.6 metres (10–12 ft) will not only ensure that the ceiling is accessible for cleaning but will also mean that extremes of temperature are unlikely to arise.

As with wall surfaces, care should be taken to avoid a suspended ceiling, which may create a breeding ground for insects or rodents. Where a suspended ceiling is provided, ready access should be available to the concealed area to enable ease of cleaning.

Doors, windows and stairs

Many parts of the food premises must, of necessity, be made of wood. Where this is so, they should be designed to prevent the accumulation of dirt and to facilitate easy cleaning. Doors should be of plain rather than patterned construction and window frames should be simple rather than complicated.

Doors should generally have finger plates to facilitate easy cleaning where hands are most likely to come into contact. A metal plate fixed to the bottom 15–20 cm (6–9 in) and metal edging strips around the sides of the door will prevent damage by people kicking it open, and by trolleys, etc. On outside doors it acts as a deterrent to gnawing rodents.

Catches, handles and other door and window fittings should be made of aluminium, which is rust-proof, does not need painting and which is obtainable in various, easy-to-clean designs. Many industrial food premises have installed polypropylene or toughened rubber doors incorporating self-closing devices. These have advantages from a food hygiene standpoint and they may be also required in connection with fire prevention.

Stairs should be designed to provide a straight access between floors with an adequate width, easy pitch (not too steep) and handrails for safety. Good natural and artificial lighting is essential and special attention should be paid to the construction and surfacing of stairs. A non-slip tread should be provided wherever possible. Carpeting should be avoided because of the cleaning and maintenance problems.

Ventilation

Ventilation is a process which provides an adequate supply of clean, fresh air, generally from the outside. It is basically dependent upon movement or circulation of air at a sufficient rate to ensure that moist, stale air is removed at regular intervals.

Adequate ventilation is essential in any kitchen, not only for the welfare of the staff, but also because high temperatures are going to promote the growth of bacteria on the more vulnerable foods. Inadequate ventilation will also contribute to the cleaning bill because, if grease and steam-laden fumes are allowed to remain in the kitchen, they will condense on to surfaces making effective cleaning much more difficult.

Ventilation can be achieved either naturally or artificially. Natural ventilation can be supplied through windows and doors although clearly, in cold weather, it may not always be convenient to have all the necessary windows open. Open windows also have the added disadvantage of admitting dust and insects, although the latter can be controlled by fitting perforated gauze coverings. Any covering will, however, restrict the circulation of air, can be difficult to clean and may be easily broken. Although a kitchen may have sufficient windows, they may not be positioned to give the most effective circulation when open and their constant opening and closing by food handlers can present an additional hazard through hands touching fitments which have become contaminated. Most kitchens therefore will need some form of mechanical ventilation, especially those which are of peculiar shape, size, below ground level, or enclosed within a building.

The caterer will need expert advice on deciding which type of ventilation is best for his premises but, as a general rule in deciding on the design of the system, it is always better to overestimate than underestimate. Although the initial cost may be higher, the long-term advantages will justify the expense. There are many heating and ventilation engineers available to give advice.

The simplest type of mechanical ventilation can be an electric extractor fan fitted into an external wall or window and operated by either a pull cord or switch. Pull cords, incidentally, are not recommended because of the difficulty in cleaning them. The positioning of the fan is important. It should be placed to pick up the majority of the fumes from the kitchen. Externally it should not be allowed to discharge at the face level of passers-by or where the discharge might carry to other rooms.

It has been suggested that one should aim at about 20 air changes per hour in a large kitchen. Although some say that this rate is too high, mechanical ventilation will still be necessary if one is to achieve 10 to 15 changes per hour.

Apart from creating a circulation and renewal of the total air within a room, one should pay individual attention to particular sources of heat, fume or steam. Cooking ranges, fryers and boilers all release large volumes of fumes into the atmosphere and special provision should be made to control this effluvia. The simplest way is to collect the fumes inside a hood which connects to a duct leading to the outside air. The ducting should incorporate a fan which will create an air current away from the source and a filter arrangement to arrest the majority of heavy material such as grease particles. The fan will normally be situated as far from the source of heat as possible to prevent damage to the motor, while the filter will be near to the source in order to absorb as much grease and dirt as possible and thereby prevent any build-up in the ducting.

In providing ducting outside the building, care should be taken to obtain approval for the installation by both the Environmental Health Officer and the local Planning Department. In certain circumstances, planning permission may be required and this should always be obtained before any works are carried out.

In a large kitchen, the best position for the cooking range is in the centre. This permits easier access for cleaning around and underneath the equipment, and also it does give an opportunity to install a canopy arrangement overhead. Canopies come in a variety of shapes and sizes but, as a rule, they should be of stainless and rust-proof metal without hidden corners and voids in which dust can collect. They should not be so high that fumes can escape into the room or so low that staff can knock their heads on them. The filter, which may be of wire wool or similar material, should be readily accessible for easy removal and cleaning. Any fan housing should likewise be accessible.

Cooking smells can give rise to nuisance. Though any filtration system will probably go some way to controlling these, the most effective measure is to install an activated carbon filter. These still need residual

A fresh air/filtration system installed in a bar

deposits of grease, dust etc. to be removed but they can be of particular use where premises are near to residential areas. Some odours can be dealt with by the installation of an oxidiser. How effective these are will depend very much on the type and extent of the odour.

Many modern buildings in this country are equipped with air conditioning which provides a balanced system of purified air into each part of the building, and a separate ducted extraction of stale air. The design should make special allowance for the catering activities.

Increasing concern is quite rightly being expressed in connection with the effects of 'secondary smoking' – that is non-smokers inhaling cigarette smoke generated by others. NO SMOKING areas are often set aside in restaurants, canteens and public places and some catering concerns even ban smoking completely on the premises. To ensure a smoke free and fresh atmosphere for the public, suitable ventilation systems are being increasingly installed in public areas, these also incorporate the necessary filtration equipment.

Ventilation is very much a specialised subject and when choosing equipment, advice from a qualified ventilation engineer is recommended.

Lighting

While premises should take the fullest advantage of natural lighting through large, well-placed windows, efficient artificial lighting is essential throughout the food premises for three main reasons:

1. to enable staff to work in an agreeable environment and to see what they are doing;
2. to facilitate adequate cleaning by revealing what might otherwise be 'hidden spots'; and
3. to prevent accidents.

Adequate lighting should not be confined to the main work areas but should also be provided in passageways, storerooms, on stairs and in those areas outside a building where staff need to go, such as refuse areas or delivery bays. The design of premises can do much to procure adequate lighting by ensuring that areas are as open as possible, without unnecessary walls or other obstructions. Wall and ceiling finishes can be chosen to enhance available light by using light-reflecting colours.

The number and capacity of lights required in any particular place will obviously depend on the size of the area to be illuminated. From a working point of view, a number of independent lights, positioned over those areas where people work, are preferable to fewer large-wattage lights, which will need to be positioned fairly high to spread the light and which may well lose intensity and cause shadows in the process. Glare from unshaded lights or working in inadequately-lit surroundings will cause fatigue and can damage the eyes. A level of 400 lux on working surfaces is recommended.

The choice of equipment is important. Fluorescent lights will give a more efficient light than the traditional bulb, besides it is easier for a tube to be covered with a shade which will disperse the light evenly. Both tubes and shades can be selected to give a light most agreeable to those working on the premises and without glare. Most designs are fairly easy to keep clean. Tubes also have a longer life and are cheaper to run than tungsten-filament bulbs.

All light fittings, including switches, should be of simple design and preferably flush with the ceiling or wall to permit easy cleaning. Press button or recessed switches should be avoided as food deposits build up on them. Electrical fittings situated near sinks, cooking ranges or refrigerators should be sealed to keep out moisture and should preferably be of either rubber, plastic or rust-proof metal. Wiring should be laid in conduits and, where possible, chased into the wall to avoid unnecessary dust traps.

In a large kitchen it may be preferable to have individual lights, or groups of lights, operated by separate switches. This not only saves electricity and offers a greater flexibility, but also eliminates the need to have a large cluster of switches which may become difficult to clean.

Some food rooms may conveniently be fitted with 'illuminated ceilings'. These consist of a series of fluorescent tubes situated behind a translucent screen. This has the advantage of dispersing the light efficiently, also the surface can be easily cleaned. The main disadvantage, however, is that dust and dirt may find its way behind the screen and create what can become a harbourage for insects.

Water supplies

The availability of a pure mains drinking water supply is taken for granted by the vast majority of people in the UK. There is, however, an increasing number of food producers who have sunk boreholes to obtain their own water supplies as a cheaper alternative to purchasing from the local water company. If food production uses water – as most surely do – the bacteriological and chemical quality of the water must be checked at frequent intervals to ensure that it is not likely to contaminate the product. Water companies are legally required to check the mains water virtually continuously, and extensive sampling programmes are undertaken, not only at the water treatment works but at supply reservoirs and from consumer's taps. The results are submitted to the local district council and to the Department of the Environment so that independent checks can be made.

As far as private water supplies are concerned, the Government introduced the Private Water Supplies Regulations in July 1991 to increase the surveillance of bacteriological and chemical quality of water used for commercial and domestic purposes. Local Councils have the responsibility for monitoring the water in the same way as for mains supplies.

Although it is desirable to use water direct from the mains for food preparation, sometimes water storage tanks are used, which are situated in the roof space. These can be a source of problem if the water becomes contaminated by, for example, insect and rodent pests and birds. Such tanks should be well constructed and fitted with a tight-fitting lid to keep out dirt as well as pests. The tanks may in any case need to be cleaned out occasionally. It *is* important is that checks on the water supply should be carried out regularly. Consult the local Environmental Health Officer if in doubt.

Refuse storage

Refuse containers must be situated ouside the building, preferably in a covered, though not totally enclosed, area.

This is because any such area will be much more difficult to clean if the refuse is wet. However, if the area is roofed and semi-enclosed, this ensures that there is adequate ventilation.

Bulk containers (SULO)

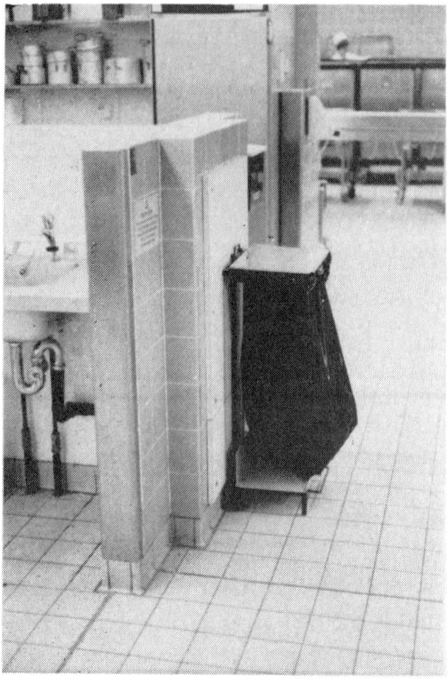

Plastic refuse sack – in hospital kitchen

Refuse can be divided into two types: dry waste, which includes paper, cardboard and boxes; and wet waste, which includes food and general kitchen debris.

The best type of container for wet waste is either a metal or plastic bin with a close-fitting lid which keeps out flies and other insects. The bins should be sited off the ground on racks to allow for easy cleaning and to make the lifting process less arduous.

Dry waste should also be stored off the ground and should, as far as possible, be compacted. This makes collection easier and ensures the maximum use of the available space. Where there are large quantities of paper and cardboard involved, a compaction unit can be installed which compresses the waste into manageable bales.

Where space is at a premium, and where there is no need to separate the refuse, it may be possible to install one of the many types of bulk containers that are marketed. These are of approximately 1 cubic metre

(35 cubic feet) capacity and can replace up to 8 dustbins. The containers are fitted with wheels and, as they are lifted and emptied by a specially-adapted vehicle, road access must be provided or it must be possible for the container itself to be wheeled to the vehicle. The local authority usually advise on the type of bulk container which fits their vehicles. Alternatively, many private waste-disposal firms operate very efficient services and provide their own containers.

Both dustbins and bulk containers need to be kept clean and should be regularly cleansed to prevent food accumulating which might attract flies or give rise to offensive smells. Many councils and private operators of bulk container systems include a steam-cleaning service and traders are well advised to pay the small extra charge for this. If flies or smells do present a problem, particularly in hot weather, various aerosols or dusting powders are available which should be applied regularly.

In all cases, refuse needs to be collected regularly by either the local authority or private contractors. The frequency will depend upon the volume of refuse generated by the business and could be daily.

The working waste generated in a kitchen during the day is best kept in either plastic bags or bins within the kitchen. These should be renewed or cleansed as necessary at the end of each working day. Waste food should never be stored within the food premises overnight.

Most wet waste can be removed by using a disposal unit. These are fitted beneath the outlet of the sink and incorporate an electrical grinding mechanism, reducing the waste to small particles, which can then be sluiced to the drain. These units have many advantages not least that they facilitate the speedy disposal of waste. Care is essential – obviously – to ensure that metal and similar objects do not enter the grinding mechanism. Although safety cut-off switches exist, to react in such circumstances, cutlery can sometimes cause serious damage.

Some drainage systems are unsuitable because of their shallow fall which would soon silt up and block the drain. Sound drainage coupled with an adequate supply of water is essential to ensure that the waste is flushed away.

The refuse area itself should have an impervious floor such as concrete, which is well drained to assist with washing down. Walls should be smooth and impervious for easy cleaning and the area generally should be well lighted, both naturally and artificially. The junction of the walls and floor should be coved to prevent the accumulation of waste.

Free-standing waste disposer – IMC

Sanitary conveniences and staff cloakrooms

All food premises should have adequate sanitary accommodation for staff and, where appropriate, separate accommodation for the public. The accommodation should be readily accessible to staff and while in smaller premises, where only one or two are employed, a single lavatory may suffice; in larger premises involving numbers of employees, it will be necessary to have separate accommodation for each sex, which should be situated at each floor level.

Sanitary conveniences must be kept clean and in efficient working order. They should be so constructed that the walls, floor and ceiling are finished with a smooth, impervious material which is capable of being readily cleaned. Every compartment should have adequate lights and should be ventilated to the outside air. In the case of a compartment not having a window, effective ventilation can be achieved by using a system of ducts, incorporating an extractor fan worked in conjunction with the light switch and an electrical overrun device to provide at least three air changes per hour.

Although lavatories must be conveniently situated within the food premises, they must not be directly entered from a food room, so as to avoid offensive odours penetrating into the latter. It is necessary to provide an intervening lobby between the food room and the sanitary convenience and this should be well ventilated. Neither the compartment containing the sanitary convenience or the intervening lobby may be used for the storage of food.

It is a requirement of the law that there has to be displayed, in a conspicuous position near to the sanitary convenience, a legible notice clearly requesting users to wash their hands after using the convenience.

Although it may be necessary to provide suitable washhand basins elsewhere in the food premises, it is important that one or more basins be situated conveniently near to the sanitary conveniences so that staff may wash their hands having used the lavatory. The wash basins can be situated within the intervening lobby and should be provided with hot and cold water supplies or with hot water at a suitably controlled temperature, soap or liquid detergent, a nail brush and suitable means for hand drying.

In the case of separate conveniences for the sexes, outermost doors should be conspicuously labelled as being for each sex. In order to

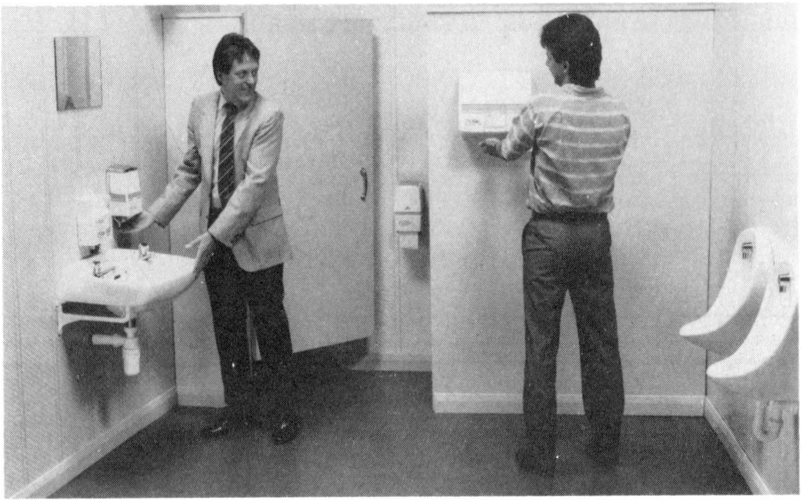

A well-designed wash room (Initial Automatic Services)

maintain an effective intervening space between the sanitary convenience and the food room, the doors should be self-closing.

Adequate accommodation for the outdoor or other clothing and footwear not worn by the staff during normal working hours, must be provided. These articles of clothing must not be stored in a food room and should be stored in separate lockers allocated to each member of staff. Although these lockers may be situated in a food room, it is recommended that a separate room be designated as a cloakroom so that clothes can be stored there conveniently. In the event of outdoor clothing becoming wet, they can be more readily dried than if contained within a small locker. Adequate washing facilities should be provided in the cloakroom, which will not only encourage staff to wash their hands before starting and after finishing their work, but will also act as a reminder that personal hygiene and washing is important. Cloakrooms should be properly maintained and the same general standards for the cleanliness of the food premises should apply.

Chapter 5

Equipment

While the design and maintenance of food premises will be a major influence on whether food hygiene standards are good or bad, the choice of equipment will also influence standards to a very great extent. The condition of equipment must be viewed in two ways:

1. Is it clean?
2. Is it worn or broken?

Both of these criteria are important because any equipment is a potential danger if, by reason of its condition, it cannot be properly cleaned. It is a danger because dirt may accumulate in cracks, hidden corners or within the material with which the equipment has been constructed and that dirt may, in turn, harbour those bacteria which could give rise to food poisoning. Equally, given the very best equipment, unless it is kept clean there is always the danger of harmful bacteria being transferred to the food.

The Food Hygiene Regulations should influence the design, construction and subsequent maintenance of any equipment. The Regulations require equipment not only to be clean but also to be in such condition that it can be thoroughly cleaned. The Regulations go further by insisting that equipment shall not be absorbent and that it shall not present any risk of contamination to the food with which it comes into contact.

In effect, these criteria mean that equipment, with few exceptions, must be made from materials that are smooth, impervious and capable of being readily cleaned. This is a golden rule for the caterer and one that can be applied both to his choice of equipment and to the construction of his premises. Looking at equipment in the form of tables and other preparation areas first, it means that wood should not be used where open food is prepared or stored, the reason being that it simply cannot be adequately cleaned. All woods to a greater or lesser degree are absorbent. The softer woods, even when new, are absorbent and tests have shown that fluids can be 'drawn' into the body of a wooden table

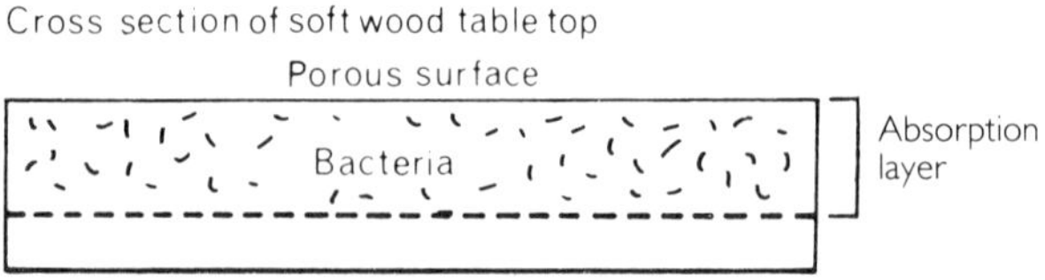

The vulnerability of wooden table tops to contamination

top to a depth of several inches. This being the case, one can assume that bacteria can likewise be drawn into the body of the wood. Once there, normal superficial cleaning, though resulting in conditions appearing clean to the naked eye, will not remove or destroy them. The result is that those bacteria can then transfer to other food which is placed on the table.

The aim, therefore, in any catering establishment must be to eliminate the use of soft wood whenever possible. This extends to the use of plastic-backed nail brushes and plastic broom handles instead of the traditional wooden ones.

The use of wood

There will be parts of equipment in the catering premises which may include wood in their construction. Wooden legs to tables, shelves in a dry store or duck boards on the floor may be used, although only as a second choice to stainless steel or similar metal. They should be sealed by using three coats of polyurethane varnish. The surface to be treated should first be cleaned of any visible dirt, then steeped in a disinfectant solution to destroy both surface and hidden bacteria. The wood should then be thoroughly dried, following which the first coat of polyurethane should be applied. This will usually be soaked up completely by the wood, but after a few hours it will form a base for the second coat. This coat will very often be soaked up again, but having allowed it to dry out, if a third liberal coat is applied the wood should end up with a glazed finish which will resist chipping or extremes of heat and which is smooth, impervious and capable of being readily cleaned. In coating table legs, care should be taken to apply the varnish to the surface in contact with the floor, otherwise moisture may be drawn up the wood and in turn may cause the varnish to peel.

There is an exception to the general rule relating to the use of wood. This is where the traditional chopping block is concerned. Although a more desirable synthetic alternative is available, the traditional block is still considered to be an essential piece of equipment by many.

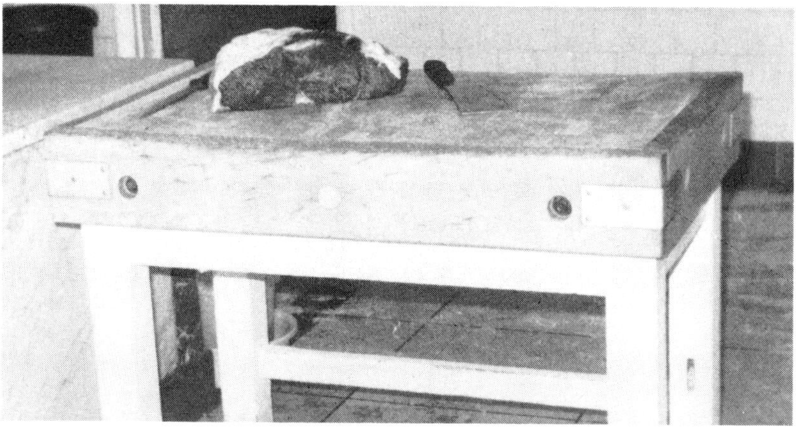

Traditional wooden chopping block

Chopping blocks

These are usually made of a denser, heavier type of wood which is less absorbent than soft wood. To give it additional strength, so that it will not split along the grain, the block is made up of a series of squares of wood which are bonded together. Although it may be dense, the fact that it is wood means that extra special care should be taken with regard to maintenance and cleaning, particularly as it is going to receive heavy treatment from knives and cleavers which, inevitably, are going to create potential harbourages for dirt and bacteria.

The important point about cleaning a block is to ensure, first of all, that as smooth a surface as possible is maintained so that dirt is not trapped unnecessarily. Having cleaned away visible dirt with a scraper and wire brush, it is then necessary to apply a disinfectant solution which will soak into the block and destroy any bacteria which have penetrated into the body of the wood and where they might multiply and provide a reservoir of infection.

Although chopping blocks are usually thick and will withstand considerable wear, there comes a time when the surface has worn too much to enable proper cleaning. The normal practice is to turn the block over and use the reverse side which is similarly constructed. It may be possible, where there is sufficient thickness, for a specialist firm to remove the top layer of wood to leave a smooth surface.

The more modern synthetic chopping tables combine the advantages of the wooden block whilst having few of its drawbacks. They usually consist of a stainless metal table base onto which the chopping surface sits. They can be turned over when necessary and some manufacturers offer a sanding/recovery service whereby worn surfaces are smoothed. These have the big advantage in that they are not absorbent and can be easily cleaned.

Cutting boards

Metal preparation tables will last for years if properly used, but one of the problems often encountered in catering premises is that handlers abuse the surface by using it for cutting or chopping to the extent that it becomes scored or broken. In this condition, it is bound to provide a harbourage for bacteria. Neither stainless steel nor laminated nor formica type surfaces are suitable for cutting or chopping. Chopping should always be confined to a chopping block, while cutting should always be carried out on a special cutting board. Although some hardwood cutting boards are available, the more modern composition or rubber based boards are better because they do not crack; most types can be put into boiling water to sterilise them. All boards inevitably become scored at some stage and when this happens the board should be discarded; although in some cases, manufacturers are able to remove the thin upper layer which is most affected to leave a new smooth cutting surface.

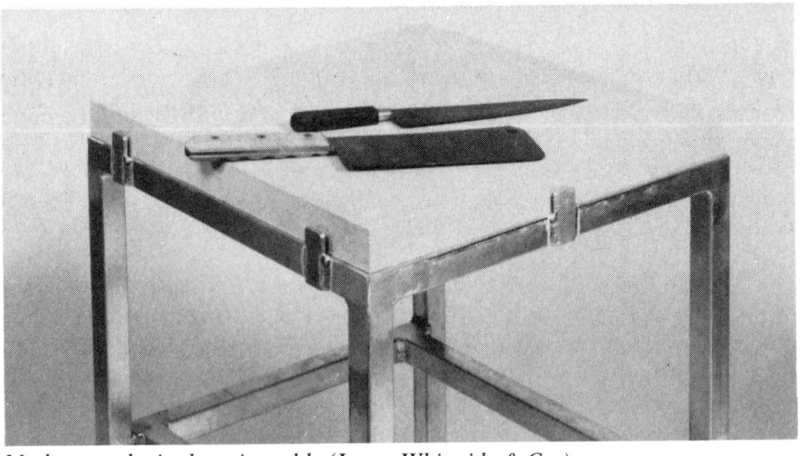

Modern synthetic chopping table (James Whiteside & Co.)

Some composition boards do not withstand high water temperatures readily, in which case they should be steeped in a disinfectant solution for cleaning purposes. If a board warps, it can be warmed until it is soft; then placed on a flat surface and weighted until it hardens flat.

The food handler must be familiar with the dangers from cross-contamination, that is the transfer of infection from one food to another via equipment or hands. There is a very high incidence of cross-contamination when using cutting boards which have been used for a variety of foods without adequate cleaning in between and very special care should be taken to ensure that boards are well maintained and thoroughly cleaned between use. On no account should the same cutting board and knives be used for both raw and cooked foods.

Cutting boards are available in different colours which can be helpful when dedicating boards specifically for raw and cooked meats. Such an arrangement will help to prevent cross-contamination. Even without coloured boards, it is possible to mark them with an approved marker or paint 'R' for 'raw' and 'C' for 'cooked'.

Food preparation surfaces

The choice of surface on which food is to be prepared is vitally important. Failure to ensure a suitable material may provide a dangerous breeding ground for bacteria.

For the reasons outlined earlier, wood should not be used, although it may be used as a base for another surface. For example, a wooden table may be covered with a non-absorbent material such as stainless steel or plastic laminate, both of which provide an excellent surface. Where this is done, however, care should be taken to ensure that there are no hidden gaps between the surface and the table which might harbour dirt. Edges, particularly, should be formed so that water and food scraps cannot work underneath.

The design of tables has improved considerably over the past few years with a tendency to simplify as much as possible to permit easy cleaning. Stainless steel tables are the best because they do not rust and, with their welded seams, eliminate unwanted cracks or open joints. Sealed tubular legs are preferable to angular iron ones because again they eliminate corners in which dirt collects. Tubular legs have often been found to

A simple, well-designed, stainless steel preparation table (Bartlett)

provide a harbourage for cockroaches and other insect pests. Tables with open sides and without drawers are best because they provide less opportunity for dirt to accumulate. If drawers are necessary, they should be of rust-proof metal and easily removable to allow thorough cleaning. Wooden drawers should not be encouraged but where they exist, they may be made acceptable by cleaning and sealing, as described above, with polyurethane varnish.

As a further measure to prevent cross-contamination, tables and other work surfaces are increasingly designated for a particular use, e.g. for raw or cooked food only. These need to be clearly labelled as with cutting boards.

Slicing machines

Effective cleaning of these is especially important because of the risk of cross-contamination of foods. The design of slicers has improved considerably over the past few years, but because of their winding gear, cutting edge and other moving parts the design is fairly complicated with numerous potential sites for dirt and bacteria to collect if the machine is neglected.

Good food practices should apply in the use of the machine and, for example, cooked meats should never be placed on a machine where raw meat may have previously been sliced without it being thoroughly cleaned first. Failure to do so may give rise to cross-contamination between the foods.

In choosing the best slicer for the job, having agreed on the size, decided whether it is to be manually or electrically operated, and checked that the necessary safety features have been incorporated to protect the operator, the best model will be that where the blade and blade housing can be readily dismantled for easy cleaning. The blade must be cleaned daily, but it may also need to be cleaned between cutting various foods and a few simple wing nuts are preferable to a complicated system of nuts and bolts for releasing covers. Thorough cleaning of the following parts is essential: the blade, carriageway, and hand-guard as well as the blade casing, which may become contaminated by pieces of food being thrown from the blade when rotating.

Most machines are made of stainless steel or aluminium. These are easily kept clean and have the advantage over metals which are enamelled, by not chipping or requiring periodic painting.

Machines tend to have the minimum number of oil or grease points but care should be taken to ensure that only oil recommended by the manufacturer is used. This will normally be vegetable oil based and certainly non-toxic. Cooking oil is not suitable.

Where electrically-powered slicers are used, they should be situated near a power point to avoid using long leads. Leads in any case should be securely fixed to the wall and not allowed to trail across the floor or equipment.

Cookers

These are inevitably going to become soiled with food particles, which may well become baked onto the sides or beneath burners. Although sufficiently high temperatures may be applied which will kill off most bacteria in the cooking process, some contamination may occur through particles dropping into the food from the accumulation that has been allowed to remain. The debris will also provide a source of food for insects and rodents.

Although a thorough and regular cleaning programme must be applied with cooking ranges, the design can make this routine less arduous. Cookers should be simple in construction with large uncomplicated surfaces rather than more fanciful designs which will make cleaning difficult. Preference should be given to stainless steel construction over enamelled metal. The inside surfaces should be easily removable and spillage plates below heating rings should also be readily accessible for cleaning purposes.

Cooking ranges should be raised 10–15 cm (4–6 in) off the ground to allow easy cleaning. If they are near the walls, they should be situated a sufficient distance away to enable a person to reach behind when cleaning. Cookers that are situated on an island site have the advantage of being able to be cleaned 'all-round'.

The storage of fuel in most cases does not present a problem, but in the case of solid fuel cooking ranges, care should be taken to ensure that the minimum dust is created when loading the hopper. Fuel must never be stored in the food area.

Today's cooking ranges – modern equipment, easy to clean

Gas ranges should be serviced periodically to check on the efficiency of the burners which sometimes become partially blocked by food particles. In the case of oil and solid fuel ranges, checks should be made of flues to ensure that they are clean and free from obstruction.

Heating cabinets and ovens

These are of metal construction. In recent years, there have been moves to make cleaning that much easier through eliminating hidden areas and difficult corners. The best ovens are those which permit one to reach every part with ease. Doors are either hinged or sliding. While the latter are more convenient in that one does not need an 'opening' area for the door, problems can arise through dirt collecting in the tracks.

Cabinets and ovens should be raised 10–15 cm (4–6 in) off the ground to permit easy cleaning. Regular cleaning of the equipment itself is necessary to prevent any spillage becoming caked, which will be that much more difficult to remove later.

Microwave ovens

These are widely used the catering industry and the home, mainly because they are able to cook, defrost and reheat food quickly, safely and economically. From a bacteriological standpoint, they are efficient in that the temperature penetrates inner areas of food more thoroughly than by conventional heat conduction. It is essential that the food manufacturer's instructions on 'standing time' are followed. During this time, a temperature of at least 70°C should be reached. The food should be piping hot when taken out of the oven.

A microwave oven is a sealed metal box. Because microwave energy cannot penetrate metal, the waves are reflected back towards the food which absorbs them. The door is also of metal, although many have a reinforced glass door so that the food can be seen. Since microwave energy can pass through glass, there is a metal grill, which is denser than the microwaves, fitted inside the glass so that energy cannot pass through. While of great value in food preparation, various safety measures must be undertaken, as shown overleaf.

1. Microwave ovens must conform to BS 3456 or BS 5175.
2. The oven should be regularly serviced and checked for leaks. Some local authorities will carry out free tests upon request; enquire at your local environmental health department for details.
3. Make sure that the door is tightly fitting and that the interlocking safety switch is in good order.
4. Ensure that the free passage of air to the oven cavity is not obstructed by dirty filters or vents.
5. Ensure that there are no loose or missing screws, etc., in any part of the oven.
6. The 'cook' light should be 'on' when the oven is being operated.
7. Metal or foil containers must not be used, neither should metal skewers. China with metal decorations should not be used.
8. Any radiation leakage should be kept below 5 milliwatts per square centimetre at 5 cm (2 in).
9. Never use scouring pads, steel wool or other abrasives inside the oven or around the door.
10. Use only an approved type of 'cling film'.

In 1989 the UK Government sponsored tests which revealed that most microwave ovens, especially the small domestic ones, did not heat food evenly, the power ratings were not compatible and the manufacturer's instructions on use were inconsistent. Since September 1990 all new microwave ovens have to be labelled with their power output using the International Standard method (IEC 705). Unfortunately, this does not overcome the real problem which is that because ovens do not heat evenly the food may not be heated thoroughly enough to kill food poisoning bacteria. It is worth following the advice of the Consumers Association:

- Read the instructions on the food packet
- Stir food if possible
- Turn food during cooking even when the oven has a turntable
- Give the food at least the recommended cooking time
- Allow the food the recommended standing time
- Use the rack supplied or place food on an upturned plate
- Do not cook a whole chicken or turkey in a microwave oven.
- Do not use a microwave oven to cook 'at risk' foods for 'at risk' people, i.e. the elderly, pregnant women or people with reduced resistance to infection through illness or drugs.

Microwave oven in a snack bar – Litton (MacDonald's Catering Equipment)

Caterers would be well advised to use commercial microwave ovens rather than the small domestic models which tend to overheat if used extensively.

The range of advice available to the caterer is commendable, not least from the manufacturers themselves. More general advice is available from The Microwave Association.

Mincing machines

The majority of catering establishments, as well as butchers and some grocers, will use a mincer for reducing the size of meat or vegetables. Most mincers are of metal and consist of a worm drive which pushes the food on to and through a series of perforated discs which determine the final size of the food. The machines are either manually or electrically driven and demand special attention because of the danger of food particles becoming lodged in the worm and associated mechanism.

Modern mincers are designed to facilitate easy cleaning by allowing the easy removal of the worm and mincing discs through one or two simple wing nuts. The actual reception hopper should be so shaped to eliminate unnecessary corners in which food may lodge. Once dismantled, all those parts that come into contact with the food should be thoroughly cleaned and steeped in a disinfectant solution.

An important point here, and this applies to all hand operated machinery, is that care should be taken to ensure that all handles are well cleaned. Plastic handles or grips are preferable to wood and the handles should be steeped in a disinfectant solution to ensure that the hidden area beneath the handle is adequately cleaned.

Potato peelers

These require special attention because inevitably they will collect dirt from the potatoes, either on the scraper discs or in the main wash tanks. They should be thoroughly cleaned at the end of each working day to ensure that peelings and dirt do not accumulate, decompose and attract pests.

Chippers

These are often neglected because of the inherent difficulty in cleaning the actual slicing grids. The grids and associated mechanism, which should be of stainless steel, must be dismantled and thoroughly cleaned at the end of each working day to ensure that there is no accumulation of food particles.

Mixing machines

Mixers may be used for a variety of different foods and thorough cleaning, especially of the bowl and paddles, is necessary between different foods. Most commercial models are relatively heavy and because of the almost inevitable problems with spillage during mixing or from flour dust, they should be fitted with rollers to allow easy removal for cleaning. If placed on tables they should be slightly raised to permit effective cleaning underneath. Electricity supply cables should be dealt

Commercial food mixer

with as for slicing machines. Care is essential to ensure that the operator's clothes do not become entangled with the paddles during operation.

Although early models used wooden paddles, these have been replaced with various designs made from stainless steel or aluminium which have the advantage of being stronger and much easier to keep clean. Bowls and containers, depending on their size, are available in pyrex or stainless steel and provided they are kept in good condition, present few problems.

Ice-cream (soft) machines

These also require special attention, not only because of the nature of the food, but also because of the intricate pipework and valves employed, which can provide a harbour for bacteria if not properly cleaned. Although pipework and the main tank are usually of stainless steel, they must be kept clean and all pipes, taps and valves should be taken apart at the end of each day, washed and steeped in disinfectant solution, then rinsed with clean water. Self-pasteurising machines must receive the same thorough cleansing each week.

Ice-cream should not remain in the machine overnight. Care should be taken not to remove drips from the tap with, for example, a wiping cloth which may itself contaminate the tap and ice-cream. Unopened cans of sterile ice-cream mix should be stored at 3°C before being opened and used in the machine. The temperature of the mix in the machine hopper should be checked by the operator to ensure it is kept below 5°C. All operatives should study the Code of Practice on Scoop and Self-service Ice Cream published by the Ice Cream Alliance and Ice Cream Federation.

Beer and other drink dispensing machines

Most of the traditional hand-pulls in public houses have been replaced by pressurised systems, whereby independent gas cylinders force the liquid from the kegs or tanks through pipes to the taps at the bar or counter. Special controls ensure that the gas used is safe and breweries take great care to ensure that the barrels themselves are clean. This has been made much easier since the introduction of metal barrels to replace those made of wood.

Although stainless metal pipework is still used, transparent plastic piping is being installed to an increasing extent both because of its lower cost and because it can be examined more readily for signs of dirt. Pipework should be regularly cleaned by flushing through with an approved disinfecting agent, followed by a rinse with clean, hot water.

Sinks

The Food Hygiene Regulations, 1970, require that, in all food premises where open food is handled, sinks or other washing facilities must be provided for washing food and equipment. These must be provided with hot and cold water supplies or hot water at a suitably controlled temperature. In planning washing facilities, care should be taken to ensure that the hot water tank is capable of maintaining sufficient supplies at a suitable temperature.

The hot water storage tank and water heater must be big enough to cope with demand, even at peak times. Both will have a marked bearing on how efficiently staff work because with only tepid water they will take twice as long to do a cleaning job than with hot water, besides which only hot water will effectively remove grease deposits (see Chapter 6).

Sinks should ideally be manufactured in high quality stainless steel (18/8) as this metal is stain resistant, rust resistant, and capable of withstanding considerable misuse. Galvanised sinks, enamel sinks and glazed stoneware sinks are all inferior, the latter two being particularly prone to chipping and consequently failing to provide a smooth, impervious surface. Whilst stainless steel is more expensive to install initially, it is a far better investment in the long term. A brief word about plumbing services might be appropriate at this juncture.

Modern plumbing materials include unplasticised polyvinylchloride (UPVC), copper and cast iron, with a tendency to use the former in place of the more traditional materials. This is partly because of initial cost and partly because of the less skilled plumbing work necessary with UPVC. It should, however, be noted that copper and cast iron withstand high temperatures and accidental damage far more successfully and should be used in preference to UPVC in food premises.

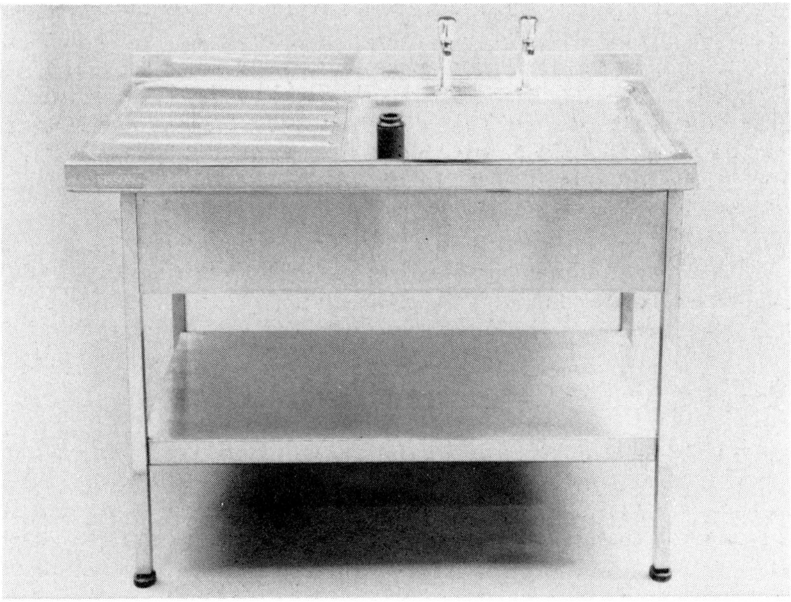

Single sink, stainless steel unit (Sissons of Sheffield)

Hand washing facilities

Washhand basins should be of stainless steel or glazed vitreous ware and should be supplied with hot and cold water, a plastic nail brush, soap or other detergent, and suitable means for hand drying. Although the Food Hygiene Regulations, 1970, refer to washhand basins, in practice the caterer will be wise to ensure that he installs a basin which is slightly larger in size to enable handlers to wash their wrists and forearms which may become soiled as well. The use of a larger basin also helps to prevent splashing on to the floor. Basins should only be used for hand washing.

Utensils

It is easy for any utensil to become a vehicle for the transfer of infection. Knives, choppers, boning tools, whisks and spoons all have access to a wide variety of foods as well as to man himself and, for this reason, special care is important. The condition of utensils must be maintained not only to ensure that they are safe – bearing in mind that a blunt knife is potentially far more dangerous than a sharp one – but also to enable it to be thoroughly cleaned. Whilst the working parts of most equipment are of metal and present few problems, some by virtue of their design do create difficulties. For example, whisks may be of metal but because of their intricate design may make cleaning difficult. Hence it is much better to choose a model which can be effectively cleaned rather than one which has hidden areas where food might lodge.

Wooden handles for utensils are slowly being replaced by plastic ones which are non-absorbent and are easily moulded about the metal part to eliminate hidden spaces for dirt and bacteria to accumulate. Although there was early opposition to plastic handles by the industry on the grounds of their being difficult to grip, modern design has produced handles which are both non-slip and easy to clean.

Wooden spoons should be discouraged because they are absorbent and quickly become worn and cracked. They are difficult to clean effectively and should be replaced with plastic or metal, the former being equally acceptable for use in connection with non-stick appliances.

Although referred to in the chapter dealing with the storage of food, the need for trays and containers to be of suitable material is important. As a general rule, wood should not be used because of the difficulty in cleaning it efficiently. Plastic, polythene and metal are preferable because they are non-absorbent, can be easily cleaned and can be so designed and constructed to eliminate hidden harbourages for dirt.

Containers used for the storage of utensils such as knives, forks and spoons should be of plastic or metal construction and should be so designed as to eliminate corners in which dirt might accumulate. Nests of individual pockets are available in plastic or metal and are designed so that each pocket is 'U' shaped. These make cleaning easier and enable utensils to be handled more quickly and safely.

Tin openers require special care, particularly table-mounted models. These can become very dirty as a result of the grease used to lubricate the column forming an accumulation with food particles. The piercing edge itself can become contaminated and, unless cleaned between use, could give rise to contamination between foods. The most effective method of cleaning is to remove the entire opener and immerse it in hot water and detergent which will remove all the grease and debris. The track, which is usually set on the table, can then be either steam-cleaned or brushed with a hot soda solution.

The common habit of keeping knives on open racks screwed to the kitchen wall should not be encouraged because they are difficult to keep clean and can also be dangerous.

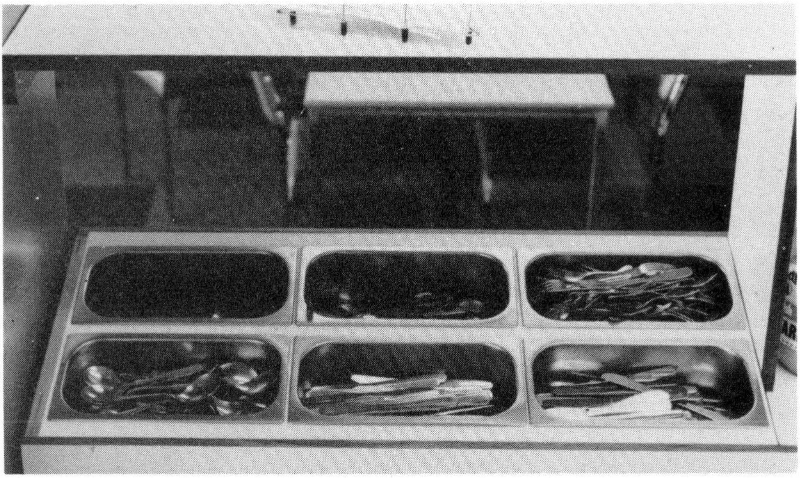

Stainless steel cutlery holder

Saucepans, pots and other similar cooking containers will invariably be of metal. Accumulations of dirt, including that on the outside, should be removed and each appliance should be regularly checked to ensure that there are no cracks which might harbour dirt. Handles should also be regularly checked to ensure that they are secure for carrying and lifting.

All those utensils which contain or are plated with metal containing lead or any other potentially harmful metal or chemical should not be used. Any coated utensil where the covering has broken or worn, should be replaced.

Chipped or damaged plates, cups or other crockery should be discarded, because of the danger from bacteria which may be present in the cracks.

Modern easy-to-clean can opener (Bonzer)

Storage

The storage of equipment needs careful consideration. Pots and pans may be stacked upside-down on metal racks near the cooking area. The

Well-designed storage racks (Bartlett)

racks should be mounted on castors to allow them to be moved. The racks themselves, of course, should be regularly cleaned.

Plates and dishes are best stored on either metal or formica-covered shelves in cupboards. They should not be placed on cloths or sponge sheeting which, although intended to provide a less damaging surface, can become a source of contamination.

Chapter 6

Cleansing Techniques

By now the reader will have gathered, if he or she did not already know, that food hygiene is all about cleanliness, and it is appropriate to examine the way in which a state of cleanliness can be achieved. As with most problems, there are a number of different aspects which need to be considered in order to obtain the best results: the nature of the equipment, its construction and situation, the type of dirt to be removed, the time available, the cleaning materials, cleaning equipment and the staff available to complete the task, are all important considerations. Each of these points will be considered, but first let us examine the various types of cleaning materials available and their advantages and disadvantages.

Soap

Manufactured from animal and vegetable oil in either hard tablet form or liquid gel. It frequently forms a scum when used in hard water supplies and is not very efficient at removing bacteria. It is mainly used for personal hygiene.

Washing cream

Made from pure vegetable oils, the cream is rubbed well into the hands prior to wetting and is very efficient, even in hard water areas, at a much lower cost than hard or liquid soaps.

Synthetic detergents

Detergents are chemicals which are capable of dissolving grease, oil and dirt in water.

1. Anionic (alkaline) detergents comprise the bulk of the common liquid and powder household detergents, used for clothes' washing and dishwashing – high foaming with good rinsing properties.

2. Nonionic (neutral) detergents are particularly useful in hard water areas, as they have less tendency to foam and dissolve mineral oils extremely efficiently.
3. Cationic (acid) detergents are complex chemicals which are capable of dissolving grease. They also provide a sterilising effect on the surface of the material being cleansed. They should never be mixed with anionic agents as they will neutralise each other.
4. Amphoteric detergents.

Disinfectants

These are chemicals which have germ-destroying properties of a proven standard (BS 2462: 1961). They may also be called sanitizers, germicides, bactericides or sterilants. They may be used in conjunction with detergents, but beware of cheap, 'pine' smelling solutions which are seldom of the required quality. So-called 'pine disinfectants' often do not possess any special cleansing quality and are intended merely to impart a 'healthy' smell. More importantly, care should be taken to ensure that this is not intended to mask unpleasant smells arising from, for example, dirty drains. Care must be taken to avoid mixing anionic disinfectants with cationic detergents.

Hypochlorites (bleach) and quaternary ammonium compounds are two examples of disinfectants which are currently available for use as sanitisers but which require special precautions to prevent misuse.

One problem does confront the purchaser of detergents and disinfectants, and that relates to the wide choice and price differentials. The Government has not, so far, produced a list of approved chemicals for the catering industry, despite the presence of a list for the dairy industry. In consequence there are a number of cheap chemicals on the market that are, frankly, little more than coloured liquid and completely useless. It is a false economy to purchase such products – always look for the well-known household names as their substantial reputations have been proven. A further check can be made to see whether the relevant British Standard Specification number is quoted on the label.

Scouring powders

These cleaning materials combine a detergent with an abrasive and frequently a hypochlorite to assist with the removal of hardened food deposits on cooking utensils. Care should be taken to avoid damaging surfaces by over-zealous cleaning with coarse powders. The use of oven cleaners should be unnecessary if routine cleaning of ovens is carried out. A weak solution of bicarbonate of soda should be used to coat the inside surfaces, as this dries and absorbs the fat from the food subsequently cooked in the oven.

Floor cleaners and polishes

A variety of liquid and wax-based cleansers and polishes are marketed to remove dirt and provide a shiny, even a non-slip, surface to tiles, stone, vinyl and synthetic flooring found in food premises.

With the wide range of chemicals available for use, it is important to obtain the correct product for the job, to follow the instructions carefully and to check with the supplier or manufacturer if in doubt. Never mix dissimilar chemicals and only use at the correct dilution rates. Weak

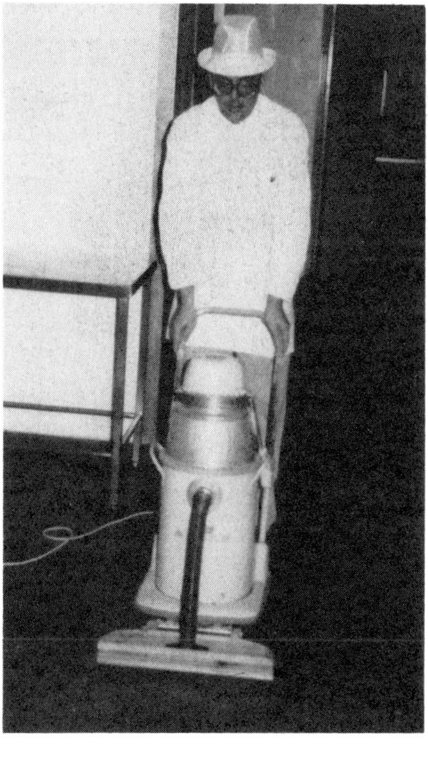

A modern mechanical floor scrubber

solutions are not effective, while strong solutions are not necessarily more effective and are merely wasteful of chemical.

Cleaning equipment

As with chemicals, there is a variety of equipment available for use in catering premises, ranging from disposable cloths to dish-washing machines, and some of this equipment will be specifically discussed later.

Dealing with the cleansing of surfaces first, everyone is familiar with the mop and bucket. These are not recommended but, if they have to be used, the mop requires daily washing and drying or soaking in a disinfectant solution. The bucket can be the breeding-ground for various bacteria unless kept clean and dry. Sponge mops are more effective and hygienic for floor cleaning but must be cleaned daily.

Mechanical scrubbing machines are efficient if used as instructed, but

Use of spray to clean a trolley (Cidelcem Industries)

again special attention should be paid to cleaning and storing the brushes and the machinery or they will act as reservoirs for bacteria. It is essential to dry the equipment before storage, even over-night storage.

The use of dish cloths and floor cloths should be discouraged. Rather disposable paper or non-woven fabrics should be used which can be used for one cleaning job and then discarded. In this way the risk of spreading dirt and bacteria is minimised.

In recent years a range of repeat-use wipers have been introduced which do not break up with use. They are available in various colours so that they can be restricted for use for certain tasks – thus avoiding cross contamination. Even so, it is essential that they are washed in-between use in a suitable bactericidal agent.

A wiping cloth for every task (Kimberly-Clark)

Planned cleaning

Before examining the particular cleansing techniques employed in catering, it is necessary to emphasise the importance of regular cleaning. It is rarely carried out enthusiastically and, by tradition, is a job done by the trainees or the lowest grade of staff. The importance of cleaning has always been underestimated and, not unnaturally, the authors place a great deal of importance on the thorough cleaning of premises and equipment. To 'lead by example' is a good principle for the proprietor or manager, because staff respond to the 'boss' who is prepared to undertake the menial tasks in order to keep the equipment wholesome. There can be no excuse for the accumulations of grease and dirt frequently seen in some catering premises, if one follows the clean-up-as-you-go-rule. This is particularly true of preparation surfaces and cooking equipment.

The premises, i.e. floors, walls, ceilings and equipment, will have to receive regular cleaning and this is where a planned routine will be invaluable. The building or department should be divided up into rooms or areas and a separate schedule prepared for each part. Every detail of the premises, including windows, outside gullies, drains, ventilation system, sanitary accommodation and offices, should be listed. The frequency of cleaning and the method and materials should be specified. Staff should be involved in the discussions on their particular cleaning responsibilities to stimulate interest and the management should carry out regular inspections to ensure a satisfactory standard is maintained. Special training in the techniques should be undertaken and, in larger establishments, records of inspection should be kept. Cleaning should be recognised as a scientific management technique.

Specialist cleaning contractors are now available to undertake heavy duty cleaning of catering premises on a routine basis. Steam or chemical solutions are used to remove encrusted material but, once the original surface has been restored, it is usually possible to maintain it by daily cleansing. Exceptions to this are the cleaning of ventilation ducting fans, degreasing of specialist equipment, servicing of grease gullies, drains and similar equipment. Staff usually respond to the incentive of working in clean premises, but the highest standards can only be achieved by constant effort on a systematic programme.

In some instances where equipment has become so encrusted, it is not possible to clean it *in situ*. An alternative is to remove the equipment and

LEVER CLEAN

CLEANLINESS RECORD *from*
Lever Industrial Limited
COMPANY

ADDRESS (or Branch)

SHEET No.

DATE

✓ SATISFACTORY / ✗ REQUIRES ATTENTION	Date of Inspection
FOOD STORAGE	
Walls Windows	
Floor	
Shelves Racks	
Containers Bins	
PREPARATION	
Walls Windows	
Floor	
Mixers	
Slicers	
Cooking utensils	
Cookers	
Working surfaces	
Meat blocks	
Refrigerator	
Cupboards Racks	
Swabbing cloths	
Fish range	
Canopies	
Sinks Drainage	
SERVERY	
Cups Saucers	
Plates	
Cutlery	
Glassware	
Servers	
Trays	
Plate separators	
Hotplates	
Cupboards Racks	
Tea urns	
Tea Coffee pots	

✓ SATISFACTORY / ✗ REQUIRES ATTENTION	Date of Inspection
SERVERY—cont.	
Swabbing cloths	
Food Display cabinets	
Trolleys	
Condiment containers	
WASHING UP	
Sinks—Washing	
Sinks—Sterilizing	
Draining boards	
Dishcloths	
Drying cloths	
MACHINE	
Interior	
Exterior	
Wash jets Brushes	
Rinse jets	
Curtains	
Overflows	
Trays Racks	
Drainage	
STAFF	
Overalls etc.	
Hands	
DINING (1)	
Tables Chairs	
Linen	
Floor Carpets	
Walls Windows	

✓ SATISFACTORY / ✗ REQUIRES ATTENTION	Date of Inspection
DINING (2)	
Tables Chairs	
Linen	
Floor Carpets	
Walls Windows	
DINING (3) (or Licensed)	
Tables Chairs	
Linen	
Floor Carpets	
Walls Windows	
Bar counter	
Glass sinks Machine	
Cellar floor Sump	
TOILETS (Public)	
Wash basins	
Towels	
Toilets Urinals	
Floor Walls Fittings	
TOILETS (Staff)	
Wash basins	
Towels	
Toilets Urinals	
Floor Walls Fittings	
GENERAL	
Drains	
Wastepipes	
Waste bins	

The Lever Clean record chart (Lever Industrial Ltd)

Heavily encrusted equipment may need special attention

send it for cleaning by specialist treatment which may involve high temperature scrubbers. Replacement units can be used in the meantime. This type of arrangement especially applies to such as grills, oven parts, etc.

In order to provide for efficient, labour-saving cleaning routines, it is necessary to examine the design of premises and equipment and to introduce specifications which incorporate all the advantages and none of the disadvantages which modern materials can produce. Some design details will be examined in the following notes which highlight various parts of a cleaning operation.

Hot water supply

Without question the first fundamental in any cleaning operation is the availability of plentiful supplies of hot water. This is not always found in catering premises, but it is absolutely essential and a legal requirement. Hot water systems are available from a variety of sources and heaters, the most efficient being via a central boiler, the poorest from a small sink-type element heater which does not provide constant hot water.

Floors

Special attention must be given to floors because of the obvious dangers which wet, slippery or greasy surfaces present to staff. Spillages must be removed immediately and the use of sawdust or cardboard should be prohibited as both encourage dirty conditions despite the alleged safety claims. Daily cleaning of floors, particularly floor channels, grids, gulleys and wall/floor junctions, behind ovens, underneath tables and cupboards is essential. The use of coving at the wall/floor junction assists in cleaning, as does the use of round legs on equipment, moveable equipment or cantilevered fittings.

Walls

These should be finished with glazed tiles, polypropylene welded sheeting or a similar smooth impervious material which incorporates the advantages of a non-absorbent, easily-cleaned surface with lower maintenance costs. Routine cleaning with hot detergent water is sufficient without the additional decorating costs which would be incurred with plastered walls.

Lighting

Windows should, of course, be subject to regular cleaning both inside and out in order to obtain maximum benefit from natural lighting. Many catering premises have to rely on artificial lighting to a large extent and it should be emphasised that this produces inferior working conditions. Light fittings need to be kept clean, especially the diffusers on fluorescent tubes. If the fittings are suspended, routine cleaning of the upper surfaces should be undertaken as these attract dirt and dust.

Freezers and refrigerators

These vital pieces of modern catering equipment are frequently abused. It is essential to defrost them regularly and at the same time to clean them thoroughly using detergent and hot water. Walk-in freezers or cold rooms should be washed out weekly to avoid accumulations of dirt and debris on the floor.

Ventilation equipment

An essential component in almost all kitchens, whether in the form of a simple extract fan or a fully ducted air conditioning system. The design of many ventilation systems is inferior, leaving too many dust and dirt collecting surfaces which require regular cleansing. Filters and ductwork need inspecting every fourteen days because of the fire risk inherent in grease and dirt. Anti-drip channels need special attention as do the special ventilation systems provided to deep-frying pans or ranges.

Preparation equipment

The food preparation stage is where the highest standards of hygiene need to be observed and therefore equipment and working surfaces need to be spotlessly clean. This means that equipment must be kept in good condition and cleaned after every use to avoid cross contamination. Suitable detergent/disinfectant solutions, not phenolic disinfectants which will taint food, should be employed and the surface thoroughly dried with a clean disposable cloth after use. This is especially important between use for preparing raw food and cooked food, particularly meat, fish or dairy products. Wiping the surfaces with a reusable cloth is not acceptable as this merely transfers the contamination.

Special attention should be given to the regular cleaning of food slicers and mincers (remember the Aberdeen typhoid outbreak in 1966), not overlooking the prohibition on untrained employees under eighteen years of age. Such equipment should be carefully dismantled to ensure thorough cleaning of all parts.

Sinks and washing-up

Ideally all crockery and cutlery should be machine-washed, and this principle is discussed in detail later on. It is appreciated that many people will continue to hand-wash not only crocks but also pots and pans, so a detailed examination of the correct procedures is necessary.

The sinks themselves should be of stainless steel construction incorporating draining boards and, ideally, a sink waste grinder. The use of enamel or glazed stoneware sinks is inadvisable because of their vulnerability to chipping or cracking which leaves an unhygienic surface. The sinks and fittings must be thoroughly cleaned after use with a fresh disinfectant solution.

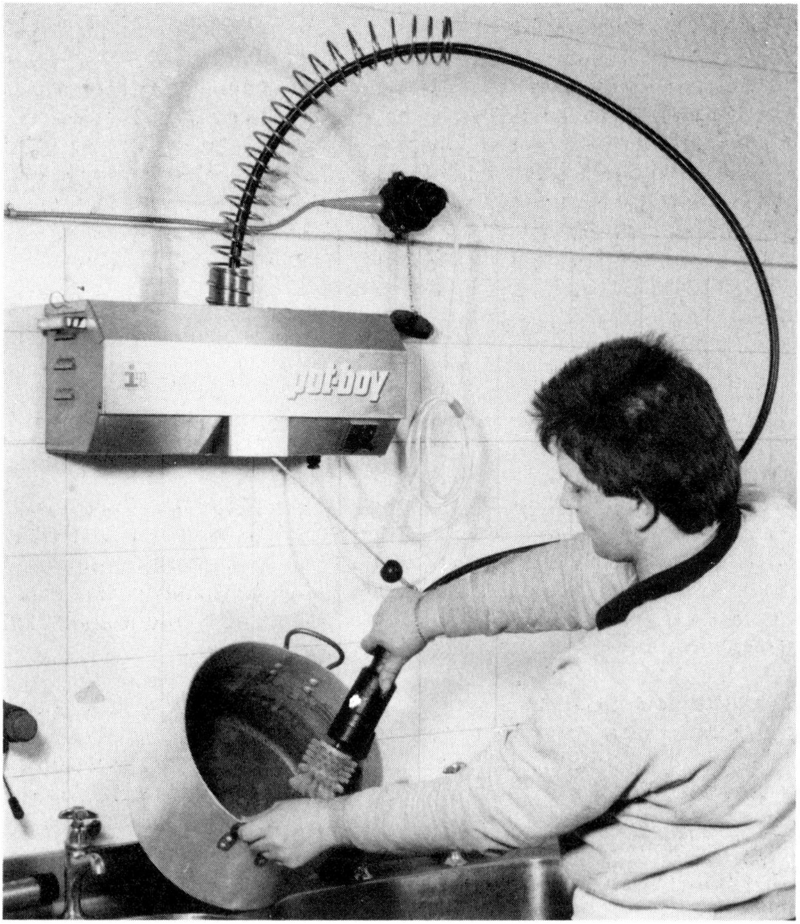

A mechanical pot boy (IMC)

One sink should be used to wash the crockery and cutlery in a suitable detergent solution in order to remove dirt and grease or fat. This solution may be controlled by the use of a tap proportioner connected to a drum of detergent, so that a measured supply of detergent automatically mixes with the water in the sink. Clean nylon brushes should be used but not dishcloths. The water should be regularly changed and maintained at 60°C.

The equipment should then be transferred for at least one minute to the rinsing sink, containing clean water at 82°C, which has the effect of destroying any remaining bacteria. As the hands will not withstand such temperatures, rubber gloves or baskets will be necessary.

Once cleaned and rinsed, the crockery, cutlery, etc., should be either air-dried, heat-dried or hand-dried using disposable paper towelling. Tea towels should not be used, even if freshly laundered each day, because of the risk of cross-contamination which would defeat the object of disinfection.

Plates should be thoroughly dried before stacking. Pots and utensils should be dried before storage. All equipment should then be stored in closed cupboards to reduce the risk of contamination from dust and dirt. Chipped, cracked, stained or broken items should be discarded immediately.

There was a time when the cleaning of pots and pans was like a punishment. Soaking and scraping was necessary and these needed time. Various mechanical cleaners are now available, based on a motorised flexible drive attached to a rotary brush. They are usually wall mounted although they can also be trolley mounted for use as a mobile equipment cleaner.

Washing by machine

Dish-washing machines are expensive pieces of equipment, especially if one accepts the manufacturers' advice to use softened water for best results. There is little doubt that the industrial models provide an efficient labour-saving service to cope with that chore which is one of the least popular in the kitchen. Most machines give a wash and rinse cycle similar to the technique described above, but their biggest fault is their inability to remove dried or encrusted dirt and grease effectively. Some pre-washing is usually necessary when stacking the crockery and cutlery in the trays. Another point to note is that manual washing-up facilities will still have to be available in the event of a machine breakdown.

Today's range of machines offers a size suitable for all needs. They can also be designed to fit into particular areas, including corners.

It is important to ensure that filters and jets are regularly cleaned as they can so easily become blocked with food debris or as a result of salts, e.g. in hard water areas. For the latter reason it is always advisable to use a softener.

Automatically metered quantities of detergent and rinse additives are part of the dish-washing system and many chemical companies offer products and servicing agreements. Until recently the chemicals have been supplied in bulk liquid containers of 5 or 25 litres capacity. However, several companies have developed concentrated solid or granular detergents supplied in compact, lightweight containers which are fitted into wall-mounted dispensing units.

Water temperatures should be checked periodically to ensure that correct levels are maintained, even under load. The temperature of the final rinse is especially important as this is used to 'sterilise' the utensils and enable them to air dry. This temperature should be in the region of 82–85°C.

Only machines constructed of stainless metal should be used.

Space-saving corner unit dishwasher (Energy Mizer)

Glass washing

Although the use of glass washing equipment is becoming increasingly popular in public houses and bars of all types, many premises still use the manual system. This should at least involve a wash sink and a rinse sink, both being supplied with hot and cold water supplies. These should be of stainless steel and incorporate suitable integral draining boards. In the restricted space beneath or behind a bar there is a tendency to install small sinks. This should be avoided, although it is important to ensure that the handler has easy access. He/she will not carry out the washing process properly if it is difficult. A detergent/bactericidal agent should always be used. Glasses should be air-dried on the draining board and should not be left to drain, upside down, on a sponge sheet or cloth, as is often the practice.

Wooden draining boards or the traditional butlers sink should not be used; although often made of hardwood, they cannot be 100% cleaned.

Glass washing equipment is available to suit all needs. They range from the smaller model that relies on revolving brushes to the larger cabinet models that rely on water jets. These also incorporate a rinse cycle. In all machines it is necessary to use the appropriate detergent/bactericidal agent. In some areas it may be useful to use a water softener.

It should never be necessary to dry glasses with a reusable cloth. Disposable cloths may be used but clear instructions need to be given to prevent them being used continuously. Needless to say, it is quite unacceptable to polish glasses by first breathing on them prior to wiping with a cloth!

As an alternative to the use of hot water for the final rinse cycle, a range of chemical agents have been introduced in recent years. These are added to the final rinse which operates at a lower temperature, thereby saving in energy costs and also avoiding steam/heat that can be a problem, especially in a confined space. These chemicals ensure that the end product is bacteriologically acceptable combining the advantages of hot water sterilisation but without its disadvantages. Perhaps the one drawback is that without the higher final temperature, glasses are slower to air dry but this is a small price to pay for the many advantages.

Ice-making machines

Ice in various forms is used to an increasing extent in the catering industry, particularly with drinks. Some ice-making machines rely simply

Glasswasher with integral water softener (Philips)

on a supply of water being frozen into a special shape in a container or mould. Alternatively ice may be made by slowly running water onto a revolving drum which is so cold that ice forms as a layer which is then scraped off into a manageable size. Such a method is often used in larger premises when the demand is for a continuous supply.

It is important to ensure that the equipment is cleaned regularly and that it is kept in good condition. Some older types of metal moulds can even give rise to metallic food poisoning. The water supply itself should be wholesome and once frozen, the ice should not be stored for too long. Remember that bulk ice can easily become contaminated as servers, tongs, etc., are used to transfer it to food or drinks. Fingers should not be used.

As with any cooling equipment, ice-makers should not be situated near to sources of heat.

Sanitary accommodation

Thorough cleaning is necessary using proper disinfectant powder or liquid; they should never be mixed together. This extends not only to compartments and the closet and basins, but also to the associated equipment such as chains, levers, door handles and light switches.

Refuse storage

Although not technically a subject requiring to be discussed in this chapter, refuse storage nevertheless needs to be mentioned because of the cleaning aspects associated with the problem. As previously mentioned, the use of a sink waste-disposal unit is to be preferred or, failing that, a paper or plastic sack system incorporating a sealing device so that the sack can be removed to the refuse storage area both quickly and hygienically. The use of plastic pedal bins and swill bins is to be discouraged because of the hygiene considerations; attraction to insect pests, vermin and smell in particular.

It is advisable to consult the local authority on the preferred methods, because some Councils prohibit the use of sink grinders due to their silting effect of the sewerage system. There is also the question of payment and frequency of the trade refuse collection service which may have a bearing on the final choice of system. All refuse storage areas must be kept neat, clean and tidy by daily attention.

Drainage

Although not a task with which the food handler or kitchen hand will usually be directly involved, it is essential to realise the importance of maintaining clean drainage facilities and to be aware of the potential abuse and expense of dealing with neglected drains. A fundamental rule is that the sink waste gullies should be checked weekly in order to ensure that there is no accumulation of tea leaves or debris likely to create a blockage and overflow. Some gullies may be fitted with special removable baskets to catch such debris from causing more serious trouble, and these baskets may have to be checked daily. Similarly, many catering premises have had grease traps fitted to prevent fat and grease congealing and blocking the drains, and these traps need to be regularly cleaned or the object of providing them is defeated! A strong (5%) bleach solution should be used to clean the waste traps and pipes, twice a week if possible. Manhole covers should be lifted and greased every three months to ensure ease of lifting. These jobs can be undertaken by a servicing contractor who specialises in hygiene services of this nature.

Contract cleaning

Recent years have seen the introduction of contract cleaning into the food/catering industry on a large scale. There are various reasons for this, not least being the difficulties experienced in the industry in recruiting suitable staff. Some undertakings, such as NHS hospitals, have found themselves in a competitive arena whereby some in-house services have proved too costly in comparison with private contractors.

In the early days many contract cleaning firms came on the scene and proved to be most unsatisfactory. Some, on the other hand, proved their worth by offering a thoroughly reliable and professional job to an industry in which hygiene is an essential element. As a means of introducing some discipline into the industry, a negotiating body was set up – the British Institute of Cleaning Science – to which most of the larger firms belong. There is a code of conduct for members who are expected to maintain certain standards. There is merit, therefore, if contractors are used, to check if they are members of the BICS.

What is important when using contractors is to ensure that a precise specification is drawn up. They can only be expected to quote on a definite programme of work listing precisely the tasks to be undertaken, where, to what extent and with what frequency. Unless contractors are quoting on a clear specification it is dangerous to assume that the cheapest tender is the best.

There is merit in clearing any specification with the local Environmental Health Officer before the tendering process is carried out.

Contracts should be reviewed periodically so as to check on performance and also to give an opportunity to make amendments in the light of experience. Some areas, for example, may be found to require greater attention. Any contract should not be too rigidly framed that variations cannot be made as and when necessary by the manager. This ensures, of course, that any revised arrangement must be agreed as part of a package of work with the contractor.

The 'clean' image

This entire book is devoted to various aspects of hygiene and we constantly return to the theme that "Cleanliness sells food". This policy applies to all facets of the food business, both in front of the customer and behind the scenes. It is important to attend to details such as clean public rooms, clean furniture, napkins and table-cloths, clean cutlery, crockery and condiments – not forgetting the sauce bottles – clean glasses and optics or measures and, above all, clean personnel!

Chapter 7

The Storage of Food

It has been said that the three golden rules for storing food are to keep it clean, keep it cool and keep it covered. Certainly the way in which food is stored, in any catering premises, can have a marked effect on its quality. Every care should be taken to ensure that the various types of food are stored correctly before, during and after preparation.

It is essential to maintain a proper check on the food by knowing how much of each particular item is present at any one time. Besides being good business management, it means that food is less likely to deteriorate through prolonged storage.

Although it is better from a food hygiene standpoint to maintain limited stocks, so that store rooms do not become congested, modern trading methods often demand that commodities be purchased in bulk. Therefore care should be taken to ensure that food storage and use is properly monitored.

Rotation of stock

Stock rotation – i.e. the control which ensures that older stock is used first – can only be achieved by a check system whereby, as food is received, it is coded. Retailers sometimes use a colour code to indicate the day/week of delivery, and there are many more complex coding systems. In catering premises, it is much simpler to use a date system.

In order to comply with a European Community Directive 89/395 the UK Government decided to repeal the requirement to mark all perishable foods with a 'sell by' date and to introduce a 'use by' date marking system from January 1991. In addition all 'long life foods', frozen foods, canned products and ice-cream will have to be date marked from June 1992. The datemarks on longer-life foods can use the phrase 'best before' followed by the end of a month, e.g. 'Best before end of January 1992'. It is an offence to sell out-of-date 'use by' foods. It is also an offence for anyone other than the manufacturer to change a datemark after it has been set.

The rotation of stock is particularly important with short life or perishable foods which, under normal atmospheric conditions of temperature and humidity, will deteriorate more readily than those foods which have been preserved, whether by canning, drying or freezing. It should be remembered, however, that no food has an unlimited life and even preserved foods require a degree of rotation.

In general terms the siting of store rooms should be such that they are reasonably accessible to delivery men from the outside, while at the same time they should not be too far from the main preparation or sales area. Ideally they should not be exposed to the direct rays of the sun, which could give rise to unacceptably high temperatures.

In large shops and catering premises, particular members of staff should be designated to supervise the stores and, as far as possible, access should be confined to specific persons rather than just anyone. It should be the supervisor's job not only to look after the cleaning of the store and the control of stock, but he should also be responsible for periodically checking the food for signs of insect or other infestation.

Dry food stores

As the name implies, these should be dry and should also be well ventilated and lit. It is not possible to suggest recommended sizes or capacities because much will depend on the type and size of the business. However the larger the area the better: crowded stores hamper cleaning, encourage pests and make stock control more difficult.

The same criteria that are applied to other food rooms should apply to the construction, namely that all parts should be capable of being readily cleaned. Walls and floors should be smooth and impervious and, where possible, walls should be coved to the floor for easy cleaning. Ceilings should also be capable of being easily cleaned and in the case of outside stores with corrugated roofs, these should be under drawn with plasterboard or insulation board to prevent condensation. In doing so, however, one should make sure that there is ready access to any void created by the installation of a false ceiling. This permits easy cleaning and also minimises the risk of any insect or rodent infestation.

Effective measures against rodents and insect pests should be taken and all holes and other openings which may allow access should be effectively sealed. This is particularly important around doors and windows and where cables or pipes enter the store. This is best achieved by cementing or plastering on a base of expanded wire, which has been pushed into the hole or gap.

Although there may be windows, these should always be covered with perforated metal screens which must be properly maintained. Air bricks should be similarly covered with perforated metal or nylon gauze.

If a dry store is to be effective it should be maintained at a cool temperature, around 8°C. This may be achieved by natural ventilation; although in summer or in an enclosed room, it is best achieved by using a mechanical fan either to exhaust the air into the open or merely to create air movement within the room. The positioning and size of the fan is important as is the need not to pack crates and boxes too tightly together, thereby obstructing the free flow of air. Goods should be stored off the ground and away from the walls. If only for reasons of safety, it is better to have a properly-guarded fan fixed to the wall or ceiling, rather than have one which is free standing with a trailing wire.

Shelving

The fitting out of the store room should be as simple as possible. Most goods will be stored on shelves which can be either open slats or plain wood. In either case they should be smooth and impervious to enable easy cleaning. Wood should be well sanded to give a smooth finish before being gloss painted or varnished to seal it effectively. If plain wood shelving is used with a formica-type surface, make sure that it is smooth and level and that the surface is firmly bonded to it. Also ensure that any strip on the edge of the shelf is well fixed. By so doing, there is less likelihood of food particles collecting and less chance of any insects being harboured as a result. Metal shelving is being used to an increasing extent. It is of long-term advantage to use rust-proof metals which require far less maintenance.

In fitting shelves, care should be taken to avoid creating corners and voids which will collect dust and dirt and be difficult to clean. Shelves should be removable and should not be so deep as to make the goods towards the back difficult to reach.

Cupboards within the store room should be avoided, but if for any reason they are required, the backs should first be removed so that the units fit closely to the wall. All cupboards and similar units should be capable of being dismantled for cleaning purposes.

The distance between shelves will depend to a large extent on the nature of the goods to be stored, but the lowest shelf should be not less than 75 cm (30 in) above floor level to permit the storage of bins below. Care should be taken to avoid storage of heavy goods above shoulder height as this creates a safety hazard.

Storage containers

The containers used in a dry store will depend largely on the type of food. Tinned goods can be stored directly on the shelves or, for convenience, in the boxes they are delivered in. However an advantage of removing cans from boxes is that they can be examined for leakage or other defects which may affect other stock.

Some foodstuffs, such as sugar and flour, are often delivered in large quantities and often in paper or polythene bags which are neither strong nor much of a deterrent to insect attack. These foods are best kept in either metal or plastic bins with close-fitting lids and which are set on roller bases for easy movement. Aluminium containers have the advantage of being both rust-proof and light weight.

A heavy duty, plastic duck-board – light in weight and easy to clean

Where smaller paper, polythene or plastic packages are used and where the turnover is relatively quick, it may be preferable to leave the food in those containers. These should be placed on a tray or in a shallow bin to prevent any spillage affecting food stored below.

Certain foods, such as vegetables, will need to be kept in a well-ventilated container which will hold any dirt or other debris that may become detached. These should be stored at floor level in either plastic or metal trays with perforated sides.

No container should be stored directly on the floor. Unless they are containers with roller bases, they should be put on either metal, plastic or sealed wooden duck-boards to ensure adequate circulation of air underneath.

Chilling rooms

Certain foods which do not need to be stored in a refrigerator, yet which may deteriorate more rapidly at atmospheric temperature, may be stored in a chilling room where the temperature is maintained at 6–8°C.

The temperature is achieved by using a chilling unit which consists of a small refrigeration unit and a fan which circulates the cold air. It is important that the unit is sufficient to maintain the low temperatures while the fan must be large enough to provide a steady but constant movement of the cold air around the food.

The same constructional details apply as for the dry store (above), except that the walls, ceiling and door should be insulated to maintain the lower temperatures.

Salad, vegetables and milk should be kept in the chilling room. It may also be used as a preliminary store for foods which are being cooled prior to being placed in the refrigerator.

Hot food should not be placed in the refrigerator because of its effect in raising the temperature. Food which has beeen cooked but is not intended for immediate use, should be cooled as quickly as possible rather than be left at room temperature which would encourage bacteria to multiply. This is especially important with the so-called 'danger foods', that is gravy, meat, fish and milk dishes. If allowed to cool slowly at room temperature, the bacteria within the food will multiply rapidly and, although it may be placed ultimately in the refrigerator when cool, the bacteria will merely lie dormant until the food is taken out for use.

The rule therefore for cooked food and particularly any of the 'danger foods' is to place it in a chilling room as soon as possible where the temperature will be reduced quickly. As soon as the chilling temperature has been reached, it can be transferred to a refrigerator for longer periods of storage.

There will be food premises where it is not possible to provide a special chilling room, in which case a cooler part of the premises may be adapted, provided there is no risk of contamination. Although a cooling unit is only practicable in a specially-designed room, some cooling effect may be achieved merely be using a fan which itself induces a lower temperature through creating a movement of air about the food. In such cases, the food should be adequately covered and placed so that the air can circulate around it. Once the excess heat has been lost, it should be moved into the refrigerator.

A blast chiller is becoming a feature in many food premises and does an excellent job in rapidly cooling food. Cold air is blown laterally across the food at high velocity to ensure fast chilling to 0–3°C within 90 minutes. The chilling time will vary with the size, shape and weight of food, also its density and moisture content. Blastchillers can be either free-standing cabinets or built-in modular units. All internal surfaces should be smooth, impervious and easily accessible for cleaning – either tough PVC coated steel or high grade stainless steel.

Cold storage and refrigeration

Few food premises – and certainly no catering establishment – can operate without adequate refrigeration facilities for storing food. We know that bacterial growth is reduced with any lowering of temperature and it follows that, if the temperature of food is lowered, it will not only extend its life, but will also keep it safer.

The extent to which bacterial growth is controlled will depend on the temperature. Refrigeration can preserve for days and weeks, but deep-freezing at sufficiently low temperatures can preserve for months or, in some cases, years. Readers may be aware of the food stores which had been abandoned by early explorers that have been discovered in ice in the polar regions and which have remained edible through being stored at sub-zero temperatures.

A well-designed blast chiller (Foster)

An O'cool 520 refrigerator counter display of food (Cidelcem Industries)

Refrigeration space in the catering premises should be readily accessible and adequate in capacity. Larger premises may need the more substantial walk-in type of refrigerator, while others may rely on small commercial, or even large domestic cabinet models. In each case the temperature must be maintained at between 1 and 5°C.

Although refrigerators should be readily accessible, they should not be positioned near any source of heat. Ideally they should be in well-ventilated areas, away from the direct rays of the sun, and, if small models, should be capable of easy removal to facilitate cleaning of the surrounding area.

Construction

The larger type of walk-in refrigerator should be constructed to allow easy cleaning. When installed against walls, it should be so positioned to avoid hidden spaces which could provide a harbourage for insects and other pests. Although motors may be positioned on top of the unit, or underneath they may create noise and collect dust and are best

Refrigerator section showing perspex containers (Cidelcem Industries)

positioned outside the main building in a properly constructed weather- and noise-proofed housing. Motors generate considerable heat in maintaining low temperatures, particularly in hot weather, and they should always be well ventilated.

Refrigerator construction usually consists of a wooden or metal exterior and a metal or plastic-coated inner skin with an insulation layer in between. The inner skin should be stainless or certainly rust-proof and shelving should likewise be of rust-proof metal on easily removable brackets.

Where existing wooden shelves are used, and assuming that they are in good condition, they should be thoroughly cleaned and scrubbed, soaked in hypochlorite solution to kill any bacteria, dried and then painted with at least two coats of polyurethane varnish to form an effective seal.

Floors should be tiled or granolithic type and should be coved to the walls for easy cleaning.

Doors will generally have a heavy rubber gasket to act as a seal. In time this can become perished and difficult to clean, so these should be checked regularly. Doors should also be fitted either with a safety handle which can be operated from the inside, or with an alarm which can be activated by anyone trapped inside.

Smaller refrigerators are usually of all steel/enamelled metal construction and are better designed these days so as to avoid hidden corners which can harbour dirt.

It is absolutely vital that the refrigerator is fitted with a thermometer so that the operating temperature can be checked each day. There are several types of thermometer which can be purchased for use in all sizes of refrigerator – one thing is for sure – the thermostats are usually unreliable.

Defrosting

All refrigerators need to be serviced regularly, and defrosted strictly in accordance with the manufacturer's instructions. Failure to do so will result in a build-up of the ice layer which will lower the efficiency of the unit. Also the motor has to work unnecessarily hard to maintain the temperature, which of course increases the electricity consumption. Many modern refrigerators have automatic defrost cycles.

When refrigerators are defrosted manually, all surfaces should be thoroughly cleaned at the same time. This includes the removal and cleaning of shelving and duck-boards. If it is intended to close down the refrigerator, it should be defrosted, cleaned and thoroughly dried to prevent any mould formation. Ideally, doors should be left open slightly to encourage a constant circulation of air.

When it is intended to defrost a refrigerator, the contents should be run down as far as possible and any remaining food should either be placed in another refrigerator, or be covered and stored in a cool place, or wrapped in several layers of clean paper to contain as much of the coldness as possible.

Using the refrigerator

The storage within a refrigerator is important and certain rules should be observed. It should not be overcrowded, otherwise it is not possible to maintain the necessary circulation of air. All food should be adequately covered and under no circumstances should raw foods – especially raw meat – be allowed to come into contact with other food. The reason is the danger of contamination from the raw food to that food which may be consumed without any further cooking. Besides protecting the food from contamination, adequate covering will also help prevent any drying out or possible absorption of odour from certain foods. Although foods from which there is likely to be any spillage, should be placed in suitable trays, it is a useful general rule to place these items lower down in the refrigerator just in case there is a mishap and blood, etc. is spilt on the food underneath it.

The most important point to bear in mind is that different foods need specific storage temperatures to maximise shelf-life and minimise risks. It may be necessary, therefore, to have more than one refrigerator in all catering premises so that foods can be kept at the temperatures best suited to them, especially if they are the 'high risk' foods which are legally required to be kept at specific temperatures (see p. 38).

It is particularly worth stressing that refrigeration does not introduce cold, it removes heat. Also it does not prevent food spoilage by bacteria, it delays it.

Hot food should never be placed in the refrigerator because it raises the temperature and the steam can cause a build-up of ice on the cooling unit, Those foods which tend to be wet or moist, should be kept in suitable trays or other containers to prevent dripping. Tin foil or one of the many cellophane wrapping materials now available provide an excellent covering for most types of food.

Although foods will keep very well in a refrigerator at the correct temperature for many days, the longer they are kept the more likelihood there will be of some loss of quality. When stacking a refrigerator with a fresh delivery, it is very important to bring old stock to the front so that it will be used first.

With the legal temperature levels established in 1991, it is necessary for periodic checks to be made. All food operators should be equipped with a suitable thermometer which should be fitted with either a rigid or flexible probe in order to test the core temperature of food. Thermometers come in various shapes and sizes. The local Environmental Health Officer can advise on choice, if necessary. Their accuracy will need to be checked on a regular basis and calibration carried out as appropriate.

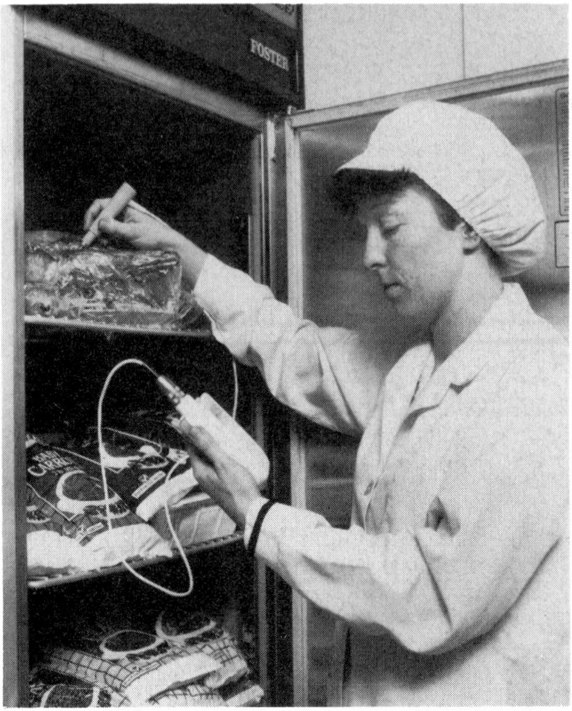

Temperature testing with a probe thermometer (Kane-May Limited)

Where temperature checks are made of storage conditions they should be taken over a period of time, representative of the working day/ environment. It is no use assuming that the inside of a refrigerator is at an acceptable temperature if in reality it is much higher because of doors being regularly opened and closed. This may well mean taking several readings over a 24-hour period. These should be carefully recorded and then examined to see if there are times when safe limits are exceeded. It will be necessary to check the temperature of in-coming goods as well as food stored on the premises.

Unless care is taken when using probes, cross-contamination can easily occur. It is important that the probe is always carefully wiped before and after use and to help the user, a range of sterilised wipes are available. These are in sachet form, one to be used each time the probe is used.

Bacterial wipes for cleaning thermometer probes (Pal International)

An open-fronted refrigerator fitted with plastic curtain (Cool Seal Ltd)

Open-fronted refrigerators are sometimes fitted with flexible plastic 'cold retainers' which help to maintain the lower temperature. These comprise a series of plastic strips that hang down over the open front, thus providing a curtain. They can be very effective although care is necessary to ensure that the strips are regularly cleaned. Customers reaching through the plastic curtain can very easily deposit dirt on the strips.

Freezers

Whilst chilling and refrigeration temperatures represent levels at which foods may be stored, an extension whereby even lower temperatures are involved is found in deep freezer storage. The temperature here is around $-18°C$, and has the effect of killing off many organisms, including some of those in the *Salmonella* group, and greatly retarding bacterial growth generally.

As with refrigerators, food must not be packed in freezers so tight that a circulation of cold air cannot be maintained.

Freezing is intended to keep sound food longer and manufacturers take great care to ensure that only sound food is processed initially. Various methods of freezing foods exist including liquid nitrogen, blast freezing and plate freezing designed to 'quick freeze'. These techniques have been developed to reduce enzyme activity, destroy bacterial cells and prevent destruction of the food cells so that the nutritional value (vitamins) and quality are maintained on thawing.

Deep freezers should be defrosted and cleaned regularly and the food itself should be examined periodically to check on damage to both itself and to wrappings. Stock rotation is essential as even frozen food has a 'shelf life'. Deliveries of frozen food should be transferred to the freezer immediately on receipt.

Many catering establishments use open-top chest freezers similar to those found in supermarkets and stores. Although the same rules for cleanliness and stacking apply as for all refrigerators, it is essential here to ensure that food is not placed above the load line. This is a red line usually marked on the sides of the cabinet, below which freezer temperatures are maintained, yet above which the temperature rises rapidly. If, therefore, the food is stored above the load line it becomes subject to these higher temperatures, which can seriously affect the quality. Apart from the vertical or horizontal cabinet freezers which can be found in many food premises, there are many types of walk-in freezers used in butchers shops, hotels, hospitals and large commercial catering premises. The construction is similar to the walk-in refrigerated store with smooth, impervious walls, floor and ceiling and moveable slatted racking.

Deep frozen food

Frozen food should be used within the time recommended by the manufacturer. As a rule, foods that have thawed should not be re-frozen because this will cause cell structure damage, loss of colour, nutritional value and quality. Food which has been refrozen and subsequently thoroughly cooked is quite safe, but the flavour and texture will be below the high quality of quick-frozen foods.

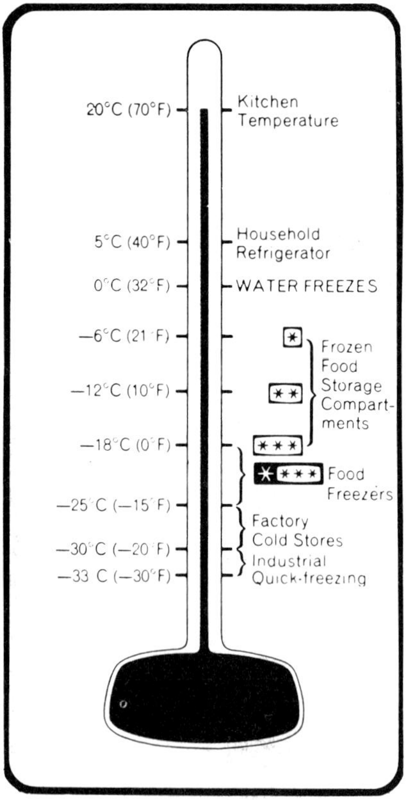

Temperature in freezing (by courtesy of Birds Eye Food Ltd)

The 'star' rating used in connection with frozen food is intended as a guide for storage and operates as follows:

- * has a storage life of up to 1 week;
- ** has a storage life of up to 1 month;
- *** has a storage life of up to 3 months.

Ice-cream is one popular frozen food which has been marketed and developed very successfully over the years. It is a useful food to take as an example of the careful handling and storage required for frozen food. Ice-cream is one of the potentially dangerous foods, because it is an excellent medium in which bacteria can multiply. For this reason, very strict hygiene precautions are taken in the manufacture of ice-cream and temperatures are carefully monitored throughout the process and its subsequent storage. In fact, if the temperature rises above −2°C (28°F), the ice-cream must be reprocessed. While wrapped ice-cream is generally safe from contamination, there is a common practice in catering of using bulk ice-cream in polythene containers. The lids must be kept on such containers and scoops or serving utensils must be kept in a suitable disinfectant solution when not in use to prevent bacterial contamination. It is not uncommon to see an old fruit can containing water being used for this purpose. The disinfectant solution must be changed regularly. Great care should be taken to ensure that the right concentrate of solution, as recommended by the manufacturer, is used. Your local Environmental Health Officer will advise you which chemical is most suitable for your needs. Some local authorities will even supply disinfectants for this purpose, at a charge.

Chapter 8

Pest Control

To most people the presence of rats, mice, flies, cockroaches and even spiders is revolting and always associated with dirty conditions. It is for precisely these reasons that extreme care must be exercised in food premises to prevent the introduction of such pests or, alternatively, ensure immediate steps are taken to exterminate them, once their presence is detected. This chapter describes the various species of pest commonly encountered in Britain, the methods of control available and the preventative measures which can be used.

It cannot be overemphasised that the presence of vermin costs money and causes trouble for the food industry. The total cost of rat and mice infestations in terms of contaminated food and damaged buildings and equipment, runs into tens of millions of pounds each year in Britain alone.

Several species of pest present a risk to human health by carrying bacteria which survive and multiply in suitable foods, and which may subsequently be the cause of illness in the consumer.

Rats and mice

These rodents are commonly encountered in urban and rural areas alike and are recognised carriers of several diseases harmful to man. In particular, they are known sources of infection for plague, leptospirosis and food poisoning.

Rats and mice are particularly attracted to food premises because of the presence of their basic requirements: food, drink and shelter. Dirty premises, poor housekeeping and undisturbed cover are ideal.

The common or brown rat is the species most encountered in this country, although the black or ship rat is occasionally found in dockland areas. The adult brown rat is about 25 cm (10 in) long, weighs 330 g (12oz) and has a blunt muzzle, small ears and a long stout tail. The colour of the coat varies from brown to grey.

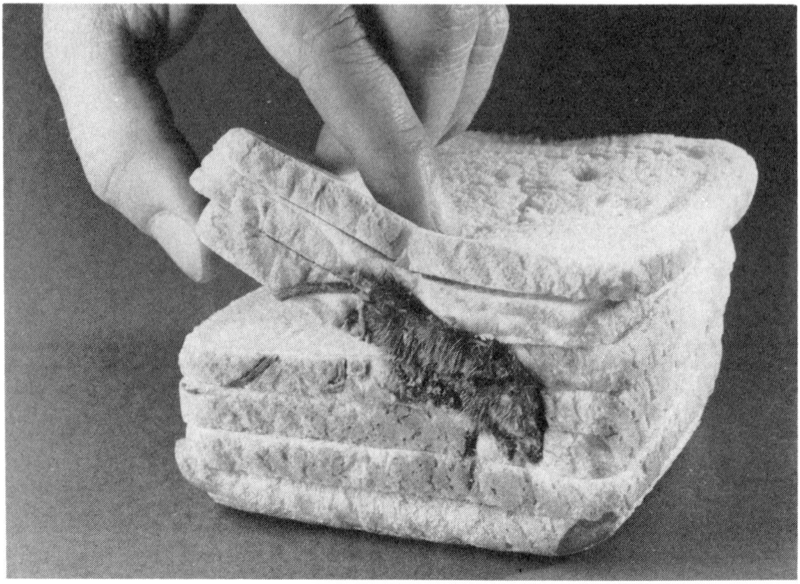

'Foreign body' – sliced mice are a rare but extreme form of contamination (Rentokil Ltd)

Rats and mice are prolific breeders; the young are born in litters of between four and ten. They reach maturity in three months and the females have three or four litters a year – one pair could produce a thousand offspring a year.

The house mouse is a cross between tame and field mice which produces a wide range of colour and size variations. The adult mouse is about 56 mm (2¼ in) long, the muzzle is pointed, it has large, hairy ears and a long tail. Mice are generally more difficult to kill than rats. The presence of droppings is the surest indication of an infestation of rats or mice. Signs of damage, such as gnawing of boxes, sacks, woodwork around doors, and even damaged lead pipes are also indicative of infestation, as are smear marks around pipes and walls.

While it is possible to eradicate a rat or mouse infestation using do-it-yourself techniques such as trapping and even poisoning, such methods are not really recommended for the food trade. Firstly there are definite techniques and 'tricks of the trade' which the amateur would not know; and secondly few people would have the time to devote to ensuring that the rodents were destroyed quickly and efficiently. It is

Brown rat – this one takes the biscuit! (Rentokil Ltd)

therefore suggested that the local Council's Environmental Health Department or a private pest control firm be employed to eradicate the pests. It is also worth considering engaging a contractor to inspect and treat the premises regularly, but this aspect is dealt with more fully later in the chapter.

Cats are often thought to be a good deterrent and may even catch an odd rat or mouse, but domestic pets should not be encouraged in food premises as they may harbour various diseases and parasites themselves. Cats are therefore not recommended.

Flies

These are probably the commonest insect pest found in food premises, and the dirtiest. There are over 3,000 different species of flies found in Britain and over 50,000 different species in the world. Flies are a potential danger to health because they are capable of contaminating food and transmitting disease. These insects are believed to spread cholera, typhoid, dysentery, poliomyelitis and food poisoning. The house fly *(Musca domestica),* the cluster fly, the blow-fly, the blue-bottle and the mosquito are the most important and frequent invaders of buildings.

Flies feed on a variety of rejected foods, refuse and the excrement of man and animals. They will feed on food, contaminate it and lay eggs on it at the same time, Many contaminated foods will be eaten without further cooking and this is why every effort should be made to exterminate flies. The most effective way of controlling flies is to prevent them breeding by efficient refuse storage, elimination of compost heaps, removal of waste, cleanliness and the storage of food in fly-proof containers.

Flies will multiply at an alarming rate; one female lays 100–150 eggs which will hatch and develop into adults in 7 to 14 days, depending on weather conditions.

Houseflies – champion germ carriers (Rentokil Ltd)

Windows can be fitted with fine mesh screens, and hanging strips of plastic can be placed across doorways effectively.

Aerosol fly-sprays can be used inside buildings, although not in food rooms. Flypaper strips are being reintroduced and insecticide lacquers can be applied to wall surfaces to provide methods of destroying flies. The installation of an ultra violet electrocutor can be very effective and certainly overcomes the old problem of dead insects falling into the food!

Cockroaches

These insects are frequently encountered in food premises of all types, from bakeries to cafes and hotels to hospitals. Like flies, these thrive in greasy, wet, dirty, warm conditions. The adults are large ugly insects whose main danger is their ability to carry disease organisms, particularly food poisoning bacteria, which can contaminate food and equipment. Cockroaches are nocturnal insects, so that an infestation can build up undetected unless the premises are used at night when there is more likelihood of the insects being seen.

There are two species of cockroach commonly found in Britain, namely the German cockroach (*Blatella germanica*), familiarly known as the 'steam fly', and the Oriental (or common) cockroach (*Blatta orientalis*), also known as the black beetle. The American and Australian cockroaches are found to a much lesser extent, these having been introduced through consignments of food from abroad in recent years. The Oriental cockroach is twice as long as the German cockroach. These insects favour

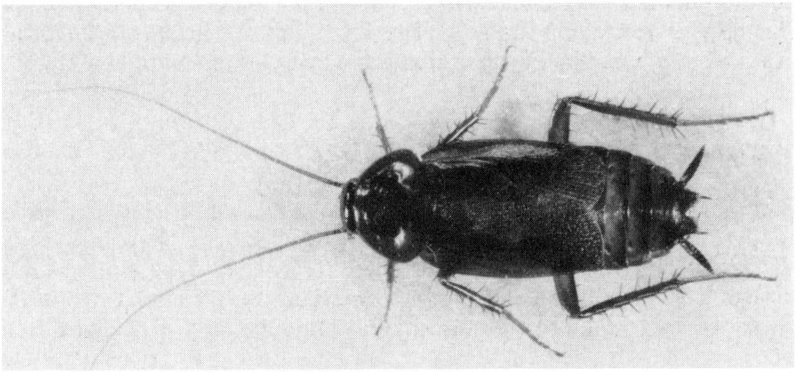

Common or Oriental cockroach – yet another enemy of the caterer (Rentokil Ltd)

inaccessible places, such as pipe ducts, lift shafts, bases of fixed ovens and cupboards, and lay their eggs in capsules out of reach of insecticides. This is why infestations cannot be immediately eradicated other than by a carefully phased programme of treatments, plus associated building maintenance works to deal with structural faults.

Strict attention to hygiene is essential to prevent food supplies being available to the insects while the efficient design, construction and maintenance of buildings and equipment will reduce the possibility of infestations occurring or being allowed to build up.

Dealing with an infestation is best left to trained staff from a commercial pest control company or a local authority. Various techniques can be used to eradicate the pests. The most effective treatment combines an insecticide to kill the young nymphs and adult insects, with a residual insecticide in the form of a lacquer sprayed or painted around the likely breeding places. The search for new and effective insecticides continues because cockroaches are particularly adept at producing an immunity or resistance to particular chemicals after a while.

Ants

These insects frequently invade food premises and domestic dwellings in search of food, particularly sugar-based products. Colonies of ants, particularly the black garden ant (*Acanthomyops niger*), are found in gardens or under paved areas; the much smaller Pharaoh's ant (*Monomorium pharaonis*) breeds in the fabric of a building, around catering equipment and heating duct pipes. The garden ant can be dealt with by tracing and destroying the nest. The Pharaoh's ant is more difficult to eradicate and needs a thorough treatment by a competent operator.

Wasps

Another insect attracted to food premises in its search for sugar-based food, fruit and beer, they are principally a nuisance. They are only a danger to human beings who may be allergic to a wasp sting. Adult insects can be prevented from gaining access to a building by fitting fly-proof screening to doors and windows. Insecticide strips may be used or preferably ultraviolet light electrocutor units which attract and kill the insects. The destruction of wasps' nests can be undertaken by purchasing a quantity of a proprietary powder and carefully following the instructions; or by employing the services of a commercial pest control company or the local authority, if it operates such a service to commerce.

Pests in stored products

Many insect pests attack not only growing crops but also stored food products in factories, warehouses and larders. A small selection of the common insects would include:

Book lice	Insects infest flour and cereals
Biscuit beetle	Larvae attack cereals, biscuits and flour
Cheese & ham skipper	A maggot or larva infesting decomposing meat, ham, bacon or over-ripe cheese
Drug-store beetle	Bread and some drugs are attacked
Flour beetles	Insects feeding on flour or broken cereals
Flour moth & Warehouse moth	Attack flour, milled cereals, dried fruits, chocolate, spices and nuts
Grain & rice weevils	Attack any whole grain
Larder beetle	Attacks most foods and materials of an animal origin
Mites	Very small insects, almost 'dust', which infest stored and packaged foods
Spider beetles	The larvae will feed on almost any food, carpets and clothing

Preventative measures include storage in sealed plastic or metal rust-proof containers and the frequent examination and rotation of food stocks. Once an infestation has been discovered it is essential to remove the foodstuffs and have them destroyed, while the premises can be disinfested using a suitable insecticide. It is recommended that the advice of the local Environmental Health Officer is obtained on the correct treatment.

Birds

Various species of birds have become an increasing problem in recent years. Apart from the damage and defacement they cause to buildings, their nests and droppings can present a serious risk to health. Pigeons, for example, are known to transmit *Salmonella* organisms. Starlings, sparrows, even finches and bluetits have become unwelcome invaders of food factories. Preventative measures include netting and sealing of access points, and the provision of gelatinous material along parapets and walls to prevent birds from perching or nesting on these surfaces.

Eradication measures usually involve extermination by narcotic poisoning, or shooting using high-powered air rifles. Once again, these measures should be left to experienced pest control companies.

The Food Hygiene Regulations have been amended to include a requirement to prevent birds gaining access to a food room.

Preventative measures

It is also possible to take certain preventative measures to reduce the risk of infestations occurring. These include erecting fly screens to open windows during the summer months; placing fine mesh behind air bricks and metal plates at the bottom of external doors and frames to stop vermin from gnawing through the wood; replacing wooden floors and skirting with concrete; keeping refuse bins off the ground; ensuring that there are no sources of water for pests to drink; sealing holes and gaps around pipes, drains and other openings in walls and floors; fixing tiles and wall coverings directly on to brick or plastered walls, not battening which provides a cavity; and keeping the building in good repair. Needless to say, obvious means of access like broken windows or ventilators should be repaired.

Although unsightly, it is better to leave pipes unlagged or uncased so that there is no harbourage for pests. Special attention should also be paid to lift shafts which can be favourite sites for infestations.

All food supplies should be kept in vermin-proof containers, preferably metal, although it is accepted that this is not always practicable. Cases of food should not be stacked against walls or into corners. The practice of painting floor/wall junctions with white paint encourages cleanliness and makes a new infestation easier to spot.

A heated trolley en route for ward kitchen – passing through insect and bird screen

Stock rotation is of vital importance, both from a food freshness and an infestation control angle. Attention to cleanliness, especially removing spillage in food rooms, will reduce the food supply and the attraction for the insect or rodent.

Control measures

As already indicated, there are three methods of eradicating vermin and pests from premises: namely

1. do-it-yourself;
2. commercial pest control companies;
3. the local authority pest control service.

Undertaking the destruction of an infestation by an amateur has the principal attraction of appearing to save money. Many chemists, ironmongers and garden-supplies shops stock entire ranges of insecticides and rodenticides.

By carefully following the instructions, it is possible successfully to deal with an invasion of mice, flies, ants – even cockroaches and rats. Mousetraps can be effectively used if flour, sugar or chocolate is placed on the spike instead of cheese, the balance finely set and the trap placed at right angles against the wall. Insects can be controlled with the use of aerosol insecticide sprays, provided care is taken not to use them where food is liable to contamination. More acceptable than aerosol sprays can be the use of insecticides in the form of residual lacquers. These are applied over the surfaces where insects crawl. They set hard with a lasting – though limited – effectiveness and the crystals are picked up by the insect. These are then either absorbed through the cuticle or taken in through the mouth when the insect cleans itself.

Although not strictly a do-it-yourself measure, the purchase or hiring of an ultraviolet light insect 'killer' apparatus does involve the regular cleaning of the lower tray and the renewal of the strip light from year to year because of the gradual reduction in the effectiveness of the light as an attraction for the insects. Incidentally these units operate most efficiently at night, when insects such as wasps are least active. Nevertheless the installation of one or more in a food room will reduce the flying insect population and thereby the risk of contamination; even the 'fly in the soup' will be less of a possibility.

An ultraviolet electric insect killer (National Pest Control)

All reputable pest control servicing companies belong to the British Pest Control Association and membership of that association is a reliable guide to the quality of the contractor. The major commercial companies have built up a reputation over many years, have extensive laboratory facilities and well-trained staff.

There are numerous companies offering pest control services, ranging from the international to the owner/operator or 'one-man band'. Prices will vary according to the overheads and care must be taken to select a reputable contractor. It is advisable to ask for an initial survey, report and estimate from a company, and possibly compare two such reports and quotations to try to assess the degree of attention which your premises will receive. Once the contract has been awarded, it is vital that a close liaison and confidence is built up between the management and the pest control operative. It is generally prudent to have a contractor calling at regular monthly intervals, to survey and deal with any minor pest infestation, than to wait until the problem reaches epidemic proportions, with the consequent risks to health and safety, not to mention the substantial bill.

Many local authorities offer a similar service to commerce and industry through their Environmental Health Department and trained staff are employed to deal with most types of vermin and pests. Inquiries should be made to the Council Offices, because some authorities prefer to leave pest control in food premises to the commercial companies; the principal reason is to avoid any conflict of interest arising with the Council's legal responsibilities to enforce the legislation in these premises.

It should be emphasised that if a contractor is employed, and especially if a contract is signed for pest control work to be undertaken, this does not absolve or indemnify the owner or proprietor of a food business from his responsibilities under the Food Hygiene Regulations to 'keep the premises free from infestation by vermin, birds or insect pests'. Few contractors call regularly enough to give an effective 'guarantee' against infestation and the costs associated with, say a weekly survey would be too prohibitive for most businesses.

It is therefore essential that persons responsible for food premises should keep a constant watch for signs of pest infestations, keep the premises in a clean and tidy condition inside and out, and maintain a cleaning standard which is linked to stock rotation and the prevention of food and refuse accumulating.

Chapter 9

Personal Health and Hygiene

Some people go through life without having a day off work through illness and are rightly proud of this achievement; other people seem prone to illness and are forever calling the doctor. Undoubtedly there are reasons why the viruses and bacteria which cause disease attack the weak person, and this is largely due to the poor resistance which such a body's defence mechanisms can put up against a massive invasion of these foreign bodies. The first line of defence is our skin. The second line of defence is the white blood cells (leucocytes) whose job is to isolate foreign bodies in the blood and kill them if possible. The third defensive system is the lymph ducts and glands which act as filters to stop bacteria spreading round the body, and finally there are the liver and spleen to act as further filters for the blood and digestive system. These defensive systems can be weakened by a general lowering of a person's health due to the stress and strain of modern living. This can either be physical, due to lack of sleep or overwork, or mental, due to worry over personal or family problems.

There are a large number of contagious or infectious diseases. Some of them are common childhood diseases, such as measles or whooping cough. Others cause severe illness, even death, such as poliomyelitis, meningitis and typhoid. Most people know that these diseases are spread from infectious persons, either by direct contact or contamination, or by droplet infection through sneezing or just breathing in the virus causing the disease. There are even people who have suffered from a disease, apparently recovered and, unbeknown to them, have retained a reservoir of infection in their bodies. Subsequently they become 'healthy carriers', continually but innocently infecting other persons. Knowledge of these ways of spreading diseases is particularly important when dealing with food hygiene because so many foods are ideal material on which the bacteria can survive and multiply, and therefore personal health and hygiene are vitally important.

Let us examine the most important diseases associated with food:

Dysentery and Diarrhoea are particularly prevalent in schools and large institutions where poor cloakroom hygiene, shared equipment and toys are all links in the chain.

Typhoid and Paratyphoid are waterborne diseases which are rare in Britain, although endemic in some countries, due largely to the lack of adequate sewerage and water purification systems.

Dermatitis is probably the most common industrial disease causing lengthy absences. Yet it is largely preventable. Bacterial or fungal infections are usually to blame, aggravated by handling chemicals or other materials (such as flour or sugar) or just by friction from continual handling of commodities.

Food Poisoning is, of course, the subject of a separate chapter in this book and is perhaps the disease most closely associated with food, as the name implies.

With the exception of dermatitis, all the diseases mentioned above, together with a further twenty five, are notifiable infectious diseases. This means that they have to be notified to the local authority by the doctor who is treating the patient. In addition, under the provisions of the Food Hygiene Regulations, if a food handler becomes aware that he is suffering from one of the infectious diseases listed, then he must notify the local authority. In this way the risk of infected food being sold to the public is minimised, but a big responsibility rests on the individual food handlers, be they in a factory or a home.

Most large food manufacturing companies take a special interest in the health and welfare of their staff; indeed, they have a statutory responsibility to do so under the Health & Safety at Work etc. Act, 1974.

Most employers will ask the prospective employees to complete a medical history of previous illness. Some companies – often the larger ones – will further insist upon a detailed medical examination which includes submitting a faecal specimen for laboratory examination. Though clearly a sensible approach, there is a school of thought that believes that medical examinations are of limited value and money spent in carrying them out would be better spent in the education of handlers. This view is also shared by the World Health Organisation.

Notwithstanding these comments the authors understand that a surprisingly large number of applicants are rejected because of poor health and personal hygiene: ear infections, septic skins, boils, dirty bodies, nits, carious teeth, bad hands, marked obesity, bronchitis, osteoarthritis, dyspepsia and severe varicose veins are some of the more common reasons. Some of these can be remedied quite easily and frequently the applicants return much improved, and are able to maintain their healthier condition when subsequently employed. This lack of interest or concern for one's personal health and hygiene is a sad reflection on the education system, which apparently fails to emphasise the basic necessities of a healthy life.

Personal hygiene

Whenever or wherever food is handled, whether in the shop, restaurant, factory or the home, one of the most critical factors is the personal hygiene of the handler. The main criterion is that any person who is suffering from any disease mentioned in the preceding paragraphs, or from attacks of diarrhoea or vomiting, skin infections, discharging ears or nose and throat infections, boils or infected wounds, should avoid handling food or utensils. Even healthy people carry some germs in the nose, throat, bowel and on the skin.

The mouth, nose and particularly the hands, are the most critical areas of the human body because these are the organs where germs can harbour, multiply and subsequently contaminate food and materials. In the 'old days', young people were taught the basic rules of hygiene by their parents and school teachers, but, as the modern generations do not appear to receive this type of education, it might be useful to review these rules and the reasons for them (as listed starting overleaf).

1. Wash your hands thoroughly before starting work, after handling raw foods, frequently whilst handling different foods, and after visiting the lavatory.
   Reasons – see the special section on hand-washing.
2. Keep finger jewellery to a minimum. Better still, have none at all.
   Reason – parts of the jewellery can become detached and fall into the food. It can harbour bacteria and prevent proper hand-washing.
3. Keep fingernails short and clean; do not use nail varnish.
   Reasons – because fingernails harbour dirt and bacteria, also nail varnish can chip off into the food.
4. Keep cuts or burns covered with waterproof dressings.
   Reasons – to prevent cuts being infected which makes them slow to heal. It also enables the hands to be washed without the dressing becoming wet and useless and prevents the food from being contaminated by septic matter from the wound.
5. Do not smoke or take snuff when handling food.
   Reasons – apart from the proven danger to health from smoking, the main risks are that these habits entail the hands being in contact with the nose and/or mouth and consequently the fingers can transfer nose and throat infections (especially *Staphylococcus*).
6. Do not lick fingers when handling food or wrapping materials.
   Reasons – as for smoking.
7. Do not pick your nose, teeth or ears, or scratch your backside.
   Reasons – various infections and bacteria can be resident in these locations and the fingers will act as the vehicle for spread of infection to other persons, materials and food in particular.
8. Do not spit.
   Reason – besides it being a filthy habit, bacteria can be transferred from the mouth and throat region to food and equipment.
9. Do not cough or sneeze over food.
   Reasons – a sneeze contains millions of bacteria which spread over a wide area by means of droplets. Contamination can best be reduced by using a paper handkerchief.
10. Do not scratch your head.
    Reasons – the scalp can be both dirty due to atmospheric contamination and full of infection such as dandruff, which is transferred to the fingernails and subsequently to food.
    Hair should be completely covered when handling food. This applies to men and women alike; no-one likes to find hairs in their food – even clean ones!

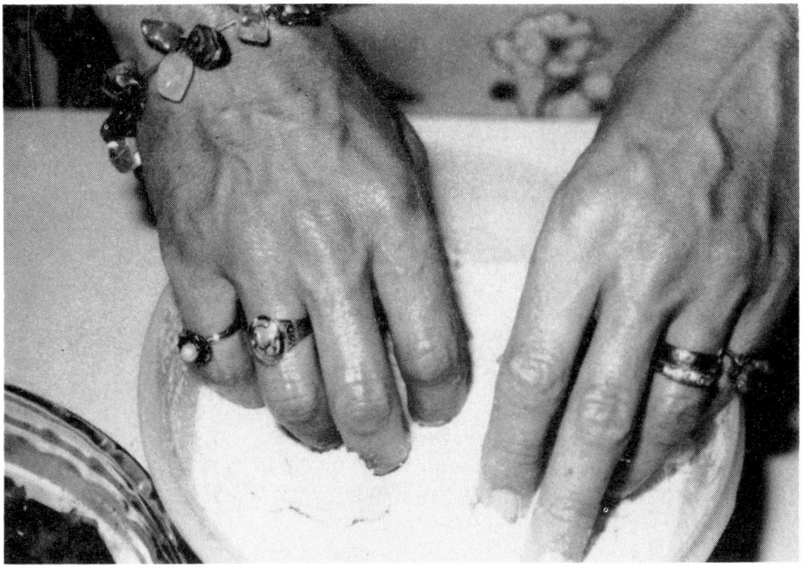

Food handlers should not wear jewellery or wrist watches

11. Do not use an overall, apron or cloth to wipe the hands. Reasons – these habits only spread bacteria and give rise to bigger risks as the bacteria or dirt accumulates. Hand-washing is the only acceptable method of keeping hands clean.

Handling food

'Food should be handled as little as possible.' This is a golden rule of hygiene but is easier said than done. There is no doubt that many outbreaks of food poisoning can be traced to bad practices which involve unnecessary handling of food. A particular danger is the practice of handling raw food, and then handling cooked or semi-cooked food without stopping to cleanse the hands and equipment in between. Poultry, meat products and pet foods are particularly prone to *Salmonella* infection and these bacteria, counted in millions, will be transferred to other foods by cross-contamination, with dire consequences for the ultimate consumers.

If possible, food should be 'handled' by clean utensils such as tongs which are to be found in most baker's and grocer's shops. Hygiene is a way of life, and it is a good habit which will be appreciated by friends and customers the world over. Of course, there are many facets of food preparation and cooking where handling is unavoidable, and this is where clean hands and forearms are vitally important.

Cleaning the hands

Hand-washing should be a very frequent habit when handling food. A washhand basin with hot and cold running water, bactericidal soap, nail brush and a paper towel dispenser or hot air dryer should be standard equipment fitted conveniently close to all preparation areas. Washhand basins should be kept exclusively for the purpose and not used as small sinks for utensils or vegetable washing. Likewise sinks should not be used for hand-washing because the tendency is to 'rinse' the hands under the tap (cold or scalding hot) with dangerous and most unsatisfactory results.

Hand-washing must be thorough, using plenty of hot soapy water and a nail brush to scrub the skin and the fingernails.

Remember that some bacteria will resist removal after five minutes' hand-washing, which is why bactericidal soaps and creams have been introduced. Heat alone will not kill some germs but the chemical sterilants will do so.

It is no use washing the hands thoroughly and then drying them on an ordinary towel or roller towel, because you will probably recontaminate your hands with the previous person's germs. Disposable paper towels or warm air dryers are the answer, as are elbow-operated taps or foot operated taps over washhand basins if one is going to be truly clinical about avoiding cross-contamination.

Most people are taught to wash their hands after using the toilet, but how many people only rinse their fingers under the cold tap as a token gesture? The human bowel carries millions of bacteria, most of which are essential to the body, but a few species of which are disease-causing organisms. Failure to observe this elementary rule exposes other people to infection, which can be picked up on the lavatory seat, chain or lever, door handle tap, towels and light switch.

Hand cleansers and hand drying

Soap itself can harbour germs and experiments have shown that many soaps are ineffective in removing bacteria; their main value is in dissolving grease and surface dirt. For this reason the installation of a

Frequent hand-washing is important

liquid or gel-type soap (containing hexachlorophane or a similar bacteria killer) dispenser at each washstand basin is recommended.

Hand creams are available to act as cleansers where soiled hands need deep cleansing prior to washing, and as barrier creams after hand-washing to protect the skin against irritants such as salts and chemicals. The use of thin polythene transparent disposable gloves may be an alternative solution in certain circumstances.

The old-fashioned roller towel is not acceptable because it means that people, after a while, begin to use the same piece of towel. Automatic roller towel cabinets are better although the mechanism can sometimes stick and one has to make sure that replacement towels are readily available. It should be noted that few laundries operate a towel cleaning service which is completely acceptable in terms of bacterial condition.

A bacterial soap dispenser (Lever Industrial Ltd)

Paper towels are commonly used today and provide a complete answer to the objections just mentioned as each person uses a separate dry clean towel. Care should be taken to ensure that the paper towels are themselves clean. It has been known for them to have been stored in places where they became contaminated by insects and rodents. Regular removal of the waste paper should not be overlooked. Electrical hot air hand dryers are usually foot operated and are found to be successful except in the event of a power cut or breakdown; an emergency supply of paper towels is the obvious reserve. The main disadvantage with hot air dryers is that they take time and the impatient user will remove the hands from the air stream and finish off by wiping the hands on either their overalls or a wiping cloth. The authors have not attempted a cost benefit analysis of the two recommended methods because of the escalating costs of electricity and paper respectively.

Sanitary accommodation

Lavatories are an essential feature of modern living, but how many people appreciate the potential hazard to health which they present? As previously mentioned, the human intestine contains quantities of harmful and harmless bacteria. These harmful bacteria may not affect the carrier but can be spread to other people by carelessness, bad habits and the water closet. The first two causes have been explained, but did you realise that even with the seat and lid closed the flushing of the WC spreads germs into the air, on to the seat, the floor, and under the flushing rim of the pan. Dysentery bacteria can live up to four weeks in faecal matter. The thorough cleansing and disinfection of lavatories and associated apparatus is essential if they are to cease to convey disease-causing organisms.

Many people, especially women, have a justifiable aversion to using public or communal lavatories because of their fear of catching diseases, such as dysentery. This disdain is well founded because of the generally poor standard of hygiene, maintenance and furnishing of sanitary conveniences in this country. It is a sad reflection, however, that it is the users who create the unsavoury conditions in the first instance. In food premises, only the highest standards of equipment and maintenance should be provided in order to reduce the risk of spread of disease to an absolute minimum. Special attention should be given to frequent cleansing of fittings, handles, walls, floors and doors with disinfectants, the provision of pilfer-proof toilet-roll holders and their replenishment.

The cloakroom should be well lighted and ventilated in accordance with the minimum standards required by the Building Regulations, 1985, the Food Hygiene (General) Regulations, 1970, and the Health & Safety at Work etc. Act, 1974. The sanitary accommodation provided for females should be fitted with an incinerator or a sanitary dressing disposal unit which is regularly serviced by one of the commercial hygiene companies now operating in the country. This is a legal requirement wherever several females are employed.

Animals

Under no circumstances should pet animals be allowed access to food preparation rooms. Cats and dogs carry a number of diseases transmissible to man, including the *Toxicaria* round-worm.

Cats are particularly prone to jumping onto preparation tables, and their paws will distribute germs whilst their moulting coats will leave a trail of hairs. Hand-washing after handling a pet animal is vital, and similarly ensuring that no animal is allowed to eat from a dish or container normally used for human food, or vice versa! Utensils and equipment, such as knives, cutting boards and saucepans should be used exclusively for animal food. Animal food stored in the refrigerator should ideally be double-wrapped.

Protective clothing

The Food Hygiene Regulations refer to 'persons handling open food to wear over-clothing', etc., and state that any person who engages in the handling of open food must wear sufficient clean and washable overclothing. The purpose is two-fold. Firstly, and more important, a person's everyday clothing may become soiled and may come into contact with the food. We all know how easily clothes may become soiled and in addition to basic dirt and dust, clothes may become soiled by animals who have been in close contact.

The second reason is to protect the worker himself from soiling his own clothes by the food which could then give rise to cross-contamination.

The Regulations require 'sufficient' clean over-clothing, which means that it must adequately cover the person to the extent of covering any part of the person's body that may come into contact with the food or equipment. It must also be clean. In the past there has been much argument over what is clean. Bearing in mind that an excellent definition of clean is an absence of dirt, you might assume that any over-clothing, however slightly soiled, should be changed. Clearly, this is intended to be interpreted sensibly and what it seeks to prevent is a coat or apron which is so soiled that it is a real source of contamination as opposed to one which has a small amount of dirt, which one must accept with the handling process.

A butcher is most likely to require a clean apron every day, whilst a grocer may only need one every two days. It is a question of degree and generalisations are dangerous.

Although the need to wear suitable over-clothing applies to most food handlers there are exceptions for those who are only handling raw vegetables, intoxicating liquor or soft drinks. This means that a person working behind a bar in a pub need not wear over-clothing, *although* it does mean that once food is handled over-clothing is necessary.

This is an aspect of the Food Hygiene Regulations which is often overlooked especially by publicans. One reason for this is that the traditional role of the publican has changed considerably since the original Regulations were introduced, to the extent that now the service of food has become a substantial part of the public house trade, especially at mid-day. While few local authorities are likely to take it literally, it is nonetheless left to the Environmental Health Officer's discretion as to whether to insist upon suitable over-clothing where food is handled. Most authorities tend not to ask for any over-clothing though there is an increasing number who do where the handling of food behind the bar is substantial.

The choice of over-clothing is important and light colours are preferable as they show up any dirt more readily. Many employers justifiably regard clean over-clothing as a psychological boost to staff. In the United States a report was issued a few years ago which stated that employers who made an ample supply of clean coats available to their staff were rewarded very often by them taking more pride in themselves and in their work which, of course, resulted in a better work performance. This practice has been copied by most of the more hygiene conscious firms in the United Kingdom. Any company policy to make clean coats available as and when necessary (as opposed to only once every two, three or so many days) clearly is desirable and should be encouraged.

Modern materials do not restrict employees to the rather clinical heavy cotton coats once available in 'all shades of white'. Modern colours as well as designs are available and have much more appeal especially to the fashion-conscious female personnel. Drip-dry fabrics tend not to absorb or retain dirt and can, of course, be laundered much more easily.

As a means of countering cross-contamination between various parts of the premises, personnel sometimes use coloured uniforms appropriate to their area or work role. This is to encourage personnel not to move too freely between different work areas. Different coloured coats, ties or hats are sometimes used.

In recent years disposable aprons have been introduced which act as an outer protection to the normal over-clothing and which are especially useful where more dirty tasks are involved such as washing up or dressing poultry. In any case, an outer rubberised or plastic apron is useful where water is involved. Aprons should also be available so that even though a handler may not normally be involved with a dirty process he should be able to put one on rather than risk dirtying his main over-clothing.

A particularly interesting introduction in recent years is that of packs containing a lightweight over-garment, gloves and a head covering. All are made of lightweight material, are disposable and are provided in very small, convenient packs, easy to carry for instant or emergency use. These can be useful in those situations where protective clothing is necessary yet not provided on site.

Protective clothing can only be as effective as the quality of the laundering process. The caterer must realise that visual cleanliness does not necessarily mean that the over-clothing is bacteriologically accept able. An apparently clean coat may contain bacteria that can be passed on to the food or equipment.

It is important to ensure that any laundry facilities are satisfactory. It is obvious to insist that white coats are not laundered with mechanics overalls. It is sometimes less obvious that any washing process should reach temperatures of at least 85°C such that pathogenic bacteria are destroyed.

A system was introduced a few years ago whereby firms that are able to offer a laundry facility acceptable to the food industry could apply for registration. Firms able to satisfy the appropriate BSI standard qualify and obviously should be patronised and encouraged.

The need for hair covering has caused much argument over the years and more especially with younger female (and not always female!) staff who object to having to bundle their hair together. The purpose of hair covering is principally three-fold. Firstly, and from the food hygiene

Disposable apron dispenser (Pal International)

point of view, it is intended to keep hair and dandruff out of the food. Secondly, it helps to keep hair dry and free from grease in a kitchen and, thirdly, and this applies to safety, keeps the hair from becoming tangled in any machinery such as mixers and grinders.

As with other over-clothing modern designs have made them far more acceptable to staff and they range from the traditional cook's hat to the turban type muslin mesh headscarves which tend to be more suitable for female personnel. What is important is that all the long hair and, indeed, most of the hair itself is covered. Needless to say, hair should never be combed in a food room.

Although there is no legal requirement in the UK for food handlers to wear gloves there is an increasing tendency to use them. Industrial rubber gloves are used for heavy duty jobs like dish washing and handling vegetables, and insulated cotton gloves for moving frozen food packs and hot dishes but these are primarily in the interests of employees health and

Men's and ladies' chefs' wear and anti-slip clogs (Alexandra Workwear)

safety. Disposable polythene gloves are ideal for use with 'high risk' foods in order to minimise the risks of cross-contamination and certainly create a hygienic impression. If worn continuously, however, gloves cause perspiration and lead to skin conditions like dermatitis which is often difficult to cure. The insides of gloves need to be cleaned thoroughly from time to time.

The choice of footwear is also important though often overlooked. While shoes are unlikely to come into contact with the food, they are nonetheless part of over-clothing and should be kept clean. They should also be practical in that they provide a safe footing for those who may be working on slippery surfaces or who are expected to climb stairs or steps.

Storage arrangements for clothing is important and the Regulations are explicit in that ' . . . subject to any certificate of exemption, there shall be provided in all food premises where open food is handled suitable and sufficient accommodation for out-door and other clothing or footwear not being worn during working hours . . . and this clothing and footwear shall only be kept in accommodation specially provided . . .'. Where no special provision is made outside the food room such clothing may only be kept in the food room if in suitable lockers or cupboards.

In most food premises a separate room is set aside, perhaps as a staff room, where mackintoshes, coats and so on may be hung. Where this is not available then a suitable locker or cupboard must be provided which allows for the clothing to be hung and which can be closed. The provision of a staff room or similar is preferable as, if outdoor clothing is wet, it has a better chance of drying than if it is hanging in the confined space of a cupboard or locker within a food room.

First aid

All food premises must provide a first aid kit which must be readily accessible to all staff. A kit kept locked in a cupboard with only one key, that is not available when the holder is away, is not acceptable. It should be kept in a staff room or at least nearby the food room so that if a person is injured he can turn to it quickly. Desirably, it should be near to a wash basin so that any injury can be washed and dressed without delay.

The containers should be suitably labelled and a member of staff should be held responsible for ensuring that it is adequately stocked. This same person should ideally have some elementary training in first aid and should be known to all the personnel. A notice indicating who this person is and where he may be contacted should be either indicated on the kit or on a notice nearby.

While the larger manufacturing and retail firms usually have a full-time nurse in charge of a sick room, most firms arrange for selected staff to undergo some training in first aid. Such courses are available in most districts and very good short courses are always available through either

the British Red Cross or the St John Ambulance Brigade. Needless to say, a first aid box without someone to use it sensibly is useless.

The contents of the first aid box are important and it should contain '. . . a sufficient supply of suitable bandages and dressings (including waterproof dressings) . . .' (Food Hygiene Regulations). The following items are the minimum recommended contents of a first aid box:

12 assorted sterilised unmedicated dressings
12 assorted adhesive dressings
1 roll adhesive plaster (1 in/25 mm wide)
2 packets sterilised cotton wool (½oz/15 g)
6 safety pins
1 pair of scissors
1 rubber finger stall

It is a good idea to use one of the coloured bandages and plasters that are available so that in the event of them coming off into the food they are easily recognisable. Some plasters are 'detectable' if passed through a scanning machine. The use of such plasters is essential in any food manufacturing process, which should incorporate an appropriate scanner.

Any break of the skin, whether it be a scratch or cut, should be washed in warm water containing antiseptic and covered with a soft dressing and, if food handlers are involved, this should be then covered with a waterproof dressing. Any cut or abrasion may harbour *Staphylococci* bacteria and the intention is to prevent any contamination to the food through a discharge. If left uncovered, towels, utensils and equipment as well as the food, may become infected and one can imagine the consequences. Fingers are the most vulnerable part of any food handler and a bandage should never be used alone but should be covered with a suitable dressing, finger stall or perhaps a rubber glove. If there is an uncontrollable discharge then the food handler must stop handling food and should immediately see a doctor.

To summarise the points made in the foregoing chapters remember the following ten golden rules –

1. Handle food as little as possible.
2. Keep your hands and nails clean, washing them in hot soapy water frequently.
3. Keep hair covered and wear clean washable clothing.
4. Keep cuts and grazes covered with water proof dressing.
5. Keep cooked and raw food separate.
6. Clean up as you go – do not leave it to the end of the work period.
7. Do not smoke when handling food.
8. Do not handle food if you are ill with diarrhoea or sickness – see a doctor at once.
9. Keep food covered, cold or very hot. *Never* warm.
10. Prepare fresh or frozen food (thoroughly defrosted) for immediate consumption. Avoid reheating food as far as possible.

Chapter 10

Health, Safety and Welfare

At first glance this chapter may seem a little out of place in a book about food hygiene. A closer study, however, will show how inextricably the two subjects are linked when one considers, for example, that the 'No Smoking' rule to prevent contamination will also reduce the risk of a fire and the clean, grease-free floor will reduce the chances of an accident to a member of the staff.

The Factories Acts and the Offices, Shops and Railway Premises Act have been with us for a number of years and set standards which give many employees reasonable working conditions. The Health & Safety at Work, etc., Act, 1974, introduced a new concept whereby everyone became involved from the employer and the employee, the self-employed and the manufacturer to the supplier and the general public. Most premises and all employees are affected by this Act, which many experts consider to be one of the most important pieces of legislation to be passed this century.

The Act involves everyone from the Managing Director to the pot boy, and each person has a responsibility to ensure that his or her actions do not put either him, her or anyone else in danger. The employer must issue a health and safety policy statement to all staff indicating the management's attitude to these matters, and staff must receive adequate training for their jobs. Suppliers of machinery and materials must ensure that these are safe to use and instructions are issued on safe working methods. It is illegal to supply machinery without proper guarding, e.g. food slicers, but the Act places the onus on an employee to use the equipment properly. If the guard has been removed, then the employee may not only have a nasty accident but may be fined in Court as well. Suitable protective clothing should be available in certain situations, and this is another link with food hygiene as is the need to wear clean, washable garments.

Some tasks may well involve the food handler wearing special protective gear. Chain mail aprons and gloves may well be necessary for the person cutting or boning meat. A knife or cleaver can maim a person in the event of an accident and it is both an obligation on the employer to provide adequate protective clothing and an obligation on the employee to wear it. As with traditional overclothing, protective chain mail is available in various forms. By its inevitably intricate construction, particular attention will need to be given to ensure that food particles/bacteria are routinely removed. Stainless metal is preferable to that which can rust and become hard to clean. It is necessary to choose a material which is light in weight and there is now a range of plastic and stainless metal gear that is both safe, durable, light in weight and easy to clean.

A fundamental concept of the legislation is that the premises must be a safe place not only for the staff but also for the customers. This means that the building itself should be sound and that furniture, flooring, machinery and equipment have to be safe to use and maintained in that condition. One company has been prosecuted because a window fell inwards on to a customer! Adequate fire precautions, equipment and emergency instructions are naturally required in all buildings as is the provision of first aid equipment and nursing staff in large organisations.

Other fundamental concepts of the Act are the emphasis on consulting employees and organising training to ensure that staff know how to work safely and what hazards and dangers may confront them. Strained muscles, especially back-ache, are a very common occurrence due to incorrect lifting, but how many people have been taught the simple rules of correct lifting? People working in the food industry are particularly prone to accidents such as cuts, burns, scalds and worse, so it is essential that staff are properly trained in correct working methods and practices to reduce the risk of injury to a minimum. Young people at the start of their careers are particularly in need of adequate instruction before they acquire bad habits and attitudes. Senior staff have a particular responsibility to ensure that safety rules are obeyed and that hazardous premises and practices are immediately corrected.

Safety representatives and notification of accidents

Since 1978, a registered trade union has been entitled to nominate Safety Representatives from among its membership at any place of employment. The TUC has arranged many training courses for these representatives and their role is set out in Regulations which entitle them to inspect premises, receive copies of reports, investigate accidents, and request health and safety improvements. They also represent their fellow employees at meetings of Safety Committees which the employer is obliged to establish on request.

If any person suffers serious injury or illness whilst at work which results in absence for more than 3 days the employer must notify the enforcing authority (i.e. Local Authority or Health and Safety Executive). Full details of the types of injury or disease are listed in the Reporting of Injuries, Diseases and Dangerous Occurrences Regulations 1985. In the event of a death, fracture of the skull or major bones, eye injury, electric shock or fumes causing unconsciousness the enforcing authority should be notified immediately by telephone and a written report on the appropriate printed form should be submitted within 7 days so that an investigation can be made. All employers must keep a record of all reportable injuries and dangerous occurrences for the enforcing authority to inspect. All insurance companies will require full details of such accidents or occurrences for their purposes too. These requirements are independent of the arrangements whereby employees are able to submit self-certification forms without a doctor's certificate when they have been absent from work for less than 7 days for whatever reason.

What is meant by health, safety and welfare in practice?

Health

This subject has already been examined in Chapter 2, dealing with food poisoning, in which it was explained how food handlers suffering from intestinal disorders, ear, nose or throat infections and skin infections can spread bacteria and ultimately cause infection in other people. Persons suffering from typhoid, paratyphoid, dysentery, food poisoning and other specified infectious diseases are prohibited from handling food until medically cleared to resume work.

Good health is of paramount importance to all persons engaged in handling food, and it is in the employers' interests to ensure that their staff are given reasonable facilities to achieve and maintain good health. Enlightened companies offer special medical facilities and schemes whereby employees can obtain specialist medical advice outside the National Health Service system. Many large factories and departmental stores employ trained nursing staff, including consultant doctors, to supervise the health of employees. Such a service may include compulsory examination of employees at regular intervals to monitor the risk of infection. Every food business must provide and maintain a sufficient supply of first aid equipment as required by law (see Chapter 9).

There are a number of industrial diseases, including dermatitis and bronchitis, which can be contracted in food premises like flour mills. The wearing of protective clothing, such as face masks, may well be necessary to reduce the risk of industrial injury or ill-health.

Damage to hearing is another health risk caused through employees not being provided with, or not wearing, ear muffs or earplugs when working at or near noisy machinery. Checks can be made to assess the noise levels and measures taken to sound-proof or insulate the offending equipment in many instances. Exposure to noise causes a gradual deterioration in the individual's power of hearing which is often not appreciated until serious deafness is a fact.

The eyesight can be damaged as a result of either inadequate artificial lighting or unshaded lights which cause glare. Both of these could and should be corrected by lighting consultants. It is not commonly realised that whereas natural sunlight gives light readings of around 5,000 lux, the average artificial lighting in a building is in the order of 500 lux. The eyes adjust to the poorer light intensity, but eyestrain frequently occurs and there is no substitute for adequate artificial lighting.

While on the subject of health, it is perhaps opportune to remember that smoking is not only a bad habit from the food contamination and fire safety angles, but also because of the proven risk of lung disease, particularly cancer, which is associated with cigarette smoking.

Safety

This subject has already been explored in various aspects, but one cannot underestimate the inherent dangers which are encountered daily in food premises. Dangers will range from slippery floors caused by grease and water in the kitchen or over-zealous polishing of the parquet flooring in the dining-room, to hot-plates, ovens, knives, dumb waiters, carbon dioxide gas cylinders, trolleys, refrigeration equipment – the list is endless. Safety rules must be obeyed in everyone's interest, and nobody should be expected to risk injury or even death through the use of dangerous equipment or practices. Dangerous electrical wiring on equipment and plugs is a common hazard. It is amazing how often people risk electrocution by using appliances with bare or loose wires which should have been firmly attached to plugs. The practice of arranging an annual inspection and testing of all electrical wiring and equipment by a qualified electrical engineer is highly recommended.

Correct lifting methods . . .

uncluttered stairs . . .

guarded openings . . .

adequate heating . . .

. . . are among the responsibilities of management and staff alike under the concepts of the important Health and Safety at Work etc. Act 1974

Today's workplace often stocks a variety of chemicals, even as part of a seemingly innocent cleaning agent. Many of these are potentially dangerous and extra care is necessary both in their handling and application. Certain cleaning fluids, for example, can react if mixed together in error to emit dangerous gases. Some agents on their own can give rise to skin burn and corrosion and it may be necessary for employers to provide special protective clothing and equipment. Employees are then obliged to wear that clothing and equipment.

The obligations of employers and their staff are set down in the Control of Substances Hazardous to Health Regulations (COSHH). Suppliers of chemical agents are also required to declare the properties of potentially hazardous materials.

Large numbers of young people are employed in the catering industry in the UK, especially in the take-away food sector and because there is a high staff turnover particular attention should be paid to their training and supervision. In 1988/89 the majority of serious accidents in kitchens were as follows:

1.	Slips, trips and falls	270
2.	exposure (inc. burns and scalds) to harmful substances	243
3.	Struck by moving objects (e.g. knives)	118
4.	Handling, lifting or carrying	104

A study of these accidents confirmed that employers were failing to train their staff, provide protective equipment, arrange safe systems of work and keep premises clean and tidy.

Taking each of the main causes of accidents in turn, the following points emerge:

1. *Slips, Trips and Falls*
   Kitchens and serveries should have a slip-resistant floor which should be kept clean, dry and free from obstruction. Only the recommended cleaning materials should be used because the wrong ones may damage the non-slip properties. If cleaning leaves the floor wet a notice should warn staff of the danger. All spillages should be cleared up immediately – it is not sufficient to cover spilled cooking oil with absorbent paper. Boxes and kitchen equipment should not be left on the floor where someone could trip over them. All kitchen staff should wear sensible footwear.

2. *Scalds and Burns*
   As might be expected, most injuries are to heads and arms but legs and feet, faces and eyes are also vulnerable. Fat and cooking oil should be allowed to cool before being filtered or drained out of fryers or saucepans. Oven cloths or gloves should always be used when handling utensils, pots and pans when cooking. Special care should be taken when using caustic cleaning products. Never use different chemicals at the same time as they can combine to give off poisonous gases.

3. *Machinery Accidents*
   Slicing machines are the most dangerous items of kitchen equipment. There are special provisions for young people involved with either cleaning or operating machinery that is potentially dangerous. Staff must keep the hand guard in place; take special care when dismantling the blade to clean it. Staff should be trained to use all kitchen equipment, how to clear blockages and why special tools are supplied to push food into the machine (not fingers!). Staff training should also include the proper use and storage of knives.

4. *Handling Accidents*
   There should be proper procedures for disposing of broken glass, crockery and empty tins. Staff should also be trained to lift and carry boxes and pans safely.

In larger organisations, there will be designated Safety Officers with special responsibility for all aspects of safety. They will be assisted by managers, supervisors and other responsible staff who have been trained to pay particular attention to safety within their department or shift.

Fire causes millions of pounds worth of damage in Britain each year and many lives are lost. The individual's knowledge of the fire exits and fire drill are particularly important and regular practices are extremely valuable. There is less likelihood of panic if the routine is established. People will also realise the importance of fire check doors and not wedge them open, if it is explained that deaths are more often due to asphyxiation from smoke than from the fire itself.

Welfare

This is one area where widely differing standards are adopted in industry. Some companies realise the advantages in providing facilities and amenities for staff, whereas others let staff fend for themselves. Common examples of such facilities would be staff canteens, concessionary shops, sports facilities and medical schemes, but some companies also offer staff hairdressing and manicuring facilities – even sauna baths are known to exist for the weary employee!

On a more mundane level, there are legal requirements governing the provision of basic welfare facilities such as sanitary accommodation, facilities for the disposal of sanitary and surgical dressings, drinking water supplies, washing facilities, cloakrooms, the provision of suitable equipment, seating, the maintenance of sufficient heating (generally 16°C minimum), the provision of adequate space in which to work, and the maintenance of clean working conditions and premises.

Training

Whilst there is a legal obligation to ensure that staff are properly trained to operate potentially hazardous machinery or carry out processes safely, there is an increasing number of more formal training courses now available especially relating to health and safety. Many employers regard the attendance on such courses as essential for all employees, with special priority given to those undertaking the more hazardous tasks. The catering and wider food industries involve many potentially dangerous tasks and besides any legal obligation to train personnel, an increasing number are being directed to courses and examinations promoted by the same Awarding Bodies involved in the food hygiene field. There are those who feel that some basic qualification in health and safety is as important in the food industry as a qualification in food hygiene and there are moves to make this obligatory. In the meantime, however, the wise employer will enquire as to what training facilities are available and in this connection the local Environmental Health Officer is a good point of contact.

Enforcement of the legislation

The duties of the two main Inspectorates currently overlap in many premises. An attempt has been made to clarify the situation, to split the types of food premises up to reduce the amount of dual inspection. The local authorities' Environmental Health Departments are responsible not only for the Food Hygiene Regulations but also the Health & Safety at Work etc. Act and Regulations in most classes of food premises: food shops, hotels, restaurants, canteens, and departmental stores. There are some food factories, however, where the Health & Safety Inspectors (Factory Inspectors) will still be responsible for enforcing the Act and the Health Officer will also visit the premises under the Food Hygiene Regulations.

Because of the additional responsibilities placed on enforcing Officers by the Health & Safety at Work etc. Act, it is possible that routine inspections will take much longer to complete. The management and the staff can demand to accompany the Officer on his/her inspection and to receive copies of any subsequent report which may be made following the inspection.

If contraventions of the Act are observed, the Inspector can choose which course of action to take. If the defect is likely to present an imminent risk of serious injury, then an Immediate Prohibition Notice can be served on the owner or proprietor. This means that the machine or procedure must cease until it is rendered safe. Alternatively a Deferred Prohibition Notice may be served if there is, or will be, a possible risk of serious personal injury. This notice prohibits something being done or used until certain safety measures have been implemented. A third course would be to serve an Improvement Notice. This could be served where a contravention is found which needs to be remedied within a specified period of time.

Finally, a prosecution may be considered if previous written or verbal warnings have been ignored and/or the contravention of the Act is so serious that the enforcing Officer feels that a fine is the only method of drawing the offender's attention to the need to take health, safety and welfare matters seriously. Inspectors always carry a means of identification, which has to be produced on request, and are entitled to enter any premises at any reasonable time without prior warning. Police officers are entitled to accompany the Inspector, who is also empowered to take samples of materials and equipment, photographs and to make sound recordings, if necessary,

If a person feels that a notice has been unjustly served on him/her, there is an appeals procedure to an Industrial Tribunal within 21 days of the service of the notice.

Good management and business practice suggests that staff will not work efficiently if health, safety and welfare conditions are below standard.

Unsatisfactory premises which create hazards to the customers or public following a prosecution will be bad for business. It must make sense to promote a bright, safe, hygienic image at all times.

The following check list has been prepared as a summary of the principal health, safety and welfare requirements which every commercial company should meet.

HEALTH AND SAFETY CHECK LIST

1. Is the accident book kept up to date?
2. Is the first aid kit properly stocked and easily accessible to staff?
3. Have the staff received first aid training?
4. What action would you take in the event of a serious accident to a member of the staff or a customer?
5. Are all staff provided with suitable protective clothing for their various jobs?
6. Is all equipment fitted with proper guards to prevent accidents?
7. Are instructions displayed and staff trained to operate equipment in a safe manner?
8. Are regular inspections of all equipment undertaken by a competent engineer or electrician?
9. Have staff been instructed in the action to be taken in the event of fire? Is suitable fire fighting equipment readily available?
10. Are the emergency services telephone numbers clearly displayed, e.g. fire, ambulance, police, gas, electricity, water?
11. Are the staff cloakroom facilities adequate and regularly cleaned and inspected?
12. Are there any potentially hazardous processes, e.g. use of chemicals?
13. Do you know where to contact the local Environmental Health Officer for advice?

Chapter 11

The Retail Food Trade

Even to begin to list the number of individual trades involved with food is a mammoth task. To try and examine the various trades from a food hygiene standpoint would require a chapter for each. Yet, if we look at the many trades that go to make up the retail food scene – and these range from the dairy to the delicatessen and from the snack-bar to the supermarket – there are certain common features to all when it comes to hygiene. The following list gives the general points of hygiene that they should all observe.

General

1. Keep all parts of the premises clean and in good condition.
2. Keep all articles of equipment clean and in good condition.
3. Make sure that there is a regular and thorough cleaning programme for all parts of the premises and for all equipment.
4. Ensure that all food is properly rotated so that older stock is used first.
5. Keep perishables in a cool place, preferably a refrigerator.
6. Where cooked food needs to be stored, cool rapidly and store below 5°C. Any reheating should be done thoroughly.
7. Keep refuse in sound containers with tight-fitting lids.
8. If you become aware that there is an infestation of rodents or insects, arrange for treatment immediately.
9. Keep raw food separate from cooked food.
10. Never prepare raw and cooked foods together on the same surface.
11. Ensure that a suitably equipped first aid kit is readily available.
12. Never allow animals into food rooms and discourage the public from taking dogs into food premises generally.
13. Ensure that you are familiar with the provisions of the Food Hygiene (General) Regulations, 1970, as amended.

Butchers

Meat is generally held in refrigerators prior to sale. It is pleasing to note the increasing use being made of refrigerated counters and window display units.

Great care should be taken not to use the same cutting boards or blocks for both cooked and uncooked foods; this is especially important, for example, where fresh poultry are being prepared. Separate cutting boards and knives must be used and, even where wholly non-absorbent surfaces like formica are used for preparation purposes, they must still be thoroughly cleaned between use. This can only be properly achieved by cleaning, and then washing or wiping the preparation surface with hot water containing a suitable disinfectant.

It is an all too common practice for butchers to keep a bucket of water and a cloth handy for 'wiping down'. If this is necessary, then the water should be regularly changed and the manufacturer's recommendation for the concentration of disinfectant strictly complied with; paper wipers are best.

The problem of slippery floors has never been completely overcome although the correct choice of surface can go a long way to making them safe. The use of a suitable detergent, followed by a clean water rinse, will also help reduce slipping. Sawdust is not recommended at all because not only does it create dust, but it can also be difficult to remove from corners where it tends to accumulate. It absorbs blood, but soon smells and encourages bacteria to multiply. In addition, it can very easily be contaminated if obtained from sawmills. Various substitutes have been tried in recent years but none have proved entirely satisfactory.

Meat, in the form of carcases, should not be hung where members of the public are likely to brush against them. It is particularly important in any display to see that the fresh meat and poultry are kept apart from foods, such as cooked ham and corned beef, which will be eaten without further cooking.

Where meat is being delivered, or simply moved around, by being carried on a shoulder, the carrier should wear a clean cap to cover the hair, and a neck apron to reduce the risk of contamination.

In all areas where blood spillages occur, the butcher should see that all drainage channels and pipes are regularly cleaned; otherwise smells will quickly appear. The waste from a butcher's shop is especially vulnerable. It should be stored in well-maintained, lidded containers and these must be regularly emptied and cleaned.

Plastic price tags and labels should be used in the displays of meat. These must be cleaned daily to avoid contamination.

The practice of customers paying a cashier for their purchases is to be encouraged. If a butcher does have to handle money, then regular hand-washing is essential if contamination is to be avoided. Cash is well known as a carrier of germs.

Farming and farm shops

Though the responsible farmer will have always had regard for good food hygiene, attention to the food chain now means that this early part of the food chain comes under even closer scrutiny. There are many ways in which food can become contaminated on the farm, smallholding or nursery, and this can be carried through the chain to cause illness in the consumer. Contamination of the soil in which plants are grown can be absorbed into the cell structure and the misuse of chemical sprays, fertilisers, etc., can also either be absorbed into the texture of the food or can remain residually on the outer surface. Not all foods are necessarily washed before they are consumed to remove such contamination. Careful attention, therefore, to anything which may contaminate the food – either below or above ground – is vital. Two of the most serious food poisoning bacteria are found in the soil – *Clostridium botulinum* and *Bacillus cereus*. *Clostridium tetani* (which gives rise to tetanus) and many other germs which are harmful to humans are also found in the soil. Beyond the actual growing stage, the farmer has a responsibility to ensure that the food is properly handled and stored because during these stages contamination may also take place. Handlers themselves may contaminate the food by not having clean hands, or they may introduce a contaminant from elsewhere – it could even be a poison with which they may have been working in connection with some completely different task on the farm. Most farms are vulnerable to insect and rodent pests. If food is to be stored in warehouses, then careful attention to pest control measures is important because pests can contaminate food through, for example, infected urine and faeces. Warehouses and storerooms may need regular fumigation to eliminate pests and careful attention to preventative measures is essential.

In an ideal world the hygienic handling of fruit and vegetables would start on the farm or in the greenhouse. We have to accept, however, that it is rather impractical to provide water closets and washing facilities out in the fields. Consequently the average agricultural worker has little or no opportunity to practice personal hygiene, except when working near the farm buildings. As a result most fruit and vegetables are contaminated with a variety of bacteria and pesticides. Once the crops have been harvested they are packaged and transported to markets and warehouses or taken to processing factories. Handling is largely by means of mechanical equipment so that potential contamination by human actions is unlikely.

The farmers' responsibility also may involve the way he manages animals. The incorrect use of drugs can result in contamination of the meat that is eventually consumed. Contaminants can find their way into milk produced by cows, and there is an obvious possibility of milk being contaminated when a cow may have been treated in the udder region without sufficient time being given for any drugs to have cleared from the system. In these cases, good animal/farm husbandry is very important and in addition to necessary guidance in connection with animal welfare that can be obtained from veterinary surgeons, there exist other agencies able to assist and advise the producer, such as the Agriculture Development Advisory Service and the National Farmers' Union.Training is also available through the auspices of the Agricultural Training Board.

Many traditional methods of farming will need to be critically examined. The quality of water used in certain processes will need to be checked to ensure that it is clean and wholesome, especially if it is not a mains supply. Some farm drainage systems may need updating and more careful attention given to the purity and quality of foodstuffs. Farmers themselves will need to ensure that their suppliers only provide goods that are of an acceptable standard and quality and unless they are able to do this then they should look elsewhere.

Many farms and smallholdings have developed the idea of a farm shop on the farm, etc., where food is marketed direct to the public. In order to maintain a supply of stock throughout the year many need to buy-in produce from other sources. It is important that the same hygiene requirements apply as for any other retail outlet.

Greengrocers

This is an important stage in the food chain especially as some of the food may be eaten without further treatment.

The variety of fruit and vegetables in Britain all the year round has improved and increased enormously in recent years. This is largely due to the availability of air cargo planes and the technology which enabled large warehouses to be built to store products in the ideal conditions of temperature and humidity. As a result we can purchase kiwi fruit from New Zealand and guava from South America; lettuce and strawberries from Israel, to name a few. Root vegetables such as potatoes, carrots, celery, turnips and parsnips need to be thoroughly washed or scrubbed before cooking and this is best undertaken at a processing plant. When these crops are handled in the market or shop it is important to practise good hand hygiene to avoid cross-contamination through touching other food. Apart from frequent hand-washing it is good practice to wear washable gloves when handling root vegetables.

Dirty hands also result from handling cash and wrapping vegetables in newspaper, so regular hand-washing is necessary. The other rules of personal hygiene set out in Chapter 9 must be observed because all food handlers – whether they are fruit pickers, market porters or shop assistants – can pass germs on to these foods and onto the consumer.

A practice which has become increasingly common in many greengrocers shops and supermarkets involves customer self-service of fruit and vegetables – the motivation is to save on staff costs but there is a real risk that customers can contaminate the produce while they are selecting their purchases.

Although most people would expect to wash all fruit before eating it there are those who believe that washing fruit introduces moisture which encourages mould growth. The answer is to wash the fruit immediately before preparation for cooking or immediately prior to eating.

With all the soil, dirt and bacteria present on vegetables, etc., it is essential that food handlers wear clean washable overclothing, practise good personal hygiene and keep the premises clean. A cleaning schedule should be drawn up which identifies all parts of the premises, equipment, the cleaning agent and the person responsible for the cleaning (and the substitute). The premises should be constructed in accordance with the hygiene principles set out in Chapter 4. Smooth, readily cleansable surfaces should be provided in all food rooms and to all counters and display cabinets. Sacks should be stored on duckboards to make cleaning easier.

Grocers

The proper storage of food is an all-too-common problem in the grocery trade, brought about by modern trading methods which rely so much on purchasing in bulk. Very often when the retailing area is increased, it is at the expense of storage room; so this merely aggravates the problem. In addition, many grocers have extended their ranges or diversified, with the result that sometimes goods are sold which are not really compatible with traditional food stuffs. This might well be objected to by the local Environmental Health Officer. For example, it has been known for grocers to sell paraffin or bulk weedkiller, with the same assistants dispensing both these and the food! Quite apart from the obvious risk of poisoning, there are many foods – such as cheese – which are tainted by strong smells.

The importance of planned cleaning of preparation surfaces, the sterilisation of bacon and food slicing machines, and stock rotation of perishable foods like meat pies, cannot be overemphasised.

The hygienic wrapping and packing of goods for customers is important and all staff should be trained in basic food hygiene.

Delicatessens

By their very nature delicatessen shops and counters in supermarkets display a wide range of ready-to-eat foods such as cooked meats, salads, soft cheeses and smoked products, all of which can be potential sources of food poisoning bacteria. Maintenance of the legal storage temperatures is therefore vital and these should be checked every three hours and recorded on a simple chart if the display unit is not fitted with a recording thermometer.

Cross-contamination is the biggest risk factor and the following food handling practices are recommended:

1. Avoid handling food – use plastic gloves, film or tongs.
2. Use separate spoons or tongs for each product.
3. Use up each product and replace it with a fresh supply – do not 'top up' the display by putting fresh food on top of old stock.
4. Use film or paper on weighing machines so that food is not placed directly on the scale.
5. Use separate knives and slicing machines for cooked and uncooked meats.

Bakery and confectionery

Many of the larger supermarkets now incorporate bakery and confectionery sections, in addition to very large numbers of bakers and confectioners involved with a range of more vulnerable foods. Many of the fillers, especially fresh and artificial cream, used in the confectionery trade are extremely vulnerable in terms of bacterial growth and it is for this reason that strict temperature control is necessary both in connection with the raw ingredients and with the finished article. Products containing meat, fish and soft cheese must be kept at a controlled temperature of 5°C maximum and displayed separately from other bakery products.

Bakery premises are vulnerable in terms of pest infestation. This is because of the warm temperatures that are maintained as a result of ovens, and the fact that there is a plentiful supply of food in the form of food debris that may be left around and flour dust that inevitably escapes into the atmosphere and finally settles in nooks and crevices. For this reason the design of bakery and confectionery premises is important and one should avoid areas which will be difficult to clean and which might become a harbourage for insect and other pests. Restricting the release of flour dust into the atmosphere is also important and a regular and thorough cleaning programme is essential.

Where bulk supplies of flour, sugar, etc., are received they need to be stored in pest-resistant containers so that infestations are avoided. Stock rotation is important, and such premises are a priority for regular visits by pest control personnel, if only in terms of a preventative measure.

Wooden trays should not be used, even with paper linings. Plastic or similar trays that are simple in design and easy to clean should be used. Some plastic trays tend to be aesthetically attractive, incorporating intricate designs and a trade name, but prove extremely difficult to clean.

Supermarkets

Most supermarkets, especially those designed more recently, are well planned and have sufficient space. However there is a tendency sometimes to have long rows of display cabinets, below and behind which dirt can so easily accumulate. These must be regularly moved for thorough cleaning. Supermarkets often rely on open-top freezers; it is important to see that food is not stacked above the load line (see Chapter 7) and that thermometers are fitted in order to check that the correct temperatures are maintained.

Supermarkets often rely on part-time labour helping out at peak business time. It should be remembered that these staff need some training in the rudiments of food hygiene, even though they may only work for a few hours a week.

The hygienic preparation of perishable food in prewrapped preweighed quantities has certain advantages over the more traditional corner shop. However there is a growing tendency to reverse the process and to introduce shops-within-shops in the larger supermarkets and hypermarkets. Instore bakeries with oven-hot bread, delicatessens, butchers, cheese shops and off-licences are common features of such stores. Throughout all such operations, strict attention to personal hygiene among the shop assistants is of fundamental importance.

Food deliveries

It is not uncommon for deliveries to be made to food premises when they are closed – either very late at night or early in the morning. These are sometimes left on the pavement in front of the premises, or perhaps somewhere more secure but equally exposed to contamination. Recent observation showed some trays of bread and other wrapped confectionery left in front of a general store, although other examples have also been noted. Such practices are unacceptable, and where food needs to be left at premises out of normal trading hours, then special arrangements must be made so that it can be left safe and secure in such a way that there is no risk of contamination. Under no circumstances should frozen of chilled foods be left outside any premises.

One large vegetable and fruit distribution company is currently looking into the possibility of installing special temperature-controlled storage bins at its outlets to overcome the problem. Access to many premises, particularly inner city ones, can pose a problem for large vehicles so if the delivery can be made in the middle of the night, for example, there is a definite advantage. Given access to a locked and temperature-controlled unit the driver is able to deliver the food and place it into totally acceptable storage facilities. The trader then transfers the food in due course to the facilities within the premises proper. Such an arrangement is widely used in other countries and there is every reason for it to be exploited more in this country. From the traders point of view, he can arrange for food to be delivered to his premises in the knowledge that it will be held safely until he is able to transfer it to his permanent store. The disadvantage is that the design of his premises needs to be such that this additional storage facility can be sited so that delivery drivers will have ready access. Certainly, those who have incorporated this trading method feel that the advantages far outweigh the disadvantages.

Dogs in retail food premises

While animals are not allowed in food rooms, it is sometimes difficult to prevent a member of the public from taking a dog into a shop. In recent years, there has been an increasing health education campaign aimed at discouraging the public from doing so, except in those cases where the animal is accompanying a blind person. Unfortunately there have been instances where blind people have been refused entry and the Guide Dogs for the Blind Association has issued their members with a card

Polite notice banning dogs (Eaton Publications)

explaining that the dogs are specially trained and are a minimal risk to hygiene in food premises. Most people respond to a simple notice that can be placed on or near to the door. Many thoughtful shop owners provide hooks or rails outside their premises so that dogs can be safely tethered.

Chapter 12

Markets, Stalls and Delivery Vehicles, Outdoor Catering and Transport

This chapter attempts to deal with food hygiene in markets, on stalls and in delivery vehicles. In many instances it is more important to observe the highest standards of cleanliness in mobile or temporary food retailing than in fixed premises. The principal reason for this is the simple construction of, say, a market stall compared to a conventional shop building with all its modern conveniences. Modern mobile shops and delivery vehicles are built to a good standard and all three categories will be examined separately in this chapter.

As with all hygienic handling of food, common sense plays a leading part. In practice, it will be found that designing and constructing mobile premises to the highest standard will pay enormous dividends, both in terms of labour saving and sales resulting from the hygienic image which the public appreciates more and more.

A special set of regulations apply to this part of the food trade, namely the Food Hygiene (Markets, Stalls & Delivery Vehicles) Regulations, 1966, which should be studied by every mobile trader and salesman. These have been amended in the Food Hygiene (Amendment) Regulations 1990 which especially introduce new temperature control provisions.

Certain regulations apply to every person engaged in handling food, whether as a stall holder, ice-cream salesman or van driver. These rules concern personal hygiene and should be familiar to readers by now. A brief reminder, however, that clothing should be clean and washable even in the depths of winter; hands should be kept clean; cuts or abrasions should be covered with waterproof dressings; no smoking or similar habits should be indulged; and all food should be handled in hygienic manner and wrapped in clean materials.

Stalls

This term covers a wide range of situations where food is handled other than in 'fixed premises', meaning shops. The traditional market stall is of wooden construction with two or four wheels, whereas the mobile ice-cream van should be constructed of aluminium, stainless steel and glass fibre/plastic laminates.

Market stalls should be constructed of impervious materials in order to make cleaning easy and efficient. Hard woods with painted finishes are commonly used, although glass fibre and metal stalls are now available. The stall must be fitted with a superstructure, because the top and three sides must be enclosed with impervious material to prevent the risk of contamination. Additionally the covering keeps the rain off in outdoor markets. The sheeting is often a lightweight plastic or durable polythene, which may be transparent to let in plenty of light. If trading is carried out during hours of darkness, then adequate artificial lighting must be provided to make sure that safe food handling is practised.

Another important rule is that every stall must conspicuously display the name and address of the person responsible for the business. This is to enable an aggrieved customer to identify the trader in the event of a complaint. Some traders have arrangements with the Health Department of the local authority whereby the stall displays the trader's name and stall number only, but this is not a universal practice.

Food on or around the stall must not be placed within 46 cm (18 in) of the ground, unless it is protected from contamination. Dirt, dust, or even dogs could cause this at any time. Refuse should be stored in suitable bins, or other containers, and these should be emptied at least daily. Rubbish should not be allowed to accumulate on or around the stall or vehicle.

On many food stalls it is necessary to provide one or more sinks with a hot and cold water supply for washing food and equipment. If the sink is only used to wash fruit, fish or vegetables, then only cold water is required. In certain circumstances, the trader can apply to the local authority for an exemption certificate; e.g. a fruiterer or greengrocer may dispense with a sink.

Washhand basins with hot or cold running water, together with soap, towel and nailbrush to ensure hygienic handling, must also be provided for the use of food handlers.

In practice these requirements have led to various difficulties because of the nature of both stalls and vehicles. A series of small purpose-built units are manufactured for mobile traders. They comprise a small insulated storage tank which can either be filled with hot water before leaving the garage or trading base, or be connected to the vehicle's radiator to provide heated water.

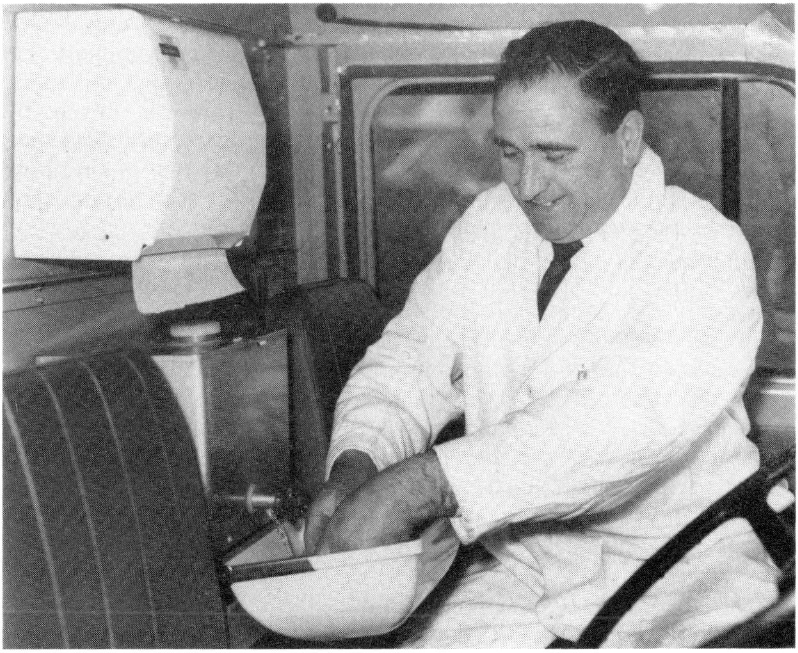

Hand-washing unit in a vehicle cab (Teal Patents Ltd)

In the case of open-air markets, the owner or local authority usually provides public conveniences to which the stall holders can resort, and the washing facilities therein can be used. Notwithstanding this, however, one of the big problems is that hands can get very dirty from handling coins. This is why washing facilities should be readily available on all stalls.

There is such a wide variety of food being sold from stalls and vehicles that it is difficult to generalise, but the basic intention is that stalls and vehicles should endeavour to comply with the same standards as shop premises. After all, the risk of contamination is equally great, if not greater.

Fast-food stalls

There are a few types of mobile trader who deserve special consideration because of their potential threat to human health if poor hygienic standards are allowed to exist. We refer to the ice-cream salesman, the hot dog stall and the roadside refreshment stall in particular. These forms of mobile food vending tend to attract their fair share of criticism, largely due to the unattractive appearance of some of their equipment. The major problems, however, relate to the types of food being handled and sold. In particular, the lack of adequate facilities for storing the perishable products at a safe temperature produces the consequent danger of unhygienic or unsound food being sold to the public. Meat products and ice-cream are two of the most likely foods to be connected with food poisoning (see Chapter 2).

Another potentially dangerous food group is shellfish, which are commonly sold from stalls outside public houses. The problem lies principally with those shellfish which are contaminated before they are harvested. Although regular sampling by the local authorities endeavours to prevent them being sold, there are numerous examples of prawns, shrimps, cockles, whelks, mussels and oysters being the cause of illness and even death amongst human beings. The problem is that no-one can detect bacterial contamination without laboratory examination, so that stallholders must ensure strict hygienic practices and equipment to prevent or reduce the risk of serious trouble.

Once again it must be emphasised that the presentation and appearance of any food retailer's equipment and sales staff produce the image which will create success. Public awareness of hygiene standards these days will readily result in dirty premises losing trade.

Outside catering

In spite of this country's variable climate, the amount of outside catering has increased considerably in recent years. Ranging from the humble barbecue in one's back garden to large-scale catering exercises for hundreds/thousands of people at a conference, agricultural shows, fetes, festivals, exhibitions, pop festivals, sporting and cultural events, all of these present their hazards. Special care is therefore needed.

Early consultation between the organisers and the Local Authority's Officers is strongly advised. The appointment of an organiser or sole concessionaire is worth considering as the best way to control the number, type and standard of food outlets. All Local Authorities will insist upon proof of registration of each food stall or caterer with their 'Home' Authority and that Authority should have checked the condition of the vehicles, stalls or premises where the food is stored and prepared.

To reduce the problems associated with washing up large quantities of crockery and cutlery most caterers use disposable cutlery, plates, cups and glasses – but remember to increase the number and capacity of refuse containers!

Invariably the facilities available for the food preparation are either limited or not always as readily available as they might be in permanent premises. Even to the family preparing a barbecue in their back garden there is the danger that hands will not be as clean as they might, besides which the food might become contaminated from dust and fire debris. Though not necessarily harmful in themselves, the latter can give rise to stomach irritation to cause great discomfort.

In terms of the location of the food preparation area, if this is in a tent or marquee the walls and roof material should be clean, weatherproof and in such condition that they do not present any risk to the food. It may be necessary to install some kind of flooring cover both as a safety measure for staff and to protect the food from contamination. Various types of covering are available, the important points to note being that it is clean and also capable of being kept clean. Reusable sacking is not acceptable, nor is unsealed wood. Food should, as a rule, be stored in any case at least 46 cm (18 in) above ground level.

Too often wooden trestle tables with a paper covering are the only work surfaces available. This becomes saturated and quite useless after a very short time. Tables with laminated plastic or similar surfaces should always be provided so as to give a smooth, impervious surface that is capable of being easily cleaned.

In addition to the need to control any bacterial growth by proper refrigeration, care should be taken to ensure that food is protected from other forms of contamination, for example dust, rain and insect pests. Domestic animals can also be a problem and should not be allowed in the food preparation areas. No food should ever be stored where it is exposed to the elements and even when stored temporarily within a marquee, etc., it should be properly protected by plastic screens, cling film or other suitable means.

With large-scale outside catering exercises, particular problems can arise unless adequate washing facilities are provided and unless proper temperature control arrangements are made. Foods prepared in advance and held in a warm marquee could mean trouble, especially if the foods are of the more vulnerable types. If foods are prepared in advance they should not be moved to the site unless they can be stored under cool conditions until ready for use. Care should also be taken with any transport facilities. There is little point in preparing the food hygienically and having refrigerators on site if it has been transported in a warm van. As a general rule 'at risk' foods should either be kept below 5°C or held at a temperature of at least 63°C.

An important requirement is to ensure that there are adequate washing facilities on site, both for hand washing and for washing food and equipment. This entails the provision of suitable wash basins and sinks which must have adequate drainage. Means of heating hot water by, for example, bottled gas must be provided to ensure that a wholesome and adequate supply of hot water is always available. It is not acceptable to have lengths of hosepipe running from an outside tap across a field or garden. It is much better to draw water from a domestic tap into a clean container which can then be taken to the point where it is needed.

Refuse storage arrangements should be readily available and if any event is intended to be held in hours of darkness, adequate lighting levels must be maintained. A suitably equipped first aid kit must be readily available.

Access to suitable toilet accommodation must also be provided for food handlers and this too should be provided with adequate washing facilities. These must be readily available – it should not be necessary to cross a field to get to the toilet!

One of the problems with outside catering is that often casual staff are employed. However well meaning they are, they can sometimes be ignorant of the basic requirements of food hygiene. If those not normally involved with food handling are employed they should be given some rudimentary training, besides which various leaflets are available that can be given to them beforehand. The local Environmental Health Officer may be able to help, but the caterer must take the ultimate responsibility for ensuring that all the employees handle the food hygienically.

If the weather is warm it is sometimes an excuse to discard protective clothing. However the need for clean, suitable protective clothing is even more important with outside catering and the rule should never be relaxed.

Some local authorities have introduced Codes of Practice which are intended as guidance for those involved with outside catering on whatever scale. Enquire with your local Environmental Health Officer; even though a special Code of Practice may not exist, the Environmental Health Officer will be in a position to advise you – in your own interest – as to what is required.

Delivery vehicles

Modern food marketing techniques invariably involve the packaging of products at the point of manufacture so that many foodstuffs are transported in protective wrappings. The nature of the product determines the type of wrapping: metal can, rigid polythene carton, vacuum package, cardboard box, waxed paper container, glass jar, plastic tub, aluminium foil, or polystyrene carton. It also determines the method of transport, namely refrigerated lorry, articulated freezer container or plain van. Naturally these variables will affect the design, construction and equipping of the vehicle, although the common theme will be of using suitable materials to provide a hygienic, easily-cleansed interior.

All fleet transport vehicles are built to high standards using stainless steel, alloyed aluminium or galvanised mild-steel welded plate. Non-slip flooring is fitted and the body is carefully insulated to prevent extremes of temperature occurring. Special attention must be paid to vehicles transporting frozen foods because the temperature of the vehicle must be maintained to match that of the cold store and the freezer unit into which the food is to be placed. Normally a temperature range of − 20°C to − 12°C is encountered. The less exposure there is to fluctuating temperatures, the longer the shelf life of the commodity. Food manufacturing companies, cold store operators and retailers should all give particular attention to the loading and unloading of frozen and chilled food. Ideally the vehicle should be pre-cooled and backed up to a purpose-built loading bay which provides an effective temperature seal between the two; this will minimise the fluctuation in temperatures which otherwise occur. Vehicles should be fitted with temperature monitoring equipment so that the driver and the recipient can check the temperature before accepting delivery.

The Food Hygiene (Amendment) Regulations require chilled perishable foods to be transported at not more than 5°C (or 8°C in some cases) with a 2°C tolerance to allow for defrost cycles and close attention to the maintenance of these maximum temperatures cannot be over-emphasised. As stressed in Chapter 2 certain food poisoning bacteria like *Listeria monocytogenes*, *Yersinia* and some strains of *Clostridium botulinum* grow rapidly above 5°C.

Meat, bread and fresh vegetables are the most common foods still transported with little or no outer wrapping to offer protection against contamination. With meat and bakery products in particular, it is therefore important that the vehicles and containers are kept clean and that the food is carefully handled on and off the vehicle. Personnel are required to wear clean, washable overclothing, including headwear in the case of meat carriers, and to observe the hygiene rules.

To assist staff to maintain personal cleanliness when handling food on vehicles, especially for direct retail sale, certain vehicles must be provided with a washhand basin, a supply of hot and cold water, soap, towel and nail brush. Such vehicles include ice-cream vans and mobile shops (unless selling entirely wrapped food).

Exemptions are allowed for delivery vehicles, provided hand-washing facilities are available at each premises at which collections or deliveries are made. This also applies to bread vans. Ideally, all vehicles should be provided with washing facilities for the delivery men.

First aid equipment should be carried on all vehicles and in the case of mobile shops at least one sink with hot and cold water supplies should be provided to enable equipment to be kept clean. The owner's name and address should be conspicuously displayed on the vehicle.

A planned routine of cleaning food vehicles should be carried out every day, using plenty of hot soapy water followed by careful rinsing with clean water. A combined detergent/disinfectant can be used to advantage as an alternative to live steam for removing grease, fat and dirt.

Vending machines

Perhaps this is a little out of place in this chapter but, nonetheless, it is a form of food retailing which is frequently encountered today. There are vending machines capable of serving most types of food, from hot beverages to instant hot meals; consequently the hygiene of the equipment needs to be given high priority.

Most modern vending machines have been designed and constructed to high standards with efficient cleansing in mind, thus quality materials such as stainless steel are often used. Automatic cut-outs are incorporated in the machine to prevent sales continuing if the machine overheats, overflows or fails to function safely. Machines are designed to prevent access by vermin or pests, and food containers are covered to prevent risk of contamination.

Cleaning instructions are normally displayed on the machine and should be closely followed. Machines should be cleaned daily. Records should be kept with the machine, detailing the date and time of cleaning. Liberal quantities of hot water with a detergent, or combined detergent/disinfectant solution, should be used to cleanse all parts of the machine which touch the food. Particular attention should be paid to tubes and containers used for milk, water and liquid beverages; water tanks should also be emptied and refilled with fresh water.

Often machines are operated under franchise. A 'middleman' may be responsible for the stocking and cleaning of the machine whether it be situated in the factory canteen, hospital or service station. This is sometimes favoured by those on whose premises the machines are situated because it relieves them of the responsibility. In such cases it is important to ensure that the terms of any agreement stipulate the frequency with which the machine is serviced – be it to stock rotate/replenish the food or to clean it. It can be useful to find out from the supplier the names of their other customers so as to enquire of them regarding their satisfaction – or otherwise – with the arrangements.

Particular care must be taken to ensure that the machine is working at the correct temperature to keep the food in prime condition. Ice-cream temperatures must not rise above −2°C; meat products, cheese, dry

A modern vending machine capable of serving full meals day or night

beverages, etc., must stay below 8°C (5°C for certain foods). Careful stock rotation and ordering is also important when selling fresh perishable food from a machine. All food should therefore be coded with the appropriate 'use by' date. Failure to observe these basic hygiene rules will result in reduced sales and, more importantly, the risk of bacterial infection from the unclean parts of the machine on which food particles are allowed to accumulate. Many modern designs incorporate 'one trip' parts so that sterile materials are fitted at least daily on all parts of the machine in contact with food.

Finally, do not forget to empty the adjacent litter bin frequently. This can be the biggest deterrent to sales, if left to overflow.

Food hygiene in transit

Whilst the majority of this book is devoted to hygiene in fixed premises we thought a short section should cover the principles for hygienic food handling on road, rail, sea and air transport.

The growth in the use of the private car has resulted in a steady decline in public transport services, notably local bus and train services. However, the long distance traveller is faced with a choice between coach, train, sea, and air services, although the latter is usually much more expensive. All four methods of transport offer some form of catering for passengers, the precise extent of the service will vary according to the distance being covered and the time of day. The inherent problems with all types of transport are the confined space, the lack of piped mains water, drainage and power. Consequently there is a high premium placed on quality equipment, labour saving design of the catering area and hygienic practices which will minimise the risk of food poisoning amongst the passengers.

Coach travel

The long distance express coach services which compete with the high speed trains tend to run non-stop along motorways using two drivers. Consequently the coach is equipped with a lavatory and a refreshment bar. The normal rules of food hygiene must be strictly observed in the confined space where the hostess or courier handles food and drink. Especially important are the refrigeration of all foods until served or cooked to order; sterilisation of surfaces and equipment and strict attention to personal hygiene. Ample supplies of hot and cold water are essential to the success of this form of catering service. The same principles apply to coaches used by holiday companies taking people to Europe. A survey by Edinburgh's Environmental Health Department in 1988 revealed some fairly unhygienic conditions on these inter-continental coaches. More recent observations by the authors suggest that though the conditions relating to food service on many coaches is good, with very many others it leaves much to be desired.

Train travel

British Rail breakfasts still have an enviable reputation amongst the travelling public of our acquaintance. Little does the afficcionado realise that a major change in catering methods has taken place in recent times. Instead of the ingredients being freshly cooked in the galley they are brought to the departure station as pre-packed cold food, or chilled food which is reheated to order in the buffet car galley. This is a modern trend which is used in many forms of contract catering these days. British Rail have the monopoly on commercial rail travel in the United Kingdom and the Travellers Fare company have their own hygiene codes and employ an Environmental Health Officer to advise on all aspects of food hygiene.

Although the catering parts of our trains are designed to a high standard, using materials that are easy to clean, the fact that one is working in a confined space makes the need for thorough cleaning all the more necessary. The very nature of the food operation on a moving vehicle can give rise to spillages and regular and thorough cleaning is vital.

There are, of course, a number of very successful private Railway Preservation Societies and companies which operate trains throughout the year. Because these lines are principally aimed at tourists and day trippers the catering service is an important feature. In addition to the station buffet many of these trains include a restaurant car and some companies promote 'diners specials' with silver service meals. Unlike British Rail, these Societies rely on volunteer help and limited financial resources to maintain and refurbish the rolling stock – much of which is very elderly. There is a conflict between the desire to retain or restore the original specification and the need to comply with modern hygiene standards using the latest materials and technology. The advice of the local Environmental Health Officer can always be sought by a Preservation Society. As with the road coach, the importance of adequate refrigeration facilities cannot be stressed too strongly. Equally important in preventing food poisoning is the provision of efficient cooking equipment which will keep the food above 63°C until it is served. The practice of pre-cooking food and keeping it in insulated containers until served can only be safely used if the food is piping hot before being placed in the 'hot boxes'.

One of the basic necessities for mobile catering is a wholesome and plentiful supply of water. Obviously this means that one or more storage tanks needs to be filled with mains water for each trip and to ensure that the water is fresh the tank should be drained at the end of each day. With old rolling stock the condition of the tank and pipework must be regularly checked to ensure it remains in perfect condition. Monthly sampling for bacteriological quality is highly recommended. Interestingly, British Rail have installed ultra violet sterilising units on 'drinks only' units and only sell commercial bottled water to passengers to minimise the risks from waterborne illness.

Sea travel

Another difficult subject to cover in a few paragraphs because of the wide range of vessels on which catering may occur. One can list roll on–roll off ferries, hovercraft, jet foils, cruise liners, cargo/cruise ships, river cruise boats and even oil rig platforms. Having had some experience as passengers on a variety of the foregoing vessels the authors sympathise with the designers and catering staff who have to contend with gale force winds and waves which send plates flying across the galley or servery.

Once again the designers have to contend with limited space, the structural limitations of a ship or boat, lack of mains water and drainage, all of which complicate the task of providing a good working environment for the caterer.

The standard of catering on a modern cruise liner tends to be as good as high class hotels thanks to the skill of the staff on board. There have, however, been regular incidents of gastro-enteritis and food poisoning in ships which have been traced to poor standards of hygiene, practices, pest infestations, especially cockroaches and structural deficiencies due to poor maintenance.

As is the case with air travel, ships often have to rely on food taken on board along the route. Some of these stops may be in hot climates making the task of maintaining ideal temperatures that much more difficult. Strict attention to quality control and the maintenance of the highest standards of hygiene is vital. Most UK based lines ensure this by having their own quality control personnel visit suppliers, wherever they may be in the world.

The application of the principles spelt out in this book, especially personal hygiene, avoiding cross contamination, proper temperature control and careful cleaning regimes will go a long way towards minimising the risks of food poisoning whilst keeping the quality of the food service at an acceptable level on all types of craft.

Air travel

If the problems of catering in cramped conditions are common to all forms of travel they are certainly at their most severe in aircraft. Whether you are travelling on a Jumbo jet or Concorde, in first class or on a holiday charter flight, the food will have been prepared in a ground-based catering unit, transported by road in an insulated container and loaded with the baggage. Because of the risks associated with flight catering and, unfortunately, the number of incidents of food poisoning over the last two decades, special attention has been given to the whole catering operation by the airline companies, tour operators and the local authorities in Britain. This supervision extends to the contractors used in other countries to supply the food for return flights but frequently the home base caterer provides both meals on the outward flight. This system places heavy reliance on the temperature control of the food over a longish timescale. Delays in schedules are not uncommon and this leads to problems of quality control and potential risks, especially if the foods are from the high risk groups such as seafood, cooked meats and dairy products. Because there are no refrigeration facilities on an aircraft all chilled foods are packed in insulated containers with dry ice acting as the cooling agent.

The staff involved in all stages of the flight catering system must pay very strict attention to hygiene and temperature control, both refrigeration at 5°C and thorough cooking at 63°C or above. This means that catering staff, porters and cabin staff should be trained in food hygiene. This can be a particularly difficult problem for the catering companies who tend to engage casual unskilled labour for some tasks. Regular quality control samples are examined for bacterial contamination by local authorities and these are usually in addition to daily testing by the catering company. It may be reassuring to know that most airlines insist that the captain and co-pilot are offered completely different food as a further precaution!

Chapter 13

Hospitals, Educational Establishments, Take-Aways, Meals-on-Wheels and Home Catering

While we have tried to incorporate references to the various types of premises and businesses involved in the food industry in the previous chapters, we have had to generalise to a great extent. Equally, because food hygiene practices are similar in their application, it is neither practical nor economic to publish separate books featuring the different sections of the industry. We have therefore included in this chapter some specific comments on food hygiene in schools, hospitals the meals-on-wheels service and for catering contractors.

Hospitals, nursing and residential homes

The basic rules of food hygiene obviously apply to catering in institutions such as hospitals, nursing homes and residential homes. With the possible exception of nursing homes, all ages from little babies to very elderly people are cared for and provided with a full catering service, including special diets. The overriding factor is that the consumers are weak and in need of appetising, nutritional food. This places the emphasis on the highest standards of hygiene, because people who are weak from illness are most vulnerable to the food poisoning bacteria and viruses described in Chapter 2.

Hospitals

Under this heading one must include the 2,000 National Health Service hospitals and the increasing number of private hospitals, hospices and clinics. Until February 1987 there was an important difference between the NHS hospitals and the private hospitals in Britain – the former were able to claim Crown Immunity and were immune from prosecution by local authorities. The protection which applied to all crown property could be traced back to the Middle Ages when the Parliamentarians defeated the Royalists and assumed most of the power from the King of England. The monarch is still the head of the Court system, and it was not possible for the Head of State to prosecute him or herself for contravening the law in the State owned property or by the State's own servants.

An increasing number of people felt that this situation was anomalous and that the public deserved to be protected by an independent enforcement agency. Not surprisingly, Environmental Health Officers were the leading campaigners for the removal of Crown Immunity. Their Institution had carried out surveys in 1975, 1977, 1985 and 1986 which revealed that 16% of all NHS hospitals catering departments were below the acceptable standard and would have been prosecuted if they had been private hospitals. A private Members Bill was promoted by Richard Shepherd MP (Aldridge Brownhills) in February 1986 and this received all party support to the extent that the Government promised to bring their own Act into law.

The National Health Service (Amendment) Act 1986, the National Health Service (Food Hygiene) Regulations 1986 and the National Health Service (Health and Safety) Regulations 1987 brought food hygiene and health and safety in NHS hospitals and other premises into full accountability for the first time.

Much could be written on the subject of food hygiene in hospitals but the authors have devoted a separate book 'Food Hygiene in Hospital Premises' (Charles Knight Publishing, 1987) to the subject and it is not necessary to reproduce all the information and advice in this publication.

Several factors which affect the catering service in hospitals are worth mentioning. Most NHS hospitals and some private hospitals are located in old nineteenth century buildings which do not lend themselves to the best hygienic standards. The financial restrictions placed on District Health Authorities by the Department of Health and the Regional Health Authorities means that managements have to choose between competing priorities. Some of the long-stay psychiatric hospitals have a long standing practice of employing selected patients to work in the catering department. If one adds the large number of nurses, orderlies, porters and volunteers who assist with the catering operation in many hospitals, some idea of the scale of the operation can be gauged. All these people should be properly trained in food hygiene. Management weaknesses were one of the major factors which contributed to the outbreak of *Salmonella* food poisoning at the Stanley Royd Hospital near Wakefield, Yorkshire in 1984 which resulted in 19 patient deaths. The NHS have now adopted codes of practice for a wide range of food handling procedures and failure to observe these can result in disciplinary action.

The Government policy on competitive tendering for public services has resulted in some Health Authorities contracting out their domestic and catering services to private companies. The problem of staff recruitment to the catering industry remains, however, whether the employer is the Health Authority or the private company. Wages and salaries in catering have been notoriously poor and usually enhanced by regular over-time.

Various modern catering systems have been introduced to try to overcome these problems, not all of which are unique to the NHS. Central production kitchens with satellite finishing kitchens are used, so are cook–freeze and cook–chill systems. Massive investment in new equipment is required, labour costs are reduced (but so is the earning power of the employee) and the utmost care and attention must be paid to hygiene.

Having touched on some of the factors affecting hospital catering we must give credit to the hospital caterers and their professional association for all their efforts in maintaining and raising the standards of the service. They have an unenviable job. The standards of catering and hygiene in many hospitals are excellent and we would not wish to create the wrong impression. However, the fact remains that only the highest standards are acceptable. Strict adherence to the correct food handling practices will minimise the risk of food poisoning in hospitals. When someone slips up there will be no shortage of publicity.

It must be said that standards of food hygiene in NHS hospitals have demonstrably improved since the removal of Crown Immunity. Surveys conducted by the IEHO in 1987/88 and 1988/89 revealed a significant reduction in the number of hospital catering departments which were found to be below the standards of the Food Hygiene Regulations. Only two local authorities found it necessary to institute legal proceedings in 1988/89 although six other authorities secured the voluntary closure of kitchens.

It is opportune at this stage to refer again to the engagement of patients in the food preparation process in psychiatric hospitals. This is often regarded as a valuable occupational therapy by hospital personnel. There is no reason why this should not be the case although it is vital to ensure that patients should not be engaged in those tasks where hygiene is of prime importance unless they fully realise what is involved. Such a policy should be adopted in the case of Assessment Units where food preparation takes place involving patients.

A further point to note in psychiatric hospitals relates to kitchen safety. Access to cleaning and other chemicals may present hazards both to the patient or to others. There are many recorded cases where food has been poisoned – intentionally and unintentionally – in such hospitals by patients. Similarly access to potentially dangerous machinery should also be restricted.

Hotel services

An interesting development has emerged in recent years in relation to the management of services in NHS hospitals. Whereas previously the catering and domestic services operated quite separately, hotel services managers are now appointed whose role embraces elements of both the domestic and catering functions with other support functions, for example, linen, housekeeping, staff residences, security and reception services. There is much merit in this move, especially as the principal departments of catering and domestic services are closely allied and their need to interface is vital in an effectively managed hospital. It is refreshing to see the NHS's encouragement in developing the hotel services and though such a major change is bound to bring its problems in the early stages, there is growing confidence that the more collaborative approach introduced through hotel services is well justified.

It has to be said that in the past, with the separation of responsibilities, problems sometimes arose and inefficiencies resulted. An example of this was in relation to food service at ward level where responsibilities were not always clear. Bringing together support services with a great deal of common interest must be commended and experience in those hospitals which have integrated their hotel services suggests that the organisation as well as the staff benefit at the end of the day – not to mention who after all is most important – the patient!

The only national training unit which provides advice and direct training for hotel services is based at the regional conference and training centre for S.E. Thames Health Authority in Kent. From here a vast amount of information is held in a resource section on many specialist and training issues of hotel services. A comprehensive range of courses and training packages are available from the centre and at locations around the country.

Most of the larger hospitals have shops or cafeteria which are intended as a commendable service for visitors and patients. These range from simple stalls from which sweets, etc., are sold to cafeteria from which one can purchase snacks. Many are staffed by voluntary organisations such as League of Friends or W.R.V.S. It should be remembered that the food hygiene requirements are equally important in these areas and the same rules apply as for any retail outlet. Staff training is necessary and catering officers/hotel services managers will need to liaise with, for example, W.R.V.S. organisers to ensure that all personnel are properly trained and periodically re-trained.

A problem area that often arises in hospital or institutional care relates to food brought onto the premises by patients and visitors. This is kept in cupboards or the ward refrigerator and it is very easy for it to be forgotten and deteriorate to the extent of it becoming unfit. It can contaminate other food too. Where food is introduced in this way, careful control must be exercised so that it does not 'go off' and it should not be stored alongside food supplied by the hospital. This is obviously a sensitive issue for administrators of hospitals and homes but unless careful attention is given, a potentially dangerous area is likely to emerge. Similarly, there should be a separate refrigerator for patient medication.

Nursing and residential homes

There has been a dramatic increase in the number of privately run nursing and residential homes in England and Wales since the start of the 1980s. This has been as a direct result of the Government's policies of: (1) caring for people in the community instead of in long-stay hospital wards; and (2) making substantial weekly payments to elderly people living in this type of accommodation as a contribution towards what is often a high charge.

Such was the escalation in numbers of homes that concern was soon voiced over the quality of care being given and as a result the law in respect of residential homes was strengthened when the Residential Homes Act 1984 was introduced. This Act made county councils and

London boroughs responsible for registering all such homes and for adopting codes of practice which have to be observed. Officers are appointed to inspect the homes regularly and the authority has powers to rescind the registration if the appropriate standards are not maintained. Before each home is registered the registration authority must consult the local authority to check that there are no objections as far as Planning, Building Control and Environmental Health requirements are concerned and that the fire precautions are acceptable. Most registration authorities have issued guidance which includes food hygiene, health and safety and fire safety requirements. Residential homes are premises which provide accommodation for more than four people of any age with some supervision and catering provided.

Nursing homes are, as the name implies, residential accommodation with an element of nursing or medical care provided. The district health authorities in England and Wales are responsible for registering and inspecting these homes under the same legislation and similar standards are applicable as for residential homes with the important addition of the nursing care being available to residents around the clock.

Most of these homes are large houses which have been converted to the required standard. Consequently a variety of problems have to be overcome and compromises agreed in respect of health and safety and food hygiene. The kitchen and dining room is the equivalent of a small hotel in terms of the catering service required each day. It must be properly equipped to comply with the Food Hygiene (General) Regulations and any local code of practice issued by the registration authority. The local Environmental Health Officer will inspect the home from time to time to check on the standards and the practices in addition to the borough or county Registration Officer. As with hospital catering, the highest standards must be maintained to minimise the chances of food poisoning which would have a serious effect on the residents.

Cook–chill catering

Cook–chill is a catering system which is based on normal preparation and cooking of food followed by fast chilling, storage in controlled conditions 0°C to 3°C and subsequent reheating immediately before consumption. The system had its origins in France in the early 1970s and has been increasingly used in the United Kingdom since 1977 with over 300 installations working by 1988. The operation of a central kitchen with satellite serveries lends itself to large scale catering such as in hospitals, schools, industrial and commercial premises. Although there is a fairly high capital cost in equipment, the manufacturers claim that the quality of the food and the savings in staffing costs provide an acceptable return on the investment.

Cook–chill enables the complete range of foods from breakfasts to banquets to be produced by skilled staff in a purpose-designed kitchen at any time of the day or week because the chilled storage will keep the food in perfect condition for up to five days before being 'finished' and served. Staff must be properly trained to use the equipment to its optimum extent and this naturally includes special emphasis on strict standards of food hygiene. Because the system requires discipline the standards can be easily monitored by management at both the central and the satellite kitchens. Unlike conventional catering systems, the cook–chill method has not caused one incident of food poisoning in its first ten years of use. This is largely due to the use of blast chillers and food storage at 0°C to +3°C at which temperature micro-organisms, enzymes and chemical reactions are slowed down. Consequently the normal risks of food spoilage and bacterial growth do not occur.

Ideally the chilled food should be transported to the finishing kitchen and reheated quickly to at least 70°C in a special 'regeneration oven' immediately before being served. This is another vital part of the fail safe system which provides the quality meal. It is important to emphasise that only a purpose-designed and equipped cook–chill system with trained staff and careful supervision can produce the correct end product. Any attempt to use conventional catering equipment will end in failure.

Because the cook–chill system is a highly specialised form of catering which needs careful planning and substantial investment it is not really appropriate to describe the system in greater detail in this book. For readers who require more information the equipment manufacturers, the Electricity Council and the Department of Health all publish guidance which is readily available.

A variation of the cook–chill system is known as sous-vide which involves freshly-prepared food being vacuum-sealed in special plastic pouches, cooked and chilled ready for reheating. The method is claimed to have the advantage of better texture, colour, flavour and aroma retention. In the United States of America this method is only allowed in licensed food production plants with laboratory facilities. In Britain the Sous-Vide

Advisory Committee has published a Code of Practice, which sets out operating principles, cooking times and core temperatures for caterers who wish to adopt this method of food production. There is another technique known as chill-vac which is a closed circuit production system where food is cooked in bulk quantities in a pressure kettle and then passed through a series of pipes to a filling station where it is pumped into gas impermeable plastic pouches. These are sealed and rapidly chilled to 3°C. Because of the high investment required in plant and equipment the system is associated with large-scale industrial and institutional catering.

It must be emphasised that cook–chill foods have been particularly associated with the high incidence of *Listeria* organisms found in various surveys. Whilst thorough reheating of these foods will destroy the bacteria, there are some dishes which are designed to be eaten cold. Therefore, food manufacturers must ensure the highest standards of hygiene during production and retailers must rely on proper temperature controls (i.e. 3°C) at all stages from production, transportation and storage for sale.

Educational establishments

There are broad similarities with the catering services provided in the whole range of educational establishments. The residential premises such as boarding schools, colleges, universities and for that matter corrective institutions (e.g. HM prisons) will have to provide the traditional catering service of 3 meals a day throughout the year. The task will be similar to catering in a hospital as regards the financial limitations, staff recruitment and working conditions. Day schools and colleges on the other hand have to cater for a large lunch trade and various changes have been taking place in the philosophy of the school meals service in recent years. Some education authorities withdrew the service completely whilst others went over to a central kitchen with satellite finishing kitchens in the individual schools or to call-order snack foods. The Government's enthusiasm for competition in the provision of local government services saw the phasing out of some direct labour catering departments in favour of commercial catering companies providing the services. Whichever method of food delivery is practised however, the necessity to produce a quality product, hygienically, is paramount.

Many premises used for educational purposes, whether public authority or privately owned, are far from modern. Some are positively ancient and historic and difficult to maintain to the highest standards at reasonable cost. Problems such as condensation, poor ventilation, unsuitable wall and floor finishes, bad drainage, pest infestations, and inefficient storage, preparation and cooking space are frequently encountered. The inability to provide sufficient refrigerated storage is another common problem which leads to dangerous practices involving the 'high risk' foods mentioned in earlier chapters.

With good advice from experienced catering officers or specialist companies these problems can be overcome, especially if the management are prepared to finance the improvements without 'penny pinching'. The advances in food equipment technology in the past 10 years means that much can now be achieved with lower levels of staffing, skilled and unskilled, than used to be the case.

Probably because of the environment in which the catering is provided, there has been a first class record of staff training in the school meals service. Senior staff have obtained the City and Guilds certificates or equivalent examinations and all grades of staff have attended training courses on catering and hygiene.

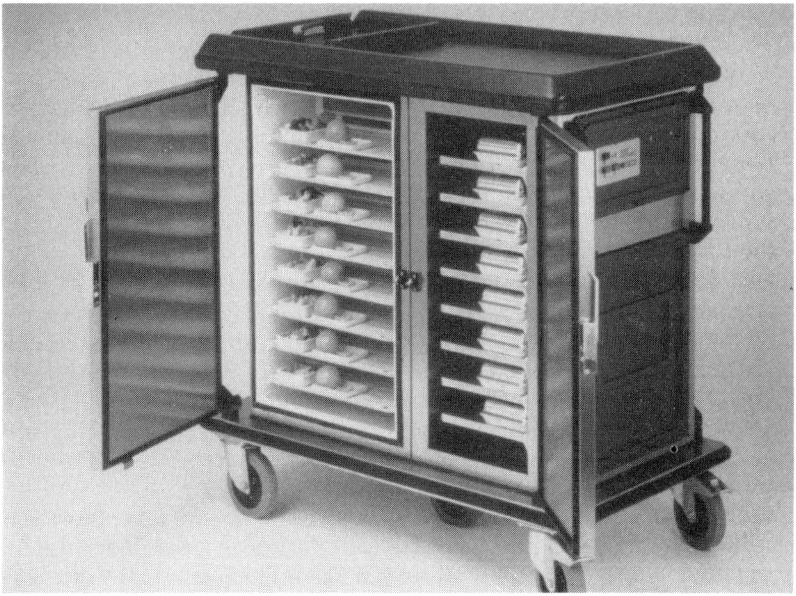

Inside a food trolley (Cidelcem Industries)

All educational establishments are subjected to regular inspection by either senior education department staff or their equivalent and by Environmental Health Officers of the local authority. A weakness arises, however, in that the Environmental Health Officer is often employed by the same education authority (e.g. London boroughs) or by the district councils who are reluctant to authorise legal proceedings against the County Education Authority for serious contraventions of the legislation. As a result the action tends to be on a 'goodwill advice' basis only.

Prison catering

Although the prison catering service has always enjoyed Crown Immunity, this is not now the case, and as with NHS hospitals and various other government establishments, they are now subject to the same legislation as any catering concern.

Many of the country's prisons are old and catering facilities within them have not been ideal, having regard to age and layout of buildings. Some prisons are able to maintain a conventional meals programme whilst with others this is less easy as they, for example, may have more of a transient population whereby prisoners may only stay for very short periods of time. All these aside, the early indications are that the prison catering service had made a commendable effort to conform with the law even before Crown Immunity was lifted, and this in spite of sometimes very substandard conditions. Although there is an active programme to improve and refurbish many of the prison catering departments, a great deal needs to be done to bring all of the facilities up to a satisfactory standard.

Most prison catering departments engage prisoners both as part of a therapeutic programme and also to provide vital manpower. This needs to be properly controlled, not least for security reasons, but in terms of food hygiene it is important to ensure that all staff, including prison staff, know the rudiments of food hygiene. Basic introductory training is vital and it is encouraging to note that the prison catering service itself places much emphasis on the training of personnel at all levels.

An important issue in this service is the need to maintain the morale of staff, for a failure to do so could easily reflect in poor food hygiene conditions. Supervisory staff are conscious of the need to motivate staff and to set an example, not least in connection with hygiene and this was noted when the authors visited a number of prisons.

Most prison catering officers have been quick to respond to the lifting of Crown Immunity and are working closely with local Environmental Health Officers. In addition to inspections of premises and advising on standards, Environmental Health Officers welcome opportunities that are emerging to promote training amongst catering personnel. Visiting Environmental Health Officers obviously respect the necessary security requirements which apply to each prison.

In some of the older prisons, pests can be a problem and firms carrying out treatments will need special security screening. This applies to suppliers generally, whether of goods or services.

In addition to the main catering areas, most prisons also operate small 'wing kitchens' or similar facilities where small- scale food preparation is carried out. Special attention is necessary to ensure that acceptable standards are maintained.

Where larger prisons are concerned, it is likely that food will need to be transported to satellite parts. This may involve food being stored and moved in insulated containers. Given this, it is vital to ensure that the appropriate temperatures are maintained throughout the food chain and regular checks should be carried out and records kept.

Contract catering

A significant part of the catering industry is involved in the preparation of food for consumption on other premises. The businesses range from supplying banqueting and ceremonial functions, dances, weddings and sporting occasions, to providing full-scale catering at schools, colleges, factories and offices. Catering services are also available on trains, aircraft and pleasure boats on inland waterways, but the Food Hygiene Regulations do not apply to international aircraft or shipping.

The actual catering often involves the finishing of preprepared foods which have been transported from the home base. This base may be a modern factory, a restaurant or even a private house. Obviously the Food Hygiene Regulations apply in all these types of premises and the greatest attention must be paid to hygienic practices. Experience has shown that the most likely problem will be the risk of food poisoning brought about by the time/temperature lapses. Unless very careful attention is paid to keeping food cold or hot, with the minimum delay between preparation and consumption, then the possibility of an outbreak is very real. Modern insulated food containers are a big improvement over earlier methods.

While the use of properly constructed and managed business premises is to be applauded, the increasing tendency to use private houses as the base of a commercial catering venture is deplored. Quite apart from the fact that private residences are not allowed to be used for business purposes under the rating and planning laws, the design and equipment of a typical kitchen is not suitable. The family washing should not be done in the same sink as the salad for a wedding party!

There are many large, efficient contract catering companies who are specialists in supplying services to schools, factories, offices, racecourses, football and cricket grounds, theatres, conferences, and open air shows. An increasing number of these contractors employ their own hygiene advisors who will ensure that acceptable standards are achieved on site. If a company or organisation is considering the use of contract caterers they should always enquire as to their hygiene standards and what arrangements there are to achieve and maintain those standards. In any contract to supply food or a catering service, it is important to ensure that a clear written statement of the contractors food hygiene policy is supplied to the client. On some occasions the facilities available on site will be minimal, so it is essential that thorough preparations are made to ensure that all necessary services like water, drainage, electricity and refuse storage/ disposal are available when required. Personal hygiene amongst temporary staff can be a problem, unless the management provide some basic hygiene training for their employees.

Take-aways and fast-food catering

This is a form of catering which has evolved in Britain and ranges from the ever-popular fish-and-chip shop, through the Chinese and Indian restaurants and take-away shops, to the American-style burger-and-chip shops which seem set to revolutionise our eating habits. Fast food outlets in the UK were estimated to have a turnover of £1.8 billion in 1990.

Fish-and-chip shops do not present any unusual hygiene problems, the normal rules apply. The biggest hazard is the fire risk associated with overheated dirty oil in the fryers. Regular filtering and renewal of the oil will reduce this risk to a large extent.

The popularity of Chinese, Indian – not to mention other nationalities – cuisine is one of the success stories of post-war years in Britain. Almost every group of shops in an urban area seems to possess an establishment specialising in an ethnic menu. There are the usual hygiene rules to comply with and particular problems to overcome, not least the language difficulty. The familiar problem of preparing food well in advance to speed the service to the customer means that storage at correct temperatures is vital to reduce bacterial growth – the outbreaks of *B. cereus* food poisoning due to reheated rice are well known to health departments. Take-away meals which are packed in foil containers should be eaten as soon as possible or thoroughly reheated.

Fast-food outlets are rapidly gaining trade in this country, which have been firmly established in America over many years. Chicken and pressed meat are the main constituents. They are served with chips or in bread rolls with a wide range of beverages, cordials and sweets which can be eaten on or off the premises. Speed is the hallmark of the service which is computerised and linked to the latest cooking equipment. Staff training is usually of paramount importance and hygiene is not overlooked. Cleaning schedules are standardised as part of the company policy and, even when the retail outlet is franchised, there are checks on quality and hygiene in order to maintain the image of the company. It will be interesting to see whether the eating habits of the British will become more 'Americanised'. The authors are starting to encounter every other person in a typical High Street walking along eating or drinking from a disposable container. That leads to the last point about take-aways – the irresponsible behaviour of some customers who flout the litter laws, thereby making the streets a disgrace.

Sandwiches

The traditional packed lunch for many workers, ramblers and holiday-makers consists of sandwiches or rolls filled with a variety of tasty fillings. Because they are prepared some hours before they are to be eaten and are carried in containers or polythene bags at air temperatures there is ample scope for food poisoning bacteria to multiple. Numerous surveys by Environmental Health Officers reveal the high levels of microbiological contamination of the 'high risk' fillings such as meats, pâté, eggs, soft cheese and mayonnaise. The Government introduced Regulations to tackle these problems in 1991 and the British Sandwich Association issued their own Code of Practice for sandwich producers to secure the highest standards of hygiene and safety for their products. Quite simply, it is recommended that all filled sandwiches and rolls should be kept in refrigerated units at 5°C and discarded if not sold within 24 hours of production. Once purchased, they should be kept as cool as possible prior to eating.

Meals-on-wheels

This service is increasingly in demand throughout the country. Although generally intended for elderly people who are unable to cook a hot meal for themselves, more local authorities and other organisations responsible for the service are now prepared to provide for the non-elderly who have a similar need. Some local authorities provide the service on a short term basis, for example, to those of any age who are convalescing or who are handicapped and have no-one to cook a necessary hot meal for them.

Meals-on-wheels are provided by a variety of organisations in addition to local authorities: these include the WRVS, Old Persons Welfare Associations or small groups of people wanting to serve their immediate community. The essence of the scheme is usually to produce a meal at a central source, then to distribute it by van or car to the recipient. The central kitchen can be a school canteen, hospital, day centre or indeed any kitchen capable of providing a number of meals at once. The meals provided fall into two categories:

Convenience Foods

An increasing number of firms in recent years have entered this field by producing either individually prepared meals or multi-portion meals which can then be divided. In both cases, these are generally provided in foil containers, pre-cooked, then quick frozen. They are then delivered in specially refrigerated lorries to the central kitchen where they are stored in freezers. When required, they are placed in ovens and reheated. There is an increasing tendency to use fan-assisted convector ovens for this purpose and care should be taken not to overload the oven and to ensure a ready circulation within the cooker. The advantage of this type of food is that all of the actual food preparation is carried out by the producer, thus obviating the need for extra kitchen staff. Where multi-portion meals are used, these will need to be divided into individual portions using special foil containers, although some authorities use returnable trays. One disadvantage with the latter is that extra care is needed to ensure that the containers are clean before reuse, especially if the onus is placed on the consumer to clean and return them through the delivery service.

Fresh Foods

This system relies on a full kitchen staff preparing individual meals from fresh foods. It involves the buying in and storage of the food, but is regarded as being more flexible in that menus can be varied more often and the quantity can be adjusted more easily. The meal is cooked and served into aluminium dishes or foil containers for delivery.

With either method, it is important to ensure that the meals, once cooked, are delivered to the recipient as quickly as possible ensuring that there is minimum heat loss. This is especially important where long distances are involved. Temperature checks should be made from time to time and, in general, the temperature at time of delivery for hot meals should never be less than 62–67°C. Meals are best transported as follows:

Polystyrene insulated containers

These rely on the property of polystyrene to retain heat. They are light in weight, easy to handle and relatively cheap to provide. A coating of polyurethane varnish or a polythene inner bag is recommended to maintain hygiene.

Heated insulated containers

These are usually of aluminium construction incorporating an insulation material. Some are pre-heated using an electric element which is plugged in for several hours before delivery. Some containers incorporate a small tray which is charged with burning charcoal beforehand and which burns

Stainless Steel insulated containers (Cidelcem Industries)

for several hours. This type of container is heavier than its polystyrene counterpart and considerably more expensive both to purchase and to operate. Its advantage however is that the container itself is heated and therefore heat loss from the food is minimal.

Home catering

This book is principally intended to offer advice to people engaged in food businesses, however there are many examples of such businesses being run from domestic premises. The Government actively encouraged self-employment and the establishment of small businesses in the 1980s with advice and financial assistance and there were many examples of cottage industries which expanded to become very successful large companies. It must, however, be emphasised that most small domestic kitchens are unlikely to be suitable for catering on any large scale, especially if it is a commercial enterprise. The reasons quite simply are that:

(1) the equipment is unsuitable in design and capacity to cope with the volume of food;
(2) it is unlikely that sufficient space is available for specialist equipment such as blast chillers;
(3) the kitchen is accessible to children or adults not connected with the business;
(4) and the use of the same sink for domestic washing and food preparation is to be deplored because of the risk of cross-contamination.

Home catering can take various forms; occasional volume catering for a voluntary organisation's dinner/dance or fete; regular cooking for WI market, pub or home bake shop; a catering service for business lunches, buffet receptions, weddings and similar functions.

Whatever form the catering takes the same principles apply, starting with the kitchen being cleared of all domestic items and pets. This should include the refrigerator if the ingredients are to be stored before preparation, because the family food should not be mixed up with that purchased for the function to reduce the risk of contamination. From the reports of incidents of food poisoning associated with domestic premises being used for volume catering it is clear that the main risks are:

(a) preparing food too far in advance,
(b) improper storage,
(c) inadequate cooking, cooling and reheating,
(d) poor transportation (unrefrigerated containers),
(e) unsatisfactory finishing/handling at the service site.

In general, the standards required by the Environmental Health Department will not permit a normal domestic kitchen to be used for commercial catering. The question of insurance cover also arises because a caterer who is the proven cause of a food poisoning incident may be sued for damages and the insurance company may have imposed conditions which have not been observed. One common factor is the lack of training in basic food hygiene. The importance of proper tuition cannot be over emphasised.

It may be appropriate to mention the legal controls (see Chapter 1) over catering from home. The Food Safety Act 1990, the Food Hygiene (General) Regulations 1970, the Food Hygiene (Markets, Stalls and Delivery Vehicles) Regulations 1966, the Health and Safety at Work etc. Act 1974 and the Planning and Building control legislation are all likely to be applicable to one degree or another.

Petrol stations and food sales

Most petrol stations sell a range of food from simple wrapped-sugar confectionery to sandwiches, pies and pasties. The very nature of the trade means that food can easily become contaminated and careful attention needs to be given to ensuring that the food is kept separate and in hygienic conditions. Strict attention to temperature control is necessary with those more vulnerable foods and staff involved with dirty tasks should not handle food – even if wrapped.

Because the food element is ancilliary to the main business it is easy to overlook cleaning and proper stock rotation. Special attention is therefore necessary in these areas.

Anyone intending to introduce such food sales should consult their local Environmental Health Officer. Some authorities restrict the range of food that can be sold if the conditions are not entirely acceptable.

Chapter 14

Licensed Restaurants, Hotels, Public Houses, Wine Bars and Clubs

The popularity of 'eating out' has risen significantly as a result of the buoyant economy, especially in the South East of England and in all the tourist areas. New catering premises are opening with monotonous regularity, fast food chains, restaurants specialising in ethnic cuisine and significantly many Brewery/Catering companies are refurbishing former public houses as family restaurants.

The consumption of wine has increased substantially and whilst much of this is for home consumption the licensed trade has been selling far more wine over the bar than ever before. Most towns have at least one wine bar where a wide range of wines can be purchased.

All this has been achieved despite the deterrent of the breathaliser test and the drink/drive law. Such is the popularity of these premises that there was general support for the Government's decision to remove the restriction on opening hours in 1988.

Some licensees are very reluctant to give up their traditional public house role of serving drinks first and foremost, others have seen the chance to maximise their income through catering. Unfortunately, many such pubs were not designed for large-scale catering and the licensees private domestic kitchen is rarely suitable for use on a commercial scale. Apart from the lack of space for storage and preparation of food there is the serious risk of cross-contamination when the domestic washing, etc., has to be done in the same sink as the lunch-time vegetables!

Fortunately the Breweries and catering companies accept this difficulty and have been spending vast sums on upgrading many hotels and public houses to provide modern catering services quite separate from the landlord's domestic accommodation. Part of this upgrading invariably sees the provision of hygienic inside toilets for customers – a much needed improvement over the old outside lavatories of yesteryear.

Some of the credit for these improvements has to be due to the activities of the Licensing Justices who, as part of their annual review of licensed premises, have taken a particular interest in hygiene and safety matters. In addition to an annual report by the Police, many Brewster Sessions receive a report from the local Environmental Health Officer detailing his Department's comments on individual premises. Objections to the grant or renewal of a licence can be made by anyone including the Police, Fire Brigade and the Local Authority Environmental Health Department.

Good food hygiene standards have always been important in licensed premises because 'food' includes drink of all kinds and food poisoning can be easily passed via dirty glasses. Unfortunately far too many bar staff ignore the 'no smoking' rules – blissfully unaware of the risks to their own and their customers health and the maximum fine of £2000 if they are caught and prosecuted.

The cleanliness of glasses is important and the authors commend the law in Scotland which requires a fresh glass for every drink. More detailed information in connection with glass washing can be found in Chapter 6.

There are probably more potential hazards as far as food hygiene, health and safety are concerned in licensed premises than any other type of catering establishment. The following list gives the basic rules for bar staff:

Personal hygiene

1. Do not smoke behind the bar or in any room where food is handled.
2. Wash hands regularly and always after using the toilet.
3. Keep any exposed cut or abrasion covered with a suitable waterproof dressing.
4. Ensure that overclothing is clean.
5. If a food handler suffers from sickness, diarrhoea or septic cuts or sores, he or she should stop handling food, advise the employer and consult a doctor immediately.
6. Do not spit.
7. Make sure that an adequate first aid kit is readily available.

Licensed Restaurants, Hotels, Public Houses, Wine Bars and Clubs

The emphasis on food hygiene standards is often greater if the local Licensed Victuallers Association promotes training courses and guidance notes in conjunction with their Local Authority Environmental Health Department.

One of the major problem areas in old public houses and hotels is the cellar or beer store. These are frequently damp, dark and unhygienic with a dangerous staircase and low headroom. The walls and floor should be treated to make them dry and washable, drainage should be installed along with adequate artificial lighting and ventilation. A sink with hot and cold water supplies should be installed to facilitate the pipe cleaning. Attention should be paid to the cellar stairs to make them safe and a handrail provided. If access is via a pair of flaps behind the servery and alternative access cannot be provided, the access must be properly guarded when the flaps are open. Special care must be taken with gas cylinders to avoid an explosion – cylinders must be chained or strapped securely.

The following list of good practices has been drawn up:

1. Oversize glasses and measured beer devices should be used.
2. The use of a clean glass on every occasion is highly desirable.
3. The overspill beer in the drip tray should be thrown away and beer economiser devices should not be used.
4. Last drawings and beer drained from pipes prior to cleaning should be kept to a minimum, filtered through clean filter paper and returned to the cask immediately.
5. Chipped or cracked glasses should be destroyed.
6. Optics should be washed and sterilised whenever the bottle is changed. Chrome-plated copper or zinc metal optics should not be used.
7. Bottle necks should not be immersed in the drink when filling glasses.
8. All food must be covered when displayed for sale. Perishable food should be kept under refrigerated conditions. Hot pies and other 'high risk' foods should be kept cool and then cooked to order.
9. The use of hot food cabinets is not recommended but if they are used then the temperature of the food must be over 63°C. If such food is not sold within two hours then it should be discarded and on no account should the food be cooled and reheated later.
10. Make regular checks for signs of pest infestation.

11. Do not allow animals into the servery or behind the bar. Animals should be discouraged in public rooms.
12. Clean all beer pipes, pumps and equipment weekly using a recommended cleansing solution.

Carveries

The carvery style of restaurant is very popular with the public and is to be found in most parts of Britain. Typically there are three or four roast meats on offer, i.e. beef, lamb, pork and turkey.

Special techniques must be used by the caterer if the carvery is to be safe, as well as a successful venture and the following paragraphs highlight the more important points:

1. *Ordering and stock control:* a carefully written specification of the size and cut of meat is essential. Stock levels should be kept to a minimum to avoid overloading the refrigerator or freezer.
2. *Proper defrosting:* ensuring that frozen meat, especially poultry, is thoroughly defrosted before being cooked is vital.
3. *Keeping raw and cooked food separate:* a classic error which could easily happen in a carvery kitchen.
4. *Use separate cutting tools and boards for each type of meat:* another common error with staff using the same knife to cut poultry and then other joints with the risk of cross contamination.
5. *Thorough cooking of the joint:* this involves careful calculation of the weight/cooking time in the special cook/hold oven. Guess work is not acceptable. Checking the oven cooks the meat at the right temperature for the right time and that the minimum four hour hold time is observed will lead to risks from *Salmonella* or *Clostridium perfringens* food poisoning being minimised.
6. *Observing correct cooking practices:* avoid opening the oven door during cooking or holding process, positioning the meat correctly in the oven, not overloading the oven, checking the oven thermostat and emptying the drip trays regularly.
7. *Maintaining at least 63°C in the carvery:* the importance of using equipment which can heat the meat from beneath and from infra red or quartz lamps overhead must be stressed. Staff should ensure that the joints are correctly positioned and that a probe thermometer is used to check the temperature of the joints during service. Ensuring that the meat is not cooled by draughts is also important.

8. *Re-use of leftover meat:* provided a cook/hold oven is available the unused meat can be put in the hold cycle from lunchtime until the evening meal service, but not from evening until the following lunchtime. Such meat should be cooled quickly and placed in a large chiller after about 90 minutes and used in cold buffet salads or sandwiches – not reheated.
9. *Using fresh gravy and sauces at each service period:* the temptation to reheat gravy or 'top up' gravy from a simmering stock pot must be firmly resisted as this presents a real risk of bacterial contamination. Fresh supplies of gravy and sauces must be made up every time.

Self-service salad bars

The popularity of restaurants operated by major retail companies which adopt a 'brand' image with a standard menu has lead to the introduction of salad bars. A wide range of vegetable, meat, fish and pasta dishes are usually available for customers to serve themselves. A Code of Practice for the operation of these bars has been issued in an attempt to achieve minimum standards for temperature control and hygienic display of the foods. Unfortunately many of the foods are susceptible to the risk of contamination by food poisoning organisms and are vulnerable to contamination by members of the public when serving themselves. We believe that a member of staff should be present at all times to supervise the salad bar to minimise the risks and to deal with any contraventions. All foods should be removed at the end of the service period and all 'at risk' foods should be discarded. This means that food on display should be kept to the minimum and replenished frequently from refrigerated storage.

Sweet and confectionery trolleys

These are widely used in restaurants, dining rooms, etc., and are used to display a wide range of sweets and cheeses some of which may be potentially dangerous in terms of supporting the growth of bacteria. Gâteaus and other cream-containing foods are often displayed at a high ambient temperature and there is a real risk of food poisoning bacteria thriving.

Notwithstanding the exemption provision that exists through the Regulations, caterers should select those trolleys where a measure of temperature control is possible. Some trolley shelves incorporate freezer tubes that are connected to a power supply from time to time and this acts as a refrigerator, keeping the shelves at an acceptably low temperature. This depends, of course, on staff ensuring that the trolley is connected and switched on!

Alternatively, some trolleys are provided with hollow shelves into which the caterer places eutectic units, these having been frozen beforehand. These impart their coldness to the food placed on top which, even in the warm ambient temperature found in a dining room, can retain an acceptable degree of coldness for several hours. This system, whilst totally acceptable, does depend on the caterer having a supply of eutectic units which can be replaced as the temperature rises, so regular checking of the temperature of the food is crucial.

It is important overall in connection with sweet trolleys that at the end of a service period the uneaten food is cleared, covered, and placed in the refrigerator. The trolleys themselves must be regularly cleaned and well maintained.

Mobile trolley for keeping hot food hot and cold food cold (Regethermic UK)

Chapter 15

Health Education

The days when health education was the sole responsibility of the nurse, Environmental Health Officer, doctor or teacher have long since gone, and it is generally accepted that all food handlers and especially those in a supervisory capacity have an important part to play. As it implies, health education is the process whereby food handlers are advised, informed or educated into realising why certain practices are necessary in food premises. Outbreaks of food poisoning are invariably the result of faulty food handling rather than faulty premises.

Staff may be educated in a number of ways but the most effective and, therefore, the most important is teaching by example. This example must be set from the top by management and supervisory staff and can only be achieved if they themselves have clean and tidy dress and they themselves practice good personal hygiene. Junior staff are much more likely to take note of how their seniors perform their duties, than by reading any amount of advisory literature. While the latter is important, it should be regarded only as a supplementary aid.

Newly engaged staff, and this particularly applies to new recruits to the industry, need some basic training in the particular techniques involved; whether it be restaurant catering, food processing or a supermarket, for each presents its own special needs and problems. No new employee should be just ‘left to pick things up’ for himself. At this stage, he needs help and guidance on how to do the job. Accepting that first impressions are often lasting ones, management should make quite sure that ample attention is given from the outset by a competent person. This will usually be a senior person, or perhaps one who is less senior but who has at least undergone some training in the subject of food hygiene.

Increasingly, new recruits are expected to undergo a short basic course on the rudiments of food hygiene, at the outset and before they are permitted into any food room. Non-catering food handlers are also required to undergo such training within a reasonable time bearing in mind that they are involved in the food chain. This category of handler can comprise many people and in the hospital context, for example, will include porters and nursing personnel. It is a good idea for the employer in these cases to issue a Certificate of Attendance as an acknowledgement and incentive for those who attend.

Staff in all types of food premises, however, need a sound basic knowledge of food hygiene and, while much can be achieved through an in-service training programme, most benefit can be gained by attending a specialist course on the subject. It should be remembered that it is intended to legally require those in the food industry to undergo the necessary training and to possess an appropriate qualification. Courses are often organised by local authority environmental health departments, either on their own or in conjunction with a local technical college. Management should endeavour to send all staff on such a course. An increasing number of private sector consultancies and training agencies now offer courses leading to recognised examinations. These organisations will sometimes have the advantage of being able to design the training more precisely to the needs of the company. Details of such agencies are available from your local Environmental Health Department.

Courses/training will either be specially designed for the people involved or will be based on a recognised training syllabus, e.g. as set down by the Institution of Environmental Health Officers, Royal Institute of Public Health and Hygiene, Royal Society of Health, etc. All of these are to be commended, especially as they are nationally acceptable qualifications. These professional bodies – also known as Awarding Bodies – offer a variety of courses, ranging from very basic 5/6 hour sessions leading to a simple examination to the more advanced Diploma type course which may comprise up to 50 hours tuition. Many larger companies regard sending senior personnel on the advanced courses a priority, especially as it then enables successful candidates themselves, subject to approval by the Awarding Body, to organise/teach the more basic levels. It is important that if any company is intending to organise a course leading to an examination of one of the Awarding Bodies, then the course must have prior approval, which will require that the Awarding Body has details of course duration, qualification of tutors, etc. In this way the Awarding Bodies are able to maintain, quite rightly, acceptable standards within the industry when it comes to food hygiene examinations.

Although the three main Awarding Bodies account for the vast majority of those who undertake more formal training and qualifications in relation to food hygiene, it is intended that other 'approved' agencies may also establish training criteria and in effect set their own training programmes and examinations. Such an approach may be preferred by those companies that employ large numbers of people where a greater flexibility through having their own programme may be more attractive. It may be too that the benefit of having a nationally acceptable qualification through one of the Awarding Bodies is less important. On the other hand, provided there is a proper regulatory mechanism, there is no reason why other qualifying agencies should not enter the arena to help satisfy what is going to be an ever-increasing demand for training and qualifications.

One of the advantages of attending a course is that while the food handler may know what his reponsibilities are, it is important that he should know why they are necessary. Knowing that you have to wash your hands after using the lavatory is one thing but knowing *why* is another. Once aware of the reasons, the handler is much more likely to observe the requirement.

Although the manager or supervisor must ultimately be responsible for food hygiene standards in any food premises, many firms have appointed a member of the staff as hygiene officer or assistant. Their job is to give basic training to staff and to keep an eye on standards generally. Such an appointment can more than justify itself and, indeed, some of the larger firms have made full-time appointments for this purpose.

The Hygiene Officer or assistant should, in the first instance, make sure that he or she is well trained and well able to advise and train others. He or she should make a point of liaising closely with the local Environmental Health Officer. Regular inspections of all parts of the premises should be made and reports made to management where there are deficiencies. Problems relating to hygiene should be discussed with staff: one should not forget that tact and diplomacy are required when one is discussing personal hygiene with an individual. It is not easy sometimes to draw attention to some deficiency regarding their personal hygiene, but equally do not forget the potential dangers of not doing so.

A few firms are available to give guidance on all aspects of food hygiene and will carry out surveys of premises before submitting a report on their findings. They will usually liaise with local Environmental Health Officers. Very often, Environmental Health Officers will also organise short courses on the premises, especially where numbers justify it.

Again management should consult their local authority to see if this is possible. The organisation of food hygiene courses will depend on a number of factors, not least amongst these being the amount of staff time which can be spared and the amount of time the local Environmental Health Officer can offer. In the knowledge that whatever time is spent in training is time well spent, the following two programmes are put forward as suggestions for in-service training courses.

Six Week – One Hour a Week – Food Hygiene Course

[*This is most suitable for supervisory staff*]

1. Introduction to food hygiene and food poisoning.
2. Personal hygiene.
3. The food handler and the law.
4. The design and maintenance of food premises.
5. Storage of food.
6. Summary of course and general forum.

Three Week – One Hour a Week – Course for Food Handlers

[*This is a basic programme for middle and lower level personnel or those who are unable to attend the longer course for lack of time*]

1. Introduction to food hygiene and food poisoning.
2. Personal hygiene.
3. The design and maintenance of food premises/the storage of food.

A number of suitable videos are available from various libraries or private firms. Advice on the choice of video is always available from your local Environmental Health Department.

Many people engaged in the catering industry have obtained qualifications ranging from university degrees in food and nutrition to diplomas in food technology. The Hotel and Catering Training Board is particularly active in promoting training at all levels. It is generally recognised that, however good thc qualifications may be, everyone benefits from receiving further training from time to time on new developments and trends. Some health authorities and companies, for example, require staff to undergo refresher training every 12 months. Comprising a condensed course, these serve as a reminder of the importance of hygiene. Some employers have commendably introduced bonus schemes for those who demonstrate a particular commitment to hygiene. It is important that training is not a 'one-off' exercise for the food handler. Employers should bear this in mind, making provision for 'old hands' to undergo some further training from time to time.

'Familiarity breeds contempt'. This is a favourite saying which has stood the test of time. Constant reminders of food hygiene and safety responsibilities are necessary; these can be both verbal from managers or in the form of posters and notices. Short sharp messages are best because these are quickly read, whereas detailed instructions often take too long to read and do not catch the attention of the worker.

Some local authority Environmental Health Officers and hygiene consultants operate education programmes that involve taking swabs from equipment, etc. These are then processed in a laboratory so that it is possible to show that bacteria are present. Although these bacteria may not be harmful, the fact that they are alive on the equipment, etc., demonstrates that pathogenic bacteria could equally be present.

Some food concerns use contact swabs as a means whereby staff themselves can test for bacteria. These involve simple preprepared swabs which are applied to the surface being tested. The swab is then kept at around body temperature for a set time following which it is possible to carry out a crude count of organisms. This self-checking must not be

Food Hygiene (General) Regulations 1970

Points for food handlers to remember . . .

1. Hands must be clean.
2. Overclothing must be clean and washable.
3. Cuts or abrasions must be covered with a suitable waterproof dressing.
4. Spitting is prohibited.
5. The use of snuff, tobacco or other smoking mixture is prohibited.
6. In the event of a food handler feeling ill, the employer should be notified and the doctor consulted.
7. Hands must be washed after using the lavatory.

Further details in connection with the Food Hygiene (General) Regulations 1970 may be obtained from the local Environmental Health Department.

Short, sharp messages are the most effective!

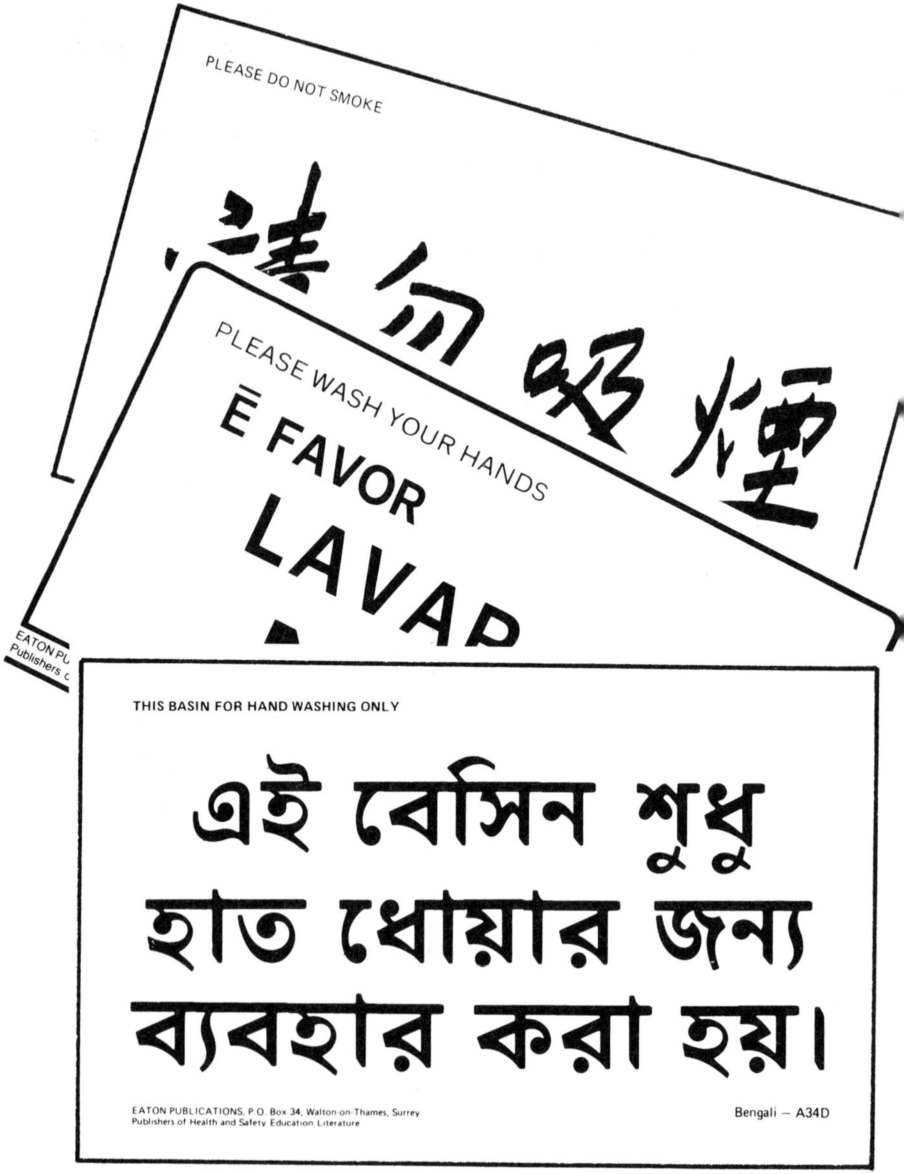

Messages in foreign languages are useful aids in the battle for cleanliness (Eaton Publications)

regarded as an accurate check of numbers or types of bacteria. It can nonetheless prove a useful aid to in-house training in proper cleansing techniques.

While training by example and attendance at specialist courses can be most valuable, a large amount of literature is available to assist the food handler in understanding his responsibilities.

The Food Hygiene (General) Regulations, 1970, are available in a simplified form and in various languages. If a food handler is to conform with the law, then he should have some idea of what the law says in the first place. Many local authorities distribute copies of the Regulations and other advisory literature free to food handlers while some firms purchase supplies themselves. Whichever the case, it is important for each food firm to have some advisory literature available covering the basic requirements and quite definitely every manager and supervisor should have a copy of the Food Hygiene (General) Regulations as a constant companion.

The following sources provide food hygiene and health and safety advisory material:

Source	**Details**
Eaton Publications. P.O. Box 34, Walton-on-Thames, Surrey Telephone 0932 229001	A wide range of notices, leaflets and posters are available, either direct or through your local authority. The Food Hygiene (General) Regulations are available in various languages.
Health Education Authority, Hamilton House, Mabledon Place, London WC1H 9TX Telephone 071 383 3833	A wide range of notices, posters and leaflets are available, usually only through the local authority.

Audio visual training aids relating to both food hygiene and health and safety are available from the following:

Health Education Authority
Central Film Library
Hamilton House
Mabledon Place
WC1H 9TX Telephone 071 383 3833

Rentokil Film Unit
View Lodge
Selcourt
East Grinstead
West Sussex Telephone 0342 87692

The Gas Consumer Council
6th Floor
Abford House
15 Wilson Road
London SW1V 1LT Telephone 071 931 9155

British Gas
Publicity Department Telephone 071 821 1444

Hotel and Catering Training Board
International House
High Street
EALING
London W5 5DB Telephone 081 579 2400

Hotel Catering and Institutional Management Association
191 Trinity Road
London SW17 Telephone 081 672 4251

Royal Society of Health
RSH House
38A St George's Drive
London SW1V 4BH Telephone 071 630 0121

Royal Institute of Public Health and Hygiene
28 Portland Place
London W1N 4DE Telephone 071 580 2731

Institution of Environmental Health Officers
Chadwick House
Rushworth Street
London SE1 0QT Telephone 071 928 6006

The following food hygiene slides are available:

Kits on hospital hygiene
1. Personal Hygiene
2. Good Catering Practices
3. Equipment – Cleaning and Maintenance

Alan Bailey (Ass. Nat. Sec.),
Hospital Caterers Association,
Clatterbridge Hosptal,
Bebbington,
Wirral L63 4JY.
051-334 4000
(For sale only)

The Electricity Association
30 Millbank
London SW1P 4RD

Telephone 071 834 2333

or your local Electricity Company

NHS Training Directorate
(Communciations)
St Bartholomews Court
18 Christmas Street
Bristol BS1 5BT

Telephone 0272 291029

Test Your Knowledge

In order to test your knowledge of the basic principles of food hygiene, see if you can answer the questions listed in this Appendix. If you score 36–40 marks in each set you are excellent; 26–35 marks you are average; 18–25 marks you are below average; and if you score only 1–17 marks – you should reread the book!

Questions

1. Within which temperature range do bacteria most readily multiply?
2. Name three foods which are most likely to be associated with food poisoning?
3. Although brightly coloured dressings are not legally required in a first aid kit, why would you recommend them for food handlers?
4. What type of protective clothing must food handlers wear, and how often should it be changed?
5. What is a suitable material for the handles of brushes and similar implements in a food preparation area, and why is the use of wood not recommended?
6. What are the physical conditions necessary for the growth of bacteria?
7. How often should a slicing machine be cleaned?
8. What causes a can to be blown?
9. Why is it important to wash hands after using the lavatory?
10. If you have some 'suspicious' food who would you contact to examine it?
11. Bacteria are able to multiply at an alarming rate under ideal conditions. How do they multiply and how long does it take?
12. What is the name of the regulations dealing with food hygiene in:
    (a) Food premises
    (b) Mobile food vehicles?
13. How do harmful bacteria gain access to food in a kitchen?
14. What problem may arise from lemonade being stored in a copper or galvanised container?
15. What facilities are required to be provided in food premises for the purpose of hand-washing?
16. In terms of wash hand facilities, what do you consider to be suitable means for hand drying?

17. What do you understand by the term 'cross-contamination'?
18. Which micro-organism would be described as thus – a rod shaped, spore forming anaerobic bacterium. The spores survive normal cooking temperatures and multiplication recur during cooling and reheating of food. It is a common inhabitant of the gut of animals and man.
19. What is the usual incubation period of the following:–
    (a) *Salmonella* food poisoning
    (b) *Staphylococcus* food poisoning
    (c) *Clostridium perfringens* food poisoning?
20. What is meant by the term cook–chill, in relation to food preparation?
21. Why is good lighting essential in a kitchen?
22. What are the usual symptoms of food poisoning?
23. Why is food with a pH value of below 4.5 considered to be safe as far as pathogens are concerned?
24. What action would an Environmental Health Officer take if he found food premises that were so dirty that they represented a danger to public health?
25. What effect does domestic refrigeration have on the growth of pathogens?
26. Why is it advisable to rinse cutlery, etc., in very hot water?
27. How should meat pies be stored overnight?
28. What would you do if a rat or mouse is seen on your premises?
29. Why should frozen poultry be thoroughly thawed before cooking?
30. What foods should not be cooked in copper vessels?
31. Why should finger jewellery be kept to an absolute minimum by food handlers?
32. What are the basic rules when choosing any material for use in food premises?
33. What are 'Codes of Practice'?
34. Why is the inside of a can of fruit lacquered?
35. What is the difference between a detergent and a sterilant?
36. What is meant by the term 'stock rotation' and to which foods does it especially apply?
37. What do you understand by the word 'hygiene'?
38. What is meant by the term 'pasteurization' and what is its purpose?
39. What food poisoning illness may result from eating smoked or stale mackerel?
40. Why are salt and sugar used to preserve food?

Answers

1. 5–63°C.
2. Meat; Fish; Gravy; Cream; Eggs; Milk; Soft Cheeses, etc.
3. For ease of recognition if the dressing falls into the food product.
4. Clean and washable outerclothing which should be changed as often as necessary.
5. Plastic coated or tubular rust resistant steel. Wood is porous and difficult to clean.
6. Food; Temperature;Moisture; Time, etc.
7. Between different foods and at the end of each day.
8. The creation of gas caused through the decomposition of the food. Also acid food attacking metal to liberate gas as a result of faulty canning.
9. To remove bacteria from the hands – bearing in mind that lavatory paper is porous.
10. The Environmental Health Officer attached to your local Council.
11. They divide into two by a process called binary fission. Under ideal conditions this process takes around twenty minutes.
12. (a) Food Hygiene (General) Regulations 1970 – as amended.
    (b) Food Hygiene (Markets, Stalls and Delivery Vehicles) Regulations 1966 – as amended.
13. (a) Food handlers – dirty hands, overalls, etc.
    (b) Animals and insects
    (c) Dust, etc.
    (d) Cross-contamination.
14. A chemical reaction could in certain circumstances give rise to chemical food poisoning.
15. Suitable wash hand basin; hot and cold water or hot water at a suitable controlled temperature; soap or other detergent; suitable means for hand drying; a nail brush.
16. (a) Warm air dryer
    (b) Disposable towels
    (c) Renewable (continuous) roller towel.
17. The transfer of pathogenic bacteria to a 'clean food' using a secondary agent, e.g. a knife being used for cutting raw and cooked poultry; the use of the same cutting board for cooked and uncooked foods, etc.
18. *Clostridium perfringens.*
19. (a) 12–24 hours (usually 18–24)
    (b) ½–6 hours
    (c) 8–24 hours.

20. A method in which food is cooked and then cooled to 3°C within one and a half hours. The food can then be kept for up to five/six days before thorough reheating and serving.
21. (a) to provide comfort and safety
    (b) to enable dirt to be easily detected
    (c) to enable thorough cleaning to take place.
22. Headache; nausea; vomiting; diarrhoea; stomach and intestinal pains.
23. The food is too acidic for most bacteria to survive and multiply.
24. He would apply to a Magistrates Court for a prohibition order.
25. It slows down the growth of the pathogens and food keeps longer.
26. To make sure it is sterilized and so that it can be air-dried rather than having to use towels, etc., that may become contaminated.
27. In a refrigerator.
28. Check all stock for contamination and contact a specialist pest control firm immediately.
29. To eliminate the possibility of a frozen area remaining in the middle which would prevent adequate cooking throughout. N.B. The high incidence of *Salmonella* in poultry.
30. Acidic foods – citrus, rhubarb, etc.
31. It prevents the thorough cleaning of hands and can itself provide a harbourage for bacteria. There is also the added danger of pieces of the jewellery becoming detached and falling into the food.
32. As a rule they should be smooth, impervious and capable of being readily cleaned.
33. Issued by the Government for the guidance of food authorities. Refer to recommended practices, enforcement, etc. Also available to the food industry.
34. To prevent metallic contamination of the fruit.
35. A detergent aids the removal of grease and dirt. A sterilant kills germs and should be used after cleaning with a detergent.
36. Using old stock before new ensuring that stock is used within its recommended 'life'. Particularly important for perishable foods.
37. Personal and workplace cleanliness.
38. It is a process whereby the temperature of the food is raised to such a level that pathogenic bacteria are destroyed. It is used to prolong the life of food.
39. Scombrotoxin.
40. They remove water from the food and as a result bacterial growth is retarded.

All of the Awarding Bodies promote advanced level qualifications. These are intended to give an in-depth knowledge of food hygiene. The examinations involve both written papers and a short oral. The following are included to give interested candidates an idea of questions that have appeared at this level in the past few years.

1. Describe a suitable method of cleaning dirty crockery and cutlery from the tables of a self-service restaurant. Assuming that a dish-washing machine is available, describe in detail the correct procedure for washing up.
2. List the different types of refrigeration, chill and freeze, used in the food trade. State for what purpose each type is used.
3. List the main principles involved in the design of food premises.
4. In relation to pest control, prevention is always better and cheaper than cure. Discuss this statement.
5. List the requirements you consider to be of importance in the transit of:
   (a) raw meat
   (b) milk
   to ensure that their quality does not deteriorate.
6. What is meant by the term 'cross-contamination'? Describe in detail how 'direct' and 'indirect' cross-contamination can and often does occur in a catering business.
7. The number of reported cases of food poisoning caused by *Salmonella* organisms continues to increase.
   (a) What are the reasons for this high incidence?
   (b) Which foods are mainly responsible for the increase?
   (c) What can be done to slow down this increase?
8. 'Dirty, unhygienic premises cost money and reputations'.
   Discuss this statement showing your understanding, as a manager, of its implications to the success of your firm.
9. The high turnover of staff in the food industry poses problems to Management regarding the requirements of food hygiene.
   As the supervisor in charge of personal hygiene in a large bakery, draw up a training programme for your staff which will bring out the requirements of the Food Hygiene legislation and which clearly shows the dangers of poor personal hygiene.
10. Some bacteria produce spores, others produce toxins and some produce both. Explain the difference between a spore and a toxin. How does the knowledge and understanding of these enable a food handler to reduce the risk of bacterial food poisoning? Illustrate your answer with examples.

11. (a) Prepare a cleaning schedule in respect of a hospital kitchen, listing main headings.
    (b) Specify in detail the materials and equipment to be used.
12. Write short notes on each of the following:
    (a) Toxins
    (b) Spores
    (c) Incubation periods
    (d) Moulds.
13. Discuss the merits of colour coding for equipment in food preparation premises; and give your views on the suitability of wood, nylon and plastic for cutting surfaces, knife handles, etc.
14. Quality Assurance is now very important in the food industry. Discuss those aspects of 'Q.A.' which affect food safety in a commercial catering business.
15. Convenience foods continue to increase in popularity.
    (a) What are the potential dangers with these foods?
    (b) Which pathogens may be a particular problem with take-away meals?
    (c) What advice would you give to a take-away retailer regarding cooked rice?
16. 'Foreign bodies in food present an increasing hazard to the consumer'. Discuss this statement giving both examples and ways in which they can be prevented.
17. Legislation gives attention to hygiene and safety throughout the 'food chain'. What is meant by this, stating the advantages of this approach as well as some of the likely problem areas?
18. You have received a consignment of meat that is both off colour and which has a strange smell. What action would you take and what might be the role of the Environmental Health Officer in the exercise?
19. 'Cook–chill' catering is being increasingly used in large-scale catering. Where might this be most appropriate and discuss the advantages and disadvantages of such a system?
20. 'Temperature control is vital, especially in relation to high risk foods'. What do you understand by this statement, giving examples of the storage temperatures set out in the Food Hygiene (Amendment) Regulations 1990.

We are grateful to the Institution of Environmental Health Officers, the Royal Institute of Public Health and Hygiene and the Royal Society of Health for allowing us to use these questions from their various examination papers.

Index

Index

Index